A REASON TO BE NOBLE

A Prequel to The Horses Know Trilogy

LYNN MANN

Coxstone Press

In memory of Marcus,
a very noble horse.

Chapter One

It was always the same. I would wake in the morning feeling relaxed and refreshed as a result of having had a break from myself, and then it would start. My heart would begin to race, my chest would tighten and my mind would start running away with me. What did I need to do that day? Would I be able to remember to do it all, or would my mind racing from one thing to another cause me to forget some of my tasks? If I could remember, was I capable of doing everything the day would throw at me, or would I crumble? Would the churning that had already begun in my stomach result in my having to keep racing to the bathroom?

My days had begun like that ever since I could remember, and today was no different. I made myself get out of bed, part of me wanting to stay there where the world couldn't reach me, the other part knowing that if I did, I would only lie there until my anxiety over the day ahead rose to such a level that I couldn't bear to be still any longer.

I shuffled along the landing to the bathroom feeling exhausted even though I had been awake for mere minutes. I washed quickly and according to my usual routine, then, feeling slightly better for the security of having slotted into my daily schedule, returned to my bedroom.

I opened my wardrobe door and looked at all of the clothes hanging on the rail and folded on the shelf above. Instantly, the churning in my stomach worsened. Which shirt should I choose? The white one would be cool in the heat of summer, but then I wasn't planning to be outside much that day, so it would make sense to leave it for later in the week when it could be hotter and I might need to be out in the sun. The pale blue one then? But the only shorts that went with it were those that I liked to wear with the white shirt, and if I were going to save the white shirt for later in the week, then it would make sense to also save those shorts. The tightness increased in my chest, which then rose and dropped more rapidly as my breaths became shallower and more rapid.

My bedroom door was flung open. 'Quinta, dear, your father and I need you to go along to Hightown this morning to collect more dye,' my mother informed me. She was by my side in an instant, putting her arm around my shoulders and giving me a quick hug before gently moving me to one side and selecting a yellow shirt and black, knee-length shorts from my wardrobe. 'You always look beautiful in yellow, it contrasts beautifully with your hair, which is a perfect match for these shorts. Here, put these on and then come on downstairs. I've packed your breakfast, so you can eat it while you walk. It's nice and early, so you're unlikely to bump into anyone. The sun is shining, the birds are singing, it's a beautiful day. Hurry along now.' She swept back out of my bedroom before I could say a word.

I smiled with relief. I knew I wasn't an easy person to be around, but my mother had spent all of my twenty-six years behaving as if I were. She always seemed to know when I was having even more trouble than normal getting to grips with a new day, and would quickly assess whichever stage it was with which I was struggling, then step in to take charge for a few minutes – just long enough to afford me the relief of having a decision taken away from me, without taking over and leaving me feeling disempowered and useless.

I put on the clothes she had selected for me, and considered the day ahead. It wasn't going to be anything like that which I had planned. Would I manage? My mother's words swept through my mind along with all of my other thoughts, and I grabbed hold of them, remembering the relief I had felt when she said them to me. It was sunny. I would enjoy the heat and the feeling of the sun's rays touching my skin, every bit as much as I would love listening to the birds in the trees and soaring overhead. It was early and if I left now, whilst most of the villagers of Lowtown were having breakfast, I was likely to be able to enjoy all of that alone, without the need to worry that I would meet people and have to think what to say.

I knew my mother had left it until the last minute to tell me that it would be me going to collect the dyes for which she, my father and I – as the Weavers of the village – were growing desperate, because if she had told me before, I would have worked myself up into such a state about it that I wouldn't have been able to set foot outside of the front door. She could have gone, but she made sure I took my turn going to collect supplies, whether it be fleece, dye, or parts for our looms, otherwise I would barely have stepped outside, let alone interacted with people other than my parents.

Warmth swept through me as I thought for the hundredth time how lucky I was to have parents like mine. I began to descend the stairs, but was barely halfway when I stopped. Although it was early, was it early enough? What if I bumped into a stranger travelling to Lowtown, or worse, someone from my own village? They were all so kind to me, which only made my need to keep them at arm's length more desperate; I knew from childhood experience that if I let anyone get close to me, they would have expectations of me as a friend and they would want to spend time with me, which was fine sometimes, but not all of the time. When it wasn't fine – when I needed time to myself to reset my worries and concerns so that I could function in our world of noise, feelings and sensations without being overwhelmed – I would have to turn them down, and then I would have to feel their confusion, their disappointment and sometimes even their anger, and I would be overwhelmed anyway. No. Better to be as standoffish as everyone thought me to be, it was easier that way.

My mother's face appeared in front of mine and I realised I was poised with my foot in the air ready to take the next step, while my body had yet to commit to shifting its weight. I was gripping the bannister so hard with my right hand that my knuckles were white, and tapping the fingertips of my left hand against the grey stone of the stairway in a rapid but steady rhythm.

'There you are, dear, you look lovely.' She smiled warmly and brushed a strand of hair away from my face, tucking it behind my ear as she had when I was a child.

I took a deep breath and smiled back ruefully. 'I look like a bumble bee.' I let go of the bannister and took the next step, then followed her down to the hallway. 'Thanks, Mum,' I said, taking the back-sack she held out to me. As small in stature as I was, she was one of the few adults with whom I didn't have to strain my neck in order to look at her face.

She hugged me. 'You're very welcome, dear. Enjoy the walk.' She hurried to the front door and opened it, then gestured for me to go outside before I could think about doing anything else.

Before I knew it, I was walking down the path that bisected

our front garden, to one of the cobbled streets of Lowtown. The clear sky was a beautiful, vivid blue and the sun was already hot, just as I liked it. The street was clear, so I took a deep breath, opened the front gate and stepped onto the street. I hurried along it, not looking at the grey stone cottages on either side that were all similar to the one I shared with my parents, lest anyone be at a window; I never knew whether to smile, wave, call out a greeting, or pretend I hadn't seen them when that happened, so it was easier to avoid the issue.

When I stepped off the last cobble and onto the grassland that surrounded our village, I released the breath I had been holding. I smiled at the birds swooping up, down and around me as they plucked bugs from the air. As I walked towards the river that flowed from Hightown and then along the valley floor below Lowtown, I held my arms out to either side of me, enjoying the warm breeze that gently eased its way between my fingers and ruffled the thin fabric of my long-sleeved shirt. For the first time since I had woken, I was glad that I had.

I reached the river and wandered alongside it, enjoying the sound of the water as it tumbled on its way. Where the bank was low and I could see that the river was shallow enough at the edge, I stepped down into the water, allowing it to cool my feet and ankles. I ate the breakfast of nuts and fruit that my mother had packed for me, and smiled as I fished out the pale yellow, wide-brimmed sunhat I found in the bottom of my back-sack; when my worries shut out my ability to think straight, my mother was always there for me, a safety net through which she never let me fall.

The hat was brand new and though my mother was a Weaver rather than a Tailor, I couldn't see how any of those trained to sew could have improved upon her workmanship. I knew it would be the perfect fit for my head even as I lowered it into place. The hat's existence and presence in my back-sack were more of the many ways my mother found to let me know that no matter how difficult I was to live and work with, she loved me, she was looking out for me, and her thoughts were with me when she wasn't physically.

I followed the river up into the hills, sipping regularly from my water flask, and refilling it frequently. I looked up often to monitor the sun's position in the sky; I knew how long the walk to Hightown and back usually took me, and I needed to know I was going to be able to do it in the normal amount of time. I didn't know whether the Dyers would keep me waiting, so I hurried, wanting to keep slightly ahead of schedule on the way there in case they did.

I grinned ruefully to myself as I heard my mother's voice in my head, saying the words she so often said to me: 'The word "schedule" only exists in your vocabulary, love, we work at the rate we work.' I loved her for telling me that, but she never really understood that it could never make any difference to how I thought, how I functioned.

When I saw smoke rising from the distant chimneys of Hightown, my stomach began to churn viciously. I glanced around for the large bush that I had utilised before at the same point in my journey, then looked ahead for bushes I could head towards at the last minute between my current position and the village, in case I could hold out now. I couldn't see any large enough, and couldn't risk not finding one – it would have to be now. I rushed to the nearby bush, reached into my back-sack for the trowel and toilet tissue I knew my mother would have packed for me, and hastily dug a hole out of sight of the riverside, finishing it just in time.

As I refilled the hole, I hated myself for being so weak-minded, so weak-bodied, so utterly pathetic as to be reduced to a panicking wreck at the sight of a village I knew so well, that represented no threat to me whatsoever, and that was filled with people every bit as kind and sympathetic as those of my home village.

'You are as you are, love,' my mother had told me over and over again as I cried into her shoulder at my powerlessness to overcome my over-reactions to, and worries about, anything and everything. It was one of the few things she would say to me that never helped.

At least I now wouldn't have to worry that I'd need to ask to use the toilet at the Dyers' workshop, as I had been mortified to have to do before. The thought bolstered me enough that I managed to get my feet moving back towards the riverside path to Hightown.

I cursed inwardly as I spotted movement ahead of me; someone was coming my way. My legs went weak at the thought that had they been a little earlier, they might have passed by when I was behind the bush. My heart thumped hard in my chest, my legs and arms tingled and I felt faint.

'But they didn't,' I told myself out loud. 'They didn't.' I began to calm down, but then the thought occurred to me that whoever was coming might also need to use the bush, and if they did, they would see the freshly disturbed earth I had left behind me.

I felt dizzy. They would know it was me. They would know what I tried so hard to keep secret from everyone – that although I might look like any other person, I was a mess. My body would have betrayed me as I never let my words or behaviour do, as I made sure they could never do by keeping away from other people as much as possible.

I wondered whether to turn around and run. No, whoever it was might run after me. Should I go back and hide behind the bush? No, I might lead them there. I began to sweat profusely at the thought. I looked about wildly for somewhere else to hide, but there were only a few other bushes, both smaller and less dense than the one that hid my shame, and a distant tree.

I must have stood rooted to the spot for longer than it seemed. I almost leapt out of my skin as a voice called out, 'Quinta, how lovely to see you.'

I turned around to see a slim, white-haired woman wearing the yellow bandanna of a Herald walking towards me, her arm lifted in greeting. When I merely stared at her, trying to slow my breathing and swallow so that I could answer her, she let her arm drop and asked, 'Are you alright?'

I managed to nod, but I couldn't remember her name through my panic, let alone say it.

'You don't look it.' The Herald held out a water flask to me. 'Is it heatstroke? Do you feel dizzy? Sick? Here, drink some of this, then we need to get you into the shade.' She looked past me to the nearby bush and I thought I would faint.

I held my hands up in refusal of the flask, and shook my head emphatically as I managed to gasp, 'No, thank you, I'm fine. It's, um, it's nice to see you too, but I'm expected in Hightown, so I'd better be on my way. Have a good journey, bye.'

I hurried past her, hoping upon hope that she wouldn't follow me. My heart hammered in my chest as I rushed towards Hightown, trying to get as far away as possible by the time the woman discovered my use of the bush, as she surely would. I strained to hear whether she was following me, calling to me or whether I could discern any noises that might indicate she was investigating the bush, but I heard nothing.

It wasn't until I was panting, pouring with sweat and in real danger of heatstroke, that I finally stopped and turned around. I could see the Herald – Janni, that was her name, I suddenly remembered – walking briskly yet unhurriedly towards Lowtown.

My eyes quickly measured the distance between her and our

meeting point, and then my own distance from it. The two distances were similar. That meant she hadn't paused at the bush, didn't it? She wouldn't have had time to divert to it and still get to where she was at her current pace. But she was going downhill and I had been walking uphill, so each of her strides would likely have covered more ground than mine. A shard of panic lanced my heart. Did that mean she'd had time to divert? What would she be thinking if she knew what I'd done? Would she, in her role as a Herald – and wearing her bandanna, so an on-duty Herald at that – feel dutybound to announce her discovery and my problem to my home village? To every village she visited?

I felt dizzy again and wondered whether it was due to panic or heatstroke. One of them, I knew from experience I could do nothing about. The other would be helped by a paddle in the river.

Thankfully, the bank was shallow nearby, so I was able to step into the water as it surged down the hillside. A conveniently placed rock provided me with a seat while the water cooled my legs, ankles and feet. I leant forward and cupped some water in my hands, which I splashed on my face. The sound of the water slapping against the rock soothed me even as I wished I could just dissolve into it and float away. I sighed. My parents would be devastated if anything ever happened to me, I knew that. I reminded myself of it whenever my head became an intolerable place to be.

I stood and waded back out of the river, then carried on towards Hightown, my feet squelching in my sandals.

Chapter Two

*I*t was nearly lunchtime when I reached the huge dam that prevented the water flowing from the mountains during spring, as well as the rain that could lash down at any time of the year, from swelling the river enough to flood Lowtown. The spillways were open, allowing water to gradually pour out of the reservoir and into the river, slowly lowering the water level in the reservoir in preparation for the autumn rains.

I walked along the bank of the reservoir, enjoying the slightly cooler breeze that blew across it even as my thoughts began to roil around in my head at an increased pace. I would be at the village within minutes. After my upset on the way there, I was in no state to converse with anyone, but I couldn't let my parents down. I couldn't go home without the dyes we needed, and that meant there was only one thing for it; I would have to pretend to be someone else.

I had done it before. When the alternatives were worse than the task in hand, I'd been forced to pretend to be someone who was calm and confident. Someone who was normal. I couldn't do it for long, it was too much effort being someone so far removed from who I was, but I could do it.

As the sounds of Hightown reached my ears – children shouting, laughing and screaming in the school playground; the low hum of voices as people chatted in the street; scraping, sawing and banging from the Carpenters' workshop at the near end of the village – I slowed my breathing, stood as tall as my short frame allowed, and relaxed the muscles in my face and neck. I was someone who could chat easily to others, who could smile and maintain eye contact whilst having a conversation, who could calmly wander into the village as if I had no cares in the world, and was in no hurry to leave. I felt the same way as I always did in those few seconds after waking, and instantly felt envious of everyone else in the world who no doubt felt like this all of the time.

I smiled and waved to one of the Carpenters, whose workshop doors were wide open. He grinned back and called out, 'Quinta, welcome. Fancy a brew?'

'In this heat? Thanks, but no thanks,' I called back and walked on past.

I exchanged pleasantries with several others on my way to the Dyers' workshop, and on arrival, wandered unhurriedly through its open door. It felt so strange to be this character I was adopting, as if the world were moving in slow motion around me instead of moving at the blistering pace it usually did, with which I couldn't keep up.

The Master Dyer looked up from the pot she had been stirring, and smiled. 'Hi, Quinta, you're just in time for lunch. Will you join us?'

A flash of panic penetrated my persona. I drew in a deep, slow breath. There was no rush to answer. I smiled back and said, 'Hi, Xanthine, that's really kind of you, but no thanks, I'm expected back so I'll take the dyes and be on my way, if that's okay?'

'Are you sure? It's one hot day out there.'

Two slow breaths. 'I'm sure, thank you. I love the heat and I have my lunch with me.'

Xanthine shook her head. 'You Fenways work too hard, I've said it before and I'll say it again. Haven't I said that, Jade?' She looked over at her Apprentice, who was crushing some bright red berries in a large bowl, with a wooden, flat-headed utensil.

Jade rolled her eyes and grinned as she looked at me. 'She says everyone else works too hard. It's her way of letting me know that she doesn't think I work hard enough, isn't that right, Master Xanth?'

'Talking of which, you know the Chandler was expecting that dye you've just about got around to, first thing this morning, don't you?' Xanthine retorted.

Jade looked back to me and shrugged. 'See what I mean?'

I couldn't think of what I should say and I almost lost my composure, but then remembered that the person I was pretending to be was calm and confident. If she didn't have anything to say then that was fine.

I nodded towards several stacks of lidded glass jars on the table by the door. 'Are those for me?'

Xanthine pointed at them with her spoon, and nodded. 'Yes, the stack nearest to you.'

I pulled a pile of thick cloths from my back-sack and began to wrap them around the jars. I could feel Xanthine and Jade watching me as they worked, and I wanted to hurry, but focused on keeping all of my movements slow and measured.

When I had wrapped all of the jars, I packed them into the back-sack, making sure to place the remaining cloths between them and the part of the sack that would rest against my back.

Then I hoisted the back-sack into place and turned back to the Master Dyer and her Apprentice. 'Thank you very much, do you have the list of colours you would like your cloth dyed, and the quantity of cloth you need?'

Xanthine put a purple-stained hand to her forehead. 'Pshhhht, I nearly forgot. Jade, pass Quinta that list on the bench there, will you? Thanks, Quinta, this heat makes my brain go to mush.'

I managed a smile. 'No problem. Are you sure you just want the cloth as is? We can ask the Lowtown Tailors to make what you need if yours here in Hightown are busy, and deliver your clothes instead of just the cloth?'

Xanthine shook her head as Jade handed me the list. 'That's kind of you, but no, I booked a slot with our Tailors here for the week after next, so as long as the cloth gets here by then, I'm sorted.'

I nodded. 'It will be, you can count on it. Thanks, Xanthine, Jade.' I lifted a hand in farewell and left the workshop.

Every part of me wanted to run, to leave the the hustle and bustle of Hightown and the friendly waves and greetings of its inhabitants behind, but I forced myself to focus on each and every footstep so that I walked unhurriedly along the street and out of the village.

As soon as I was alone, I let out a breath and increased my pace. Immediately, my mind flew back to everything that had happened from when I set foot in Hightown to when I left it. I went over it all repeatedly in the minutest detail. Had I given an acceptable account of myself? Had I caused offence by refusing the Carpenter's offer of a cuppa, and Xanthine's offer of lunch? In my effort to appear calm, had I walked too slowly so that people thought I had some sort of problem? Where had I put Xanthine's list? I patted my shorts pocket and was relieved to hear the crinkling sound of paper. Had I packed the jars well enough that they wouldn't break? We needed that dye, and if anything happened to it, I wouldn't be able to get back to Hightown for more in time to dye Xanthine's cloth and get it to her in good time for the slot she had booked with the Tailors, let alone meet all of our other orders.

I stopped and unpacked the jars, checked their wrappings and then repacked them all again. As I hoisted the back-sack onto my shoulders, I worried that where the jars had been packed perfectly well before, now they would jostle as a result of having been repacked while my back-sack rested on uneven ground. Ought I to find a flat piece of ground and unpack and repack them again?

A bead of sweat ran down my nose and dripped off, followed by another. The sun was at its highest in the sky and the heat would only continue to build during the afternoon. I didn't have time to panic, I needed to move; I needed to be near water so that I could cool myself and rehydrate, and I needed to get the dyes home, else we wouldn't be able to meet our order deadlines regardless of whether the jars made it back intact.

I shook my head in frustration. If I could just spend less time fretting and more time acting, I wouldn't have to feel like I had to hurry everywhere in order to keep up with the day. I took a swig of water from my flask and hurried to the banks of the reservoir. It felt good to be moving at my usual pace, but strangely, I felt a sense of loss for the calm, collected person I was leaving behind me.

The breeze that was still blowing across the reservoir cooled me slightly, enough to feel a little less concerned that I might yet get heatstroke. I lifted a packet of sandwiches out of the top of my back-sack and munched on its contents as I walked.

As always, the return journey seemed to pass more quickly and easily than the outward one. I was on a well-trodden path and walking downhill, I was fed and hydrated and I was going home. I felt a slight dread about who, exactly, I might meet on the way back and whilst making my way through Lowtown, but I felt lifted by having navigated through Hightown without making any mistakes that I could think of, so even that didn't dampen my spirits. For now.

When I topped a hill and caught sight of the bush that caused me so much anxiety a few hours before, I stopped in my tracks. For a moment, I thought I was imagining things, but the more I stared, the more I realised I wasn't. There must have been about twenty horses milling around between the bush and the river, some stopping to snatch mouthfuls of grass before moving again, others walking and trotting here, there and everywhere, as if they didn't know what to do with themselves. A small, brown horse was in the river, as was a larger grey one. The grey jumped out and then spun around to peer back down at the one still in the river as the rest continued to dart around.

My heart was in my mouth. How would I get past them all? I had seen horses before – over the years, many bonded horses had visited Lowtown with their human Bond-Partners and I had once seen a wild herd from a distance – but none had behaved as these were; they seemed... unsettled about something. Maybe my sudden appearance had startled them? No, surely they would have just run away from me. What, then?

I walked towards them very slowly, hoping they wouldn't notice me. As I got closer, I could see that most of them had water running down their sides and dripping from their bellies, and they all had wet legs. So, they had been in the river, I assumed to drink and cool down. Why weren't they leaving now that they had done so?

I came to a stop, too afraid to move any closer. What should I do? I couldn't go back to Hightown – I would never get my thoughts in order to try to explain to everyone why I had returned, and I had no idea what I would do there anyway – I had to get home. I decided that I needed to move in case the horses ran in my direction; I had nowhere to go except into the river, and they could always follow me in there and trample me, or I could be swept away by the current. What to do? Where to go? Sweat trickled down my back and my heart pounded in my chest as I turned around and around on the spot, trying to figure it out.

I gasped involuntarily as the horses nearest the river suddenly shied away from it. The small, brown horse had jumped out onto the bank and was spinning around, flinging water everywhere and making the most awful noise. She was scared. I'd never before heard the noise she was making, but I knew what it meant as surely as I knew the significance of a human scream. She was afraid – but not for herself. She was worried for another. A high-pitched squeal shuddered through me. Where had that come from?

The brown horse moved and I saw something on the river bank at her feet, right at the edge. I squinted. Was that a head? Flaming lanterns, it was, but it was tiny, maybe that of a foal? Understanding dawned; the brown mare's foal was in the river.

For once, there was no room in my head for any thoughts that could persuade me I was wrong, confuse me, or hold me back. I ran.

The mare called down to her baby again. She was encouraging him, pleading with him to jump out of the river and onto the bank, I knew it, without having a clue how I knew.

The foal screamed back to her and its head bobbed up and down as it tried and failed to jump up onto the bank. The river appeared shallow enough at the edge that the foal was safe where it was, but I could see from the colour of the water that the riverbed fell away sharply from the bank and the fast-moving water quickly deepened. The mare knew as well as I did that her baby was in terrible danger.

As I neared the horses, gasping and running with sweat, they seemed to calm down. They stopped milling around and gathered together to watch my passage past them, to where the brown mare was now stretching her head down to her foal and whickering as she nudged him, trying to get him to take action and escape the river that could sweep him away from her.

I shrugged out of my back-sack and dumped it on the ground without a care, then walked slowly closer to the mare. A thought entered my mind that she might see me as an additional threat to her baby, and attack me, but I couldn't stop myself walking closer. It was as if I had suddenly transformed into someone else – someone confident and capable.

The foal whinnied shrilly and his fear, far more intense than any I had ever felt, went right through me. The mare watched my approach and when I was close, whickered to me. She trusted me, I knew it. She wanted me to help. And I would.

I knelt down beside her front feet to get a better look at her foal, not even considering that although she was a lot smaller than most of the others in her herd, she could still trample me dead in an instant. She lowered her head to her foal and whickered, then turned her head and looked at me.

'I'll do what I can,' I said softly to her.

I reached a hand down to the foal, who was standing knee-deep in water alongside the riverbank, facing upstream. He flinched away from me and almost lost his footing. His mother whickered to him as he fought to regain his balance, which he managed.

'There now, little one, I'm going to need to touch you,' I said to him whilst keeping my hand held out towards him. 'Aren't you fluffy? You're not very old, are you? Only a few days, I think, way too small to jump down there, but I guess you followed your mother, didn't you?'

The foal went rigid as I gradually moved my hand closer until I was touching him. His mother nuzzled him next to my hand, and he relaxed.

'That's it, little one, I'm going to help you. I've no idea how, but I'll think about that while you're getting to know me. Okay?' I gently rubbed the soft, dark brown – almost black – fur of his neck. He had brown hair around his eyes and nostrils, and dark brown eyes which were open so wide that circles of white were visible around their irises. His tiny ears – the left of which had a small patch of white at its base – flickered back and forth rapidly and I could actually hear his heart thumping as fast as mine often did.

In that instant, I felt a connection with him that almost had me toppling into the river beside him. I knew exactly how he felt, and nothing mattered more than taking his fear, his all-consuming panic, away from him.

I lay down on my stomach so that I appeared as small to him as I possibly could, and eased my legs down into the river, landing with a gentle splash by his shoulder. I kept my hand on his neck all the while so that I wouldn't have to shock him by replacing it.

'Now, how shall we do this, hmmm?' I murmured to the foal. 'You're not very big, but neither am I. I bet we weigh about the same, don't we? The water isn't deep enough here to make you any lighter, so that won't help, but you know, I think you can jump up onto the bank if you face it instead of trying to jump up sideways as you have been, it's only shoulder height to you. But how do I get you to face the bank without the river sweeping you away? Hmmm, little one?'

It came to me what I needed to do. All of a sudden, I was flooded with doubt. Could I do it? If I failed, the foal would be swept away and he would probably die. I felt him trembling beneath my hand, and my heart went out to him all over again. I threw my doubts aside. It was this or nothing. If he were down there much longer, he could go into shock or he might panic and end up in the current anyway.

I looked up at the brown mare. 'I know you don't understand what I'm saying to you, but I need to pretend you do. When he tries to escape me, encourage him like you did before. Okay?'

The mare stared at me, and I could have sworn her dark brown eyes were seeing the thoughts in my head as well as the small, hot, sweaty woman standing in the river below her. She blinked slowly and calmly, whickered to me and then looked back at her foal. I was stunned at the confidence I felt as a result.

'Here we go then.'

Without giving whatever spell she had cast on me a chance to break, I crouched down low and scuttled beneath the foal's neck. As I stood up on his other side, I launched into his flank with my shoulder, shocking him and throwing him off balance. I dug into the silty river bed with the toes of my sandals, and pushed as hard as I could. My heart was in my mouth as he almost keeled over sideways, but he got his footing and swung his rear end into the river. Here went all or nothing.

The mare whickered urgently to her foal as I plunged into the river behind him and once again dug my feet into its bed even as it fell sharply away beneath me. Spluttering water out of my mouth, I pushed with both hands against the foal's hindquarters. The mare continued to whicker to him, and I saw her trot a few steps away and then spin and trot back to us before trotting away again. I stood firm as the current tried to take me, pushing down into my toes as hard as I could and hoping upon hope that the silt would hold me in place long enough for him to escape.

'Go on, little one, go to your mother,' I shouted, and raised a hand, bringing it down as hard as I could on his rump.

All of a sudden, he leapt up onto the river bank. His mother welcomed him with a deeper, softer series of whickers, and immediately nudged him to her teat. The relief I felt that he was safe was short lived as one of my feet began to slide down behind me in the soft riverbed, then the other. I tried to bring my legs forward underneath me so that I could stand up, but the water impeded my movement and without the foal in front of me to lean against, I fell face first into the water. My fingers touched the silt that had let me down at the worst possible moment. I tried to push against it, but it gave way under my touch. I felt the current tug at my legs... and then take me.

Chapter Three

*B*ubbles left my mouth in place of the scream I tried to discharge as, now that the foal and his mother no longer filled my mind and senses, I was free to feel all of the panic that usually came so easily and continually to me.

The river pulled me along feet first, water pounding against my nostrils and only held at bay by my refusal to take a breath. I had to get my head above the water, I had to. I flailed with my arms and the water in front of my eyes lightened in colour, encouraging me to keep going.

When my head broke the water line, I coughed and heaved but managed only a few breaths before I was dragged under again by the current. I thrashed my arms about until I got my head back up above the water, and caught a breath as well as a glimpse of a rapidly approaching rock. I was below the water line again when my feet hit the rock, and managed to use it to push myself off to one side towards the bank... but not far enough. The current took me sideways. When I managed to get up above the water to take another few breaths, I paddled hard with my right arm and was just about able to turn so that I now faced downstream.

My relief at going along with the current instead of fighting it was short-lived. I swam to the surface and managed to stay there, only to see not one but a whole host of rocks looming in front of me. I swear I saw each and every glistening droplet of water that rose up into the air as a result of being slammed against the rocks, before they all rejoined the mad, untameable beast of a river as it hurtled its way onward.

I just had time to realise that however hard I swam, I wouldn't make it far enough towards the bank before hitting the rocks, when I hit one. My hand bent back on itself as my wrist and then my arm shattered. I was turned sideways as the relentless current tried to take me around the rock, and my shoulder was next to be slammed against it, followed by my head. I heard as well as felt my collarbone crack under the impact just before everything went black apart from what appeared to be a myriad of stars in front of my eyes.

It was as if I stepped apart from myself; from my terror, my rapidly breaking body and my pain. I knew that if I didn't do something very constructive very soon, I would die.

Gasping and spluttering, I managed to turn so that my back was against the rock. The current curled my legs up in front of me, so I took a deep breath and then flung myself to the side of the rock, kicking against it with everything I had as I went past. I sped through the water on my back, kicking with my legs and backstroking the water with my undamaged arm until I felt the current begin to release its hold on me. When a branch appeared in my blurred vision, I reached upwards, hoping to catch it before I went under. I grabbed it and held on tightly, screaming at the pain in my chest and other arm. The branch held, so I put my feet down hopefully. Relief flooded me as they came into contact with the river bed. I pulled on the branch and pushed with my feet, and stood up in water that was shoulder deep.

I turned towards the riverbank and pulled my way along the low-hanging branch to it, only letting go of the branch to take a hold further along it when I was sure I was stable on my feet. When I reached a narrow strip of shingle, I almost collapsed with a combination of relief, dizziness and pain.

The bank was too high for me to clamber up, so I looked left and right, and spied what appeared to be a small beach butting up to a much lower section of the bank some distance upstream. I took a deep breath and began to trudge towards it, cradling my shattered arm with my good one, and letting out sobs and gasps of pain with every footstep. My head pounded and I felt sick. I tried to ignore the blood that trickled down my cheek and dripped onto my shirt, and the fact that my hand looked as though it had been pulverised with a hammer.

I wondered how far the river had taken me. I didn't recognise my surroundings, but supposed that could be down to the unfamiliar viewpoint. I remembered dropping my back-sack where the herd of horses had been, and panic lanced through me. Had I broken the jars? Had the horses trampled them since the river had taken me from there? Would anyone find them and take them to either Hightown, Lowtown, or somewhere else? What had got into me to make me abandon them like that?

The foal. I saw him in my mind's eye, standing trembling by the bank as the river hurtled past him. I hoped he was okay and not suffering any after-effects of his trauma, but then I remembered that he had a good mother who would take care of him, just like mine had always taken care of me. But she wasn't here now. I was goodness knew where, injured and alone.

My sobs got louder as the shock of what had happened began to wear off, and the pain from my injuries became more of me.

My mind insisted on going back to the beginning of my near drowning and reliving the whole sorry event, second by second.

By the time I had reached the beach, knelt on the riverbank and shuffled away from it on my knees, I had relived the whole terrifying episode twice over. I looked over my shoulder towards the river and a fresh wave of terror caused me to shiver even as the hot sun beat down on me from above.

I cried and cried until I had exhausted myself. It didn't change anything. I was still alone, in excruciating pain, and too weak and dizzy to do anything about either. My sunhat had been swept away by the river and the sun was beating down heavily on the top of my bleeding head. I needed to get to my feet and either walk home or get into the shade of the tree that had saved me.

I managed to stand up and look around myself, flinching and blinking with every beat of my heart as it forced blood through my pounding head. Immediately, I realised where I was, and cursed. It would take a good half hour to walk back to where I had dropped my back-sack, and several hours to walk home. The thought of doing either exhausted me. I staggered to the tree, sat at its base and leant back against it in the shade. I closed my eyes, and sighed at the relative comfort of blackness.

'Quinta? Quinta, oh, thank goodness. What on earth happened?'

I didn't think my mother was shouting, yet her voice seemed to be coming from a long way away. How could I hear her then? Maybe I was just imagining I could hear her because I wanted so much for her to be with me. Why did I need her though? I was in my twenties, I shouldn't be so desperate for my mother. Desperate for my mother. A dark brown, practically black foal appeared from nowhere. His eyes were rolling and he was screaming for his mother, just like I wanted to.

Something took hold of my arm and began shaking me.

'Quinta, wake up, come on, love, you're scaring me. She's over here, someone bring a lantern, quickly, mine's nearly out.' My mother's voice seemed closer, yet I still couldn't see her. I remembered that I was imagining she was with me, and stopped trying to see her. All of a sudden, the blackness that surrounded me lightened slightly. 'Flaming lanterns, Quinta, oh, my daughter.' I tried to close my eyes to protect them from the light, but found that I couldn't since they were already closed. I opened them to see that my mother's eyes were wide as she peered into mine. 'Oh, thank the light, you're back with us.' She turned away from me. 'Nethin, HURRY!'

'I'm right here,' said a woman's voice. 'Just shuffle a little to the side, Sabrina, would you? That's it.'

'Oh, Nethin, I think we need a Bone-Singer too, look at her hand and arm. Where's Gable?'

'He's standing behind you, and has already begun work. Try to stay calm, we've got her now.'

I closed my eyes again as humming sounded nearby; a low, harsh tone, more like a tuneful growl, which began to gradually soften to a far more pleasant sound. The pain in my head lessened. Another harsh tone sounded, more nasal than the previous one, and also gradually changed to a smoother tone as the broken pieces of my collar bone were drawn back together and then fused to become whole.

I could have cried with relief, but couldn't find the strength. Now, Gable's humming was higher-pitched and almost a screech. I swear I felt the broken bone in my arm vibrate along with the noise Gable was so skilfully, so masterfully producing to resonate with the wrongness of my injury, giving him a connection with it along which he could send his healing intention so that the bone fragments realigned and fused back together. He adjusted his tone all the while so that it continued to resonate with the bone in its various and continuous stages of healing.

When he hummed with a tone and pitch that a mother might use to sooth her infant, I knew my arm was whole. My hand took a lot longer. Judging by the number of different tones that emanated from Gable before changing to smoother, more pleasant ones, most of the bones in my hand had shattered on impact with the rock.

Eventually, Gable said in his deep, soothing voice, 'One skull fracture, one broken clavicle, one broken ulna, six broken carpals, three broken metacarpals and nine broken phalanges all whole and strong once more. Well done, Quinta, you're a strong lass.'

My mother's voice sounded by my ear. 'Can we have that in plain words please, Gable?'

'Her head, collar bone, arm and hand are all sorted. Nethin, you're up,' Gable replied.

More humming followed, and the pain in my head disappeared completely, followed by that in my shoulder, arm and hand. I breathed a sigh of relief. 'Thank you, Nethin,' I whispered.

She chuckled. 'I'm a Tissue-Singer, it's what I do. You do know you're a Weaver and not a fish, don't you?'

I managed a smile and tried to sit up, but couldn't find the strength. Immediately, Gable's strong arm enfolded me and lifted my upper body from the ground. 'Steady there, Quinta, you're going to be weak for a while after all that healing,' he said softly.

'Thank you,' I whispered and reached out a hand to my mother, who knelt at my feet, her tear-streaked face tinted orange in the lanternlight. 'I'm sorry. The dyes. I left them on the bank upstream. There was a foal stuck between the river and the bank and I had to get into the water to help him jump out. The current took me and I hit a rock.' There was murmuring and whispering, and I noticed more faces peering down at me from behind my mother and Nethin.

'A foal? A baby horse?' my mother said. 'Where?'

'Upstream. It was just after lunch. He'll be gone by now, they all will. Long gone.' Any strength I had left fled at the realisation.

The horses were gone. For the few minutes I had been with them, I'd felt that I could do anything. I'd seen it in their eyes, I'd felt it from them in the way they regarded me, the way they behaved around me. They'd had confidence in me, I had believed them and as a result, I had done something I could never have otherwise done. And now I was just me again. How had they done that to me? And how had they then just carried on their way as if nothing had happened? They could easily have followed my journey from the riverbank, but they had got what they wanted from me and then left me to die. I had been one of them when they needed me, and now I was alone in my head again; alone with my worries and my fears and my weariness of both.

Gable, as tall and muscular as I was small, lifted me easily. 'Let's get you home.'

Chapter Four

*I*t was a week before I was back on my feet. A whole week of lying in bed, worrying what Xanthine thought of me now that her cloth order would be late, and feeling guilty at the extra work I had given my parents now that they were not only a pair of hands short in the workshop, but even further behind due to my mother having had to go to Hightown to collect the dyes which had thankfully been found and handed in to the Dyers at their workshop.

Over and over, I pictured the faces of those who had peered down at me out of the dark as I explained what had happened to me, and for each person, I thought about all of those with whom they were friendly, and then all of those with whom those people were friends. It didn't take long for me to prove to myself that which I should have known without having to prove it – everyone in Lowtown and Hightown would know what had happened. I couldn't decide why it mattered that they did, but whenever I thought about it, I panicked.

I had always tried so hard to keep my life simple so that I

didn't feel overwhelmed by its content, but the events down at the river had spiralled it out of control. While it was normal for me to feel exhausted within minutes of waking up, now that exhaustion followed me into sleep and even into the nightmares that plagued me, one after the other, night after night.

Sometimes, I was trying to rescue the foal but was too tired and weak to succeed; he tumbled along in the river with me and was swept away to his death while I survived. Other times, I didn't reach him before the river took him, and I would try to run along the riverbank as he screamed and flailed around in the current, but couldn't make my legs work and so was forced to watch the river take him away from me. The worst nightmares were those in which I relived the trauma almost exactly as it happened, but as I hadn't in real life, I saw the foal and his mother walk away from the river – from me – without a backward glance as I was swept away. It was those dreams from which I would wake screaming and crying, 'Noooooooooooooooo!' It was those dreams that left me feeling as if I never wanted to get out of bed again.

But I did eventually. I stayed in the house or its adjoining workshop, either working flat out to try to make amends for my absence, or resting when my parents forced me to.

'You can't carry on like this, Q. You know that, don't you?' my father said over dinner one evening.

My heart began to thump in my chest. 'Like what?'

He reached a hand over to me and rested it on the arm I had broken, his eyes, as dark as my own, full of concern. 'You're as white as a sheet and you have bags under your eyes. You don't sleep well, you're barely eating, you're working far too hard and you won't go out at all. I know how much you need your own space and company, and I know your accident has affected you but this isn't the way to recover from it. You need the sun on your face and you need to be out in the countryside; that always does you so much good. Then, hopefully, you'll sleep more soundly and the nightmares will begin to fade.'

'But everyone will want to talk to me about what happened, you know what they're like. The minute I set foot outside, I'll be the centre of attention. There'll be people wanting to walk with me, and invitations to tea, to dinner that I won't want to take up but won't be able to turn down because I can't handle upsetting anyone or even worrying I might have. It's all too hard.' My words tumbled out faster and faster so that by the time I had finished speaking, I was out of breath.

'Thinking and worrying about something is exhausting in itself and usually far worse than it actually happening, Quinta, you know that,' my mother said.

I blinked tears away and shook my head.

My mother tried again. 'How about you and I go for a little walk just as it's getting dark, when the rest of the village will be preparing for bed? Just for some fresh air? We don't have to go far.'

'I can't go near the river,' I said quickly.

'That's fine, we'll go out of the back door, then out over the back fence of the paddock. You won't even be able to see the river. How does that sound? We'll just go as far as you want to, and then we'll come back.' Her voice was so gentle, so soft, and her eyes so warm.

I felt myself calming down, and nodded. 'Okay, but I have a few more hours to do in the workshop first.'

She smiled. 'I'll come and fetch you when it's time.'

'It's been such a hot day but there's a lovely cool breeze now, this is going to do you the world of good,' my mother said, handing me a lantern. I looked at it in panic. 'Just take it,' she said, 'we can be no more than ten minutes if you like, but even so, it's nearly dark.'

I took a deep breath and accepted the lantern. I trusted my mother. If she said we would turn back whenever I wanted to, then we would. I followed her out of the back door, straining to hear any voices that would undoubtedly be directed towards me if I were detected outdoors. All I could hear were the infrequent sounds of sheep calling to one another, the rustling of leaves as the summer breeze wove its way through the branches of the trees that lined the back fence of our paddock, and the chirping of birds, a constant throughout the day but seeming louder in the tranquillity of twilight.

The tingling in my hands and feet that often accompanied my thoughts when I was panicking, began to subside, and I closed my eyes and breathed in the warm summer air. I smiled as I smelt the honeysuckle and jasmine with which the air was laced.

'Come on,' my mother whispered. I opened my eyes and followed her across the paddock, between the rails of its fence and out onto the grassland.

Twilight soon gave way to darkness and as my vision gradually became less reliable, I loved the fact that my senses of hearing, smell and touch became ever more heightened, their feedback overloading my mind with the gentle sounds, scents and caresses of the night.

Grasses and wildflowers brushed up against my legs as I searched for the next secure footstep with the toes of my sandals. An owl hooted very close by and I heard both the creak of the branch on which she had been resting as she pushed against it in order to take flight, and the sweep of her wings as she took to the air. A vixen called to her young, who squeaked in reply, their scent causing my nose to wrinkle in both disgust and delight.

We reached a field that had recently been scythed for hay, and I was assaulted both by the sweet smell of the cut grass and by the rustling sound of hundreds of tiny bodies negotiating their way through it, no doubt collecting fallen seeds.

When we found ourselves sheltered from the breeze, I revelled in the warmth of the air that embraced me, soothing my nose and airways before the cool breeze found us again, eager to share with us the scents it had picked up on its wanderings.

When my mother stopped to light the lanterns, I found myself desperate for her not to. 'We can see more in the dark than you think we can, Mum, and we can feel where it's safe to put our feet. Leave the lanterns out, please?'

I heard her take the breath that would precede her reply, but then sensed her hesitate beside me. 'I'll, um, I'll give that a go,' she said finally.

We walked for miles. I held my mother's hand as I had when I was a child, only now, it wasn't because I couldn't bear to be separated from her, but because I was so entranced by the beautiful, amazing and – as they felt to me – safe sensations of the night, I couldn't be sure to stay in her company.

When I heard water flowing nearby, it seemed far removed from the river that had nearly taken my life.

My mother stopped beside me. 'I'm sorry, love, I seem to have lost my bearings in the dark. We'll just turn around.'

I shook my head, though she couldn't see me. 'No, it's okay. I'm okay.'

We stood there for some time, listening to the river. It began to assault my senses every bit as much as when I had been submerged in it, and I found myself squeezing my mother's hand tightly. She rubbed my arm, bringing me back to the riverbank, back to myself. I clung to the sound of my shirt rubbing against my skin, to my mother's scent, to the feel of her hand, warm and soft in mine, and thought of the foal as his mother reassured him. I calmed as had he.

I wondered whether any of the water flowing past had touched the mare and foal or any of their herd before it reached where I was, or, if not, whether it might somewhere later on its journey. I shook my head as I felt the now familiar pain of loss that assaulted me whenever I thought about or dreamt of the horses who had included me as one of their own and then left me for dead. I would never know how they were, where they were, or whether the foal was okay after his ordeal. And I would never, ever go in that river again. With both subjects resolved in my mind, I felt a little stronger than of late.

'Shall we go back?' I said. 'I think I'll be able to sleep a bit better now.'

I did indeed sleep more easily from that point forward. But while my nights were less fraught, there was no improvement in my ability to negotiate my days. One merged into the next and before I knew it, years had passed during which I rarely left the house in daylight, and never to go back to Hightown; I had too many fears, too many worries to lay to rest in order to be able to get myself to go back along the riverside path.

I was happy in a funny sort of way. Up until my near-death experience, I had always fought myself and how I felt inside; I had tried to carry on with as near a normal life as I could, despite my inability to do any task, however small, without thinking of every possible way of doing it and every possible outcome, before I could actually get on and do it. I had struggled my way through interactions with other people, as a child remembering the manners my parents taught me and sticking to them when my every fibre wanted to escape and be by myself or with my parents, and as an adult avoiding people when I could, and keeping interactions as brief as possible when I couldn't.

Once I had physically recovered from being battered by a rock and almost drowning, I found myself unable to care what normal was. I just wanted to feel safe and free from as many of the things that worried or frightened me, as possible. It didn't bother me that I was the only one of my school year – in fact of any of those who had been at school during the years I was – not to have found a life partner and married. It didn't bother me that I still lived in the same house in which I had been born, and that I would likely die there. I worked the same hours every day, doing the same jobs on a revolving basis, week in, week out, so that I didn't have to think about what I was doing.

I walked every night, occasionally with my mother but usually on my own. It was the only time during my waking hours that my thoughts ceased their usual tumultuous battering of my mind, and I felt at peace. I slept for seven hours each night, and as the weeks, months and years passed, my nightmares receded. When they did manifest, it was always the same one; I saved the foal from the river and then watched him and his mother walk away from me. The pain was always worse than the terror of the river subsequently taking me, and each time I woke from it, I would feel a physical pain in my heart at their loss.

Four years, almost to the exact date, after they had left me for real, the nightmare returned with a vengeance. I topped the hill and saw the horses milling around in slow motion below me. Their muscles bulged and relaxed as they trotted around one another, tossing their heads in agitation. When they came to a brief halt to look towards where the mare nudged her foal as she tried to encourage him to escape the river, their nostrils flared and their ears flickered back and forth. I saw every single droplet of water as it dripped from those standing still, or was flung through the air by those in motion. I heard every snorted breath, every shuddering whicker of concern, every thud of hooves on the ground, as if I were standing among them, which suddenly, I was.

Heat radiated off their bodies to such an extent that I felt enclosed and suffocated by it, yet safe in a way I never did when I was awake. I could smell their sweat, their anxiety, and I knew I had to act. I was part of them. I could help them.

I tried to walk towards the bank but my legs were so heavy, I dropped to my hands and knees and crawled. Even then, it took forever and all the while, the horses shifted, sweated and snorted around me.

Suddenly, I was kneeling alongside where the brown mare stood looking down at her foal. He was dancing about on his feet, and I sensed that it helped him to feel as if he were moving, even though he wasn't going anywhere. When he saw me, he calmed as if he had been waiting for me. He reached for me, sniffing my hands as they rested on the bank, then looking up into my eyes. Just like when his mother had looked at me during the real event, it was as if he saw right into me and knew exactly what I was thinking.

I was by his side in the water, then I was pushing his hindquarters out into the river and throwing myself after them to lean into him, supporting him so that he could jump out. When he did, rather than going to his mother, he turned to face me. I stood in the river, solid on my feet while the water lashed around me, trying to take me with it. I was calm. I was strong. As long as the foal looked at me with such love, such trust in his eyes, I knew I could withstand anything. I could do anything. Then he turned and walked away with his mother.

Pain and devastation took my strength from me. I was immediately swept off my feet and taken by the evil, tumultuous water. To begin with, terror ensured that I fought it with everything I had, but then I realised that I didn't have very much. I didn't want to fight it. The horses had left me too many times now. I stopped struggling and flailing around, and let the water do what it would.

All of a sudden, I was aware that I wasn't alone. Something was pulling at me from the inside out, as if my body were irrelevant and all I had to do was allow myself to go with it and my body would somehow follow and be safe.

My eyes flicked open. I couldn't move, and realised that I was tightly wrapped and tangled in my bedsheet. I was also drenched in sweat, so much so that for a moment, I actually believed I had been in the river. As I came to properly, I recognised the stone walls, the bedside table, desk, wardrobe and chest of drawers of my bedroom, all tinted pale blue in the moonlight that streaked in through my uncurtained window.

I untangled myself from my sheet and sat up, feeling strangely calm. Why was I so calm? I'd just had my worst nightmare, and usually that resulted in me either being shaken awake, screaming, by one or both of my parents, or waking up with a start, sobbing and shaking and feeling like the world had just ended. Either way, I was always heartbroken all over again at having been deserted by the horses, then angry at them for being so selfish, so heartless as to take what they wanted from me before leaving me to die. Yet this time, I didn't feel abandoned, even though I clearly remembered the horses leaving me as they always did. I felt included, as if they were still with me.

I suddenly realised why; the pulling sensation I had experienced in the dream was still there. The instant I became aware of it, it strengthened. I put a hand to my forehead, to my chest, to my heart, to my stomach, trying to decide which part of me was feeling the sensation, but I couldn't decide. Whatever was pulling at me wasn't pulling my body, I suddenly realised. It was pulling my mind.

Everything I had ever learnt, dreamt, felt and experienced collided in my head. Where normally that would have left me confused, overwhelmed and fearful, this time I found myself more certain, more confident and more ecstatic than I had ever been about anything. I was being tugged. By a horse.

Chapter Five

My euphoria lasted mere seconds. This couldn't be happening to me. I couldn't leave my parents, my work, my home, my life, to go on a quest to find the horse who was tugging me. Where would I sleep? What if I couldn't sleep? What if I injured myself on the way? What if I had to cross a river, or even walk near one for any length of time? What if the tugging receded and I didn't know where to go? What if I never found the horse? What if I did and we bonded, what then? I couldn't be one of the Horse-Bonded; where they travelled between the villages, passing on their horses' wisdom to those who asked for it, I was barely able to look anyone other than my parents in the eye. And I certainly couldn't go to The Gathering, home of the Horse-Bonded, and live with people I didn't know, wouldn't be able to talk to, and would have to avoid; it would be like having bees buzzing around my head all of the time with nowhere to go to escape. I couldn't be at home there but I couldn't come and live back here with a horse in tow, so what would I do? Where would I go? What would my life be? What should I do?

I was still sitting up in bed with my thoughts lashing around in my head, beating me from the inside out, when the sky lightened. I heard my parents rising and moving around, but jumped when my mother poked her head around my bedroom door.

'Time to… oh, you're awake. Quinta, what is it, love? Another nightmare?'

I couldn't move. If I did, my feet would want to follow my mind to the horse, I knew it, and I couldn't go. I was as certain of that as I was that I was being tugged in the first place. I managed to move my eyes so that I looked up at my mother, and as always, felt a little calmer.

'I'm being tugged,' I whispered to her. 'By a horse. But I can't go. I can't.'

She rushed to my side and sat on the bed, taking both of my hands in hers. 'You're being tugged? Quinta, that's wonderful, I'm so happy for you, so happy, so proud, so… wait a minute.' She ran to the door and called, 'Birch, come quickly, something marvellous is happening.' She hurried back to sit by me and put an arm around my shoulders. 'I know this will be difficult for you, but we'll get everything ready together, we'll talk everything through and we'll find a way for you to leave on your quest. You do see that this is the best thing that could have happened to you, don't you?'

I shook my head almost imperceptibly, not trusting myself to move any more than that. 'It's the worst. I can't leave here, Mum. I can't even get dressed by myself most mornings, you know that. I've only managed to get through as much of my life as I have because, between us, we've removed as many things from it as we can that cause me a problem, and you and Dad help with the rest.'

'But your horse will do all of that for you and more. You know what the Horse-Bonded are like when they pass through here with their horses – they're wise, confident, capable…'

'Everything I'm not,' I whispered as my father knocked on the door.

'Come on in,' my mother said. 'Quinta's being tugged, isn't that fantastic?'

My father appeared with toothpaste around his mouth, which widened into a foamy grin. 'It is indeed. Congratulations, Q, you'll be the pride of Lowtown.'

Panic wouldn't allow me to remain still any longer. I flung my legs out of bed and stood up, my fear causing the pulling on my mind to be of secondary prominence within it for a moment. 'I don't want to be the pride of Lowtown. I don't want to be anything, I can't cope with being anything more than a Weaver who lives quietly with her parents, you both know that.'

'What I know, love,' my mother said, 'is that this isn't enough for you. We aren't enough for you.'

I opened my mouth to argue, but she said, 'Hear me out. You're clever, you're warm, you're compassionate and you're sensitive to the point that you get overwhelmed easily. If you hadn't worked yourself into a frenzy about being tested for the Skills, you would have shown aptitude for at least one of them, probably more. Instead, you chose to apprentice to us as a Weaver because it was the safest option, but it wasn't the best. Your father and I have tried to create an environment in which you can flourish, but all we've succeeded in doing is the opposite. We've watched you shrink further and further inside yourself and we've been powerless to help you.

'I see the look in your eyes when you talk about the wild horses you met. Even when your memories and dreams terrify you, the horses within them don't. They're the only ones who light the spark in you that brings you, the real you, out of yourself. Imagine being with a horse all the time, and not just being with one, but being bonded with one, so that the two of you can communicate mind to mind. It'll be the making of you. It'll ensure that you become everything you can be, I know it.'

'Well, I know that horses can't be trusted. I trusted a whole herd of them. They made me feel included and safe while I was of use to them, then as soon as I'd done what they wanted, they left me alone to die. How do you know the horse tugging me won't do the same? How do you know that if I survive long enough by myself to find and bond with this horse, I won't be abandoned again the moment I've fulfilled my purpose?'

'How do you know a horse is tugging you?' my father asked.

'I can feel it. It's like everything I am is being pulled out of my body in that direction.' Without turning, I pointed behind myself. 'It started while I was dreaming and it continued after I woke up. It's getting stronger, but I can't follow it, I just can't.'

'Were you afraid in the dream? When the tugging started, I mean,' my mother asked.

I thought back. 'I was afraid beforehand. The horses had abandoned me again and I was drowning again. Then I felt the tugging and I felt… safe.'

'And then you woke up and started worrying until you panicked,' my mother said gently. 'What happens if you concentrate on the tugging? How do you feel then?' She smiled. 'You don't even need to answer. Your eyes have gone soft, just like when you talk about the horses. You're worried that your Bond-Partner might leave you, but what if that never happens? What if you find one another, you bond and you just have an amazing time being Bond-Partners? Think about the mare and foal. Can you imagine anything more magical than spending every single day with one of them?'

Despite myself, my heart went out to the two who had touched me so deeply, and I felt as if all I wanted to do was throw on some clothes – any clothes, not necessarily those upon which I finally decided after considering the consequences of each and every eventuality – and run towards the horse who was tugging me. But then panic pierced through my enthusiasm, shattering it into tiny pieces, none of which I could grab hold. 'What if the horse who is tugging me is nothing like those I met?'

'What if he or she is?' my father said.

I considered. If only I could know for sure what the horse was like, before I left. But I kind of did. Safe. It was the word I kept coming back to when I thought back to how I had felt when the tugging started in my dream. 'Would you come with me? In case it all goes wrong and I need to come home again?'

My mother and father looked at one another and I could sense the unspoken words carried within their gazes. 'No, love,' my mother said. 'We've hindered you for long enough. It's time for you to fly. You can do it, I know you can.'

I sighed. 'Even if I go, I can't have a Quest Ceremony. I can't have the whole village turning out to see me on my way, I'll never be able to leave the house. If I go, I'm going once it's dark.'

'Everyone will be disappointed once they find out...' my mother began, but stopped suddenly at a glance from my father. She nodded. 'We understand, and everyone else will too. You'll be needing to go tonight before the tugging on your mind becomes unbearable, which by all accounts it will if you linger. Birch, will you be okay in the workshop on your own while Quinta and I gather together everything she's going to need?'

I shook my head. 'You have a huge order to fulfil, you'll need my help, I can't go, I'll ignore...'

'You'll do no such thing,' my mother said gently. 'Orders can always wait, especially for something this important. You needn't worry about us, Quinta, it's the summer, remember? There are Apprentices looking for placements. We'll take on a couple and see where we go from there, and all the while, we'll have our pride in our daughter to keep us going.'

My father hurried over to me with his arms out wide. 'You too, Sabrina,' he said, beckoning to my mother with his fingers. He easily enveloped us both in a hug. 'Wherever you go, whatever you do, we're right behind you,' he said in my ear. My mother's arm tightened around me in agreement. My father released us both. 'Now, set to it, you two, you have a midnight Quest Ceremony for three to organise.'

Three times during that day, I ran to my room, shut the door and barricaded it with my bedside table. Three times, the pulling on my mind strengthened considerably until my mother managed to talk me back out. Each time, she reminded me how I had felt when I was with the horses, how I appeared when I spoke of the mare and foal, and how I would feel when I was with my Bond-Partner. The tugging on my mind reinforced every word she spoke.

The third time, I needed only minimal persuading to find my way to the memory of the horses I had met in the past, and to my hope for the horse awaiting me in the future. I was relieved to follow both the tugging and my mother back downstairs to where we finally had everything gathered together that I would need. We packed it all into a back-sack that I could just about carry, and then began preparing the celebratory evening meal she insisted the three of us would share before I left.

It was my favourite; a myriad of different roasted vegetables, each one seasoned differently so that the meal as a whole was a delightful assault on my taste buds. My mother always cooked it for me when I was struggling to eat due to a worry through which

I had been unable to work my way however much I obsessed about it, and usually, it meant I managed to eat a decent meal.

That evening, however, I struggled to finish my plateful. The tugging on my mind had increased to a level that made it difficult to remain still, let alone sit down and eat, even obliterating the fears that could still have prevented me from leaving. While it was a relief to have a break from the mental gymnastics in which my mind usually engaged, the desperation to move in an unknown direction whilst forcing myself to be stationary and eat, and whilst also trying to hold what might be my last ever conversation with my parents, was anything but.

When darkness finally fell, I was desperate to get going, even though my stomach began to churn and my heart to pound as I pulled on my boots.

'You'll still be able to feel the tugging through everything else that normally fills your mind when it's dark?' my mother said.

I almost laughed. 'It's pretty much all I can feel at the moment. I can barely think straight, it's so strong.'

She smiled and nodded. 'Perfect. This horse of yours knows what he's doing. Or she. Do you know which?'

I shook my head. 'No. Only that the longer I stand here, the less capable I'm going to be of even speaking. I really have to go, don't I? I'm really going to do this.'

She pulled me into a hug. 'Yes, love, you are.'

My father hugged me too and then helped me on with the back-sack that was full to the brim with clothes and food, and adorned with cooking utensils and also hunting gear that I was terrified I might have to use. Then he reached into his pocket and handed some of its contents to my mother before turning back to me.

'I made these for you today,' he said. 'They carry all of our love for you, and our wishes that your quest to find your horse goes well. Take them with you and know that we're with you every step of the way.' He hung a tiny horseshoe made of green, twisted fabric and suspended from a thin metal wire, through the arm of my shirt. My mother began to hang more of the tiny ornaments, of all different colours, to my shirt, shorts, back-sack and even a few in my hair.

When the two of them had finished, they each took one of my hands in both of their own. My mother smiled at me even as tears poured down her face.

My father blinked his own tears away and nodded. 'You'll never know how proud we are of you. Go on, Q. Fly.'

My mother kissed my cheek and gave me a gentle push towards the back door. 'Go,' she whispered.

And I did.

If I had thought the pull on my mind was strong before, it was nothing to that which beset me the very second I moved away from my parents. Any beliefs I'd had that my mind was confined to my head were obliterated as my body moved all of its constituent parts with a strength and purpose I'd never before experienced, without any conscious effort by me.

The very tiniest part of my mind that was left to observe what was happening to me, was fascinated. I marvelled at the freedom from worry I experienced as I strode across the grassland, away from Lowtown. The sounds, scents and feel of the night that had always calmed me seemed even more intense than normal now that the immediate and urgent task of finding my horse was leaving me no room to consider, to ponder, to even think. Never before had I experienced such total peace of mind, and I didn't want it to stop, not even for a minute.

I didn't hesitate to step away from the moonlit grassland, into the absolute darkness of the woods; I trusted my other four senses to form a picture of that which surrounded me in the darkness when my eyes couldn't tell me, and I was rapidly becoming used to feeling strong and capable in the absence of any ability to think about anything else.

I wasn't surprised when I stepped out of the forest with not a scratch on me, and was only marginally shocked as I sank a little into soft, sandy soil. I recognised the grey outlook before me as more grassland, however the softness beneath my feet was very different from the clay soil – rock solid in the summer, deep and cloying once the rains fell – with which I was familiar. The tiny part of me that still observed my actions, feelings and progress marvelled at my immediate acceptance of the unfamiliar territory and conditions underfoot. I strode onward, weary in body now, but exhilarated in mind.

When the sun appeared over the horizon in front of me, I stopped briefly to take off and pack my overshirt in place of the white, wide-brimmed sunhat I placed on my head and pulled down to my brow. I took out a food parcel and made sure my water flask was still hanging in place on the outside of my back-sack, which I then re-shouldered. I marched on my way, enjoying the sensation of fluid bursting into my mouth as I chewed on summer berries, and the smell and crunchiness of the nuts that completed my breakfast. Everything was brighter, louder, stronger smelling and more colourful when I was free from thought.

I walked through the heat of the morning without stopping, until the chance presented itself to refill my water flask just as it was nearly empty. I smiled at the fact that the stream flowing out of the hill before me, from which I cupped water in my hands to wash my face and drink before dunking my flask, had appeared without me having to search for it in a state of high anxiety and drama. Maybe I didn't have to worry everything into resolution?

A useful observation.

I nodded in agreement with the thought before I realised that it wasn't mine and that further, my mind was suddenly my own again.

My heart began to pound in my rapidly tightening chest, and my mouth and throat became dry. I tried to swallow but couldn't. My stomach churned and I felt an urgent need to empty my bowels. Why had the tugging stopped? Had I been abandoned in the middle of nowhere, just as I had feared? Where should I go? What should I do?

Remember your observation.

I stood frozen to the spot. What was happening?

I am happening. We are happening. Everything is happening regardless of concern or lack of it. The words appeared in my mind in the same way as those before them – as if I had thought them myself even though I knew I hadn't.

Movement caught my eye and I glanced up towards the brow of the hill to see a horse cantering down the hillside towards me.

Chapter Six

It couldn't be. It was impossible. Of all the horses in the world, it couldn't be him. But it looked like him – at least the horse hurtling down the hillside towards me looked just like I had always imagined he would when he was fully grown; small and dainty like his mother, but darker, black where she was brown, with brown around his eyes and nostrils. I squinted into the distant hills to see if I could spot his mother, his herd, anything that would confirm my suspicion, but everything was still apart from the horse who was now almost upon me.

You need no other confirmation than that which you feel.

I don't trust how I feel. I felt safe when I was with horses before but they used me and then left me to drown. I frowned, wondering how it was that I found it so easy, so natural to think a thought to someone, let alone to be confident that they would both receive and understand it.

The horse slowed and then skidded to a stop in front of me so that a wave of sand sprayed my legs. *We left you to learn.* He was blowing hard, and sweat ran down the black hair on his face and flanks. He stood still as I stepped to the side so that I could see the back of his left ear. The circular patch of white hair at its base that I had seen over and over in my dreams as I crouched on the bank, looking down at him, was also damp with sweat.

'It is you,' I breathed, my heart melting. Then it hardened. 'Why did you tug me? You left me four years ago, you and your mother and your herd, and now you want me again? What is it you need me for this time?'

The time has come for you to continue your learning. In time everything will make sense. The horse blinked and then turned to walk towards the pool of water.

'That's it? After all this time, that's it? No gratitude to me for saving you? No apology for what happened to me, that could so easily have happened to you if I hadn't stepped in? Nothing?'

The horse swished biters away from his hind legs as he lowered his head to drink. *Your perception of events is merely that.*

My perception? 'MY PERCEPTION?' I yelled. 'So I just PERCEIVED that I almost drowned, did I? I PERCEIVED that I broke my hand, my arm, my collarbone and MY HEAD?'

Water dripped from his chin as he looked back at me. He hadn't yet quenched his thirst, I could feel it without having the remotest idea how, every bit as easily as I could feel his determination that I would understand the importance of what he was about to tell me next. *Your memory of the event is dominated by the negative emotions you chose to feel. It will serve you to place your focus on other aspects of the episode for they will lead you to the lesson you have chosen to learn. Once you have identified the lesson you will progress.*

He turned back to the pool and continued to drink, leaving me staring at him in astonishment and confusion. I went over and over his thought in my mind as I was so adept at doing with details that were usually trivial, however on this occasion were anything but –

a fact that I knew in my very core. It wasn't just that he had stared at me while imparting the information, it was the sense I'd had from him as he was doing it. He knew its importance to me. He didn't believe, he didn't think, he didn't suppose, he one hundred percent knew, leaving me in no doubt that what he had told me was true, and only adding to my confusion, since I had no clue what he meant.

I went over and over it all until I hit upon the only part I thought I could achieve. *Focus on other aspects of the episode.* I was just about to go through it all again to check and then double check I was still in agreement with myself when I felt strong, unequivocal approval. My mind fell strangely silent, pulled up short by the unexpected but welcome intrusion.

The horse finished drinking and began to graze without looking at me. I shrugged out of the straps of my back-sack and lowered it to the ground, then blinked and shook my head at my complete lack of consideration as to whether that would be a good thing to do. The horse raised his head and stared at me, bringing me back to his instruction before my mind could wander further.

I sat down and leant against my pack, reaching back to push a ladle hanging from it to one side so that it ceased digging into my back. *Focus on other aspects of the episode. Okay.* I took myself back to when I had first caught sight of the horses, as I had done so many times before. I experienced all over again the fear of them while I was at a distance, and then the feeling of total inclusion and security once I was among them. I tried to move on to what had happened next, but found I couldn't. It was as if I were frozen in place in my memory of being a member of the herd. One of them. Safe. Regarded. Included. Protected. Secure in who I was, in my strength, my capability, my confidence.

I frowned. How had I never considered how peculiar that was? Not just the fact that I had felt all of those things whilst amongst the horses when I'd never come close to feeling that way amongst people, even my parents, but that the herd had given me the opportunity to do it. I had learnt about horses and the Horse-Bonded at school, as did all children of The New, but I had never heard of people interacting with horses other than those who were Bond-Partners to the Horse-Bonded. Wild horses kept themselves to themselves until the odd one left a herd and selected a human with whom to bond and impart their wisdom. Nowhere had I read or heard of a single wild horse, let alone a whole herd, tolerating a human in their immediate vicinity.

As soon as I reached my observation, my mind unfroze and I was free to move on to the knowing I had experienced that the brown mare wanted me to help her baby, that she understood what I would do, and that she would help me by keeping her foal – who now stood grazing in front of me – calm and in position until I was myself in place to support him so that he could jump out. She had seen right into me, I remembered that now. She had seen everything she needed to know and had trusted me, giving me confidence in myself as a result; confidence that had enabled me to forget how frightened I was of everything and save her foal. Confidence that I had forgotten about since then.

I didn't need the horse to hold my mind in place while I considered how that was possible. How on earth could I have neglected to remember that I hadn't done what I did by accident, or by thinking it through until I had nothing left to distract me from acting, or even because someone told me to, but by being full of confidence to act upon the solution I saw straight away?

I remembered the strength my determination had given me as I held firm against both the current and the struggling foal, until he was safe on the river bank. I remembered the clarity of thought I'd experienced that had allowed me to escape the river even after the atrocities it had inflicted upon me. Even without the horses near me, even without the mare to give me confidence, I'd seen what I needed to do and done it. I'd never done that before or since, yet on that day, I'd done it twice in little more than twenty minutes.

The injuries I had sustained, the pain – both physical and emotional – I had felt, the trauma of the event all paled into insignificance as my mind flitted between the horses and the river. Both had, in their own way, enabled me to see that I was capable of far more than I had ever supposed.

The horse continued to graze. *While that is true it is not the lesson.*

So what is?

Where was your attention when you acted to help me out of my predicament? When you acted to escape your own?

I thought back. *It was with the herd to begin with, then with your mother, then with you. When I was in the river, it was on my injuries, my body and the rock.*

What were you thinking?

I wasn't, really, there wasn't time. You were in danger and then I was. I acted on instinct. On how I felt.

The horse looked up from his grazing and directly at me, and I waited for the momentous thought that I assumed must be about to come from him. It never arrived.

Did I miss something?

You did. But not from me.

Do you ever give a straight answer?

Always. If you find yourself confused then adjust your interpretation.

I felt exhausted all of a sudden. *I haven't slept in more than twenty-four hours. Can't you just tell me what I need to know?*

You would no more hear it than anything else anyone has ever told you. You have the answer. Your mind resists acknowledging it because of the change it heralds but acknowledge it you must for only then can we move forward.

But I'm so tired.

Your body indeed requires rest but that is not what prevents you from understanding. Focus. You have the answer.

He knew I did, I could feel it just like before. He was as confident that I would arrive at it as he was that the grass he had eaten would give him energy and the water he drank would sustain him. I thought back to our conversation, glad for once of my ability to rerun situations over in my mind in minute detail. My tiredness evaporated when understanding dawned.

You were in danger and then I was. I acted on instinct. On how I felt.

There is the lesson. Feel more. Think less. Confidence comes not from ensuring you have removed all risk from your existence but from knowing that you have the solution inside of you to whatever presents itself.

But I don't know that. Just because I saved us both, it doesn't mean I can deal with anything and everything.

You did not save us both for in truth we did not require saving. You merely set yourself on a path to learning the lesson you have now identified.

We didn't require saving? Are you for real?

In one sense I am. In many others I am not. The same applies to you.

I put my hands to my face and sighed into them. I decided that his latest assertion would have to wait for another time. *Please explain why we didn't require saving. We could both have died. You were terrified and so was I.*

Everything occurred as was necessary for your learning. It is a human tendency to attach emotion and commotion to situations that are merely steps on the path towards greater understanding.

The horse turned and began to walk across the bottom of the hill. *We will find shade in which to rest.*

It wasn't an instruction, a suggestion, even, but a simple statement of fact. Pleasure flushed through me at his inclusion of me in his future, however confusing and uncertain that future may prove to be.

Already you are changing, he noted. Then he added, *Already I am changing.*

You are?

Now that you have acknowledged our bond it has settled into place. Your energy affects mine as surely as mine affects yours.

I reached his side and walked by his head. *That can't be good for you, I'm a mess.*

The patterns within you that seem substantial and insurmountable affect me little. It is the adjustments I make in order for us to coexist to which I refer. I welcome them as I welcome our bond. As I welcome my time with you.

He was so sincere, so beautiful, so utterly incredible that I thought my heart would burst. *And I welcome my time with you.*

As I walked beside him, I settled into my habit of going over everything that had happened recently. Where normally I felt compelled to do it as a way of assuring myself that I had left no loose ends about which I needed to worry, and my mind would race from one part of my experience to the next and then back again to check I really had examined everything that had happened, before I could move on, I now found myself stopping at each and every moment since I had first heard the horse in my head, and slowly, carefully perusing everything I had experienced. I even had the mental space to sense that he was with me in my mind, observing my thoughts as I thought them, reminding me that he was with me in mind as well as body and helping me to accept the change in myself; reassuring me that it was a positive one.

I jumped when the heat suddenly became less intense and I no longer had to squint at the glare from the grass and sand in front of me. The horse wandered to the trunk of the enormous larch tree to whose shade he had led us both, and rubbed his neck up and down against it.

I stood and watched him, fascinated that I could feel both the itch on his neck, and his relief as he scratched it. I immersed myself in my sense of him and discovered that he was sore too.

You have a cut on your heel, I told him. *May I have a look? I can help.*

That would be beneficial. He stepped away from the tree and watched me as I approached him.

I went straight to his left hind leg and crouched down by his foot. Sure enough, there was a cut that ran almost the width of his heel. It had scabbed over but the scab had split, and blood and pus were leaking out.

It doesn't look deep, but it's infected, I told him, not sure if he knew what that meant. *I'll clean it and then I have some unguent I can put on it that will kill the infection and help it to heal. There's sand in it, which won't be helping, I'll have to try and wrap it to stop more getting in.*

The horse didn't respond, but I sensed his trust in me. Anything I did would be fine. Absolutely anything. My mind wanted to race, to examine all of the different choices that anything included, but the sense I had of him stopped me. *Feel more, think less,* that was what he had told me to do. It was a wrench, remaining in the quietness of my mind when it was all for running away with me – like not blinking when I needed to, or holding my breath for longer than was comfortable – but the longer my mind was still and just sitting with the fact that I already knew what to do, enjoying it almost, the less I felt the need to do anything else.

I stood up. *I don't know how you're doing this to me, but thank you,* I told him and reached a hand out, intending to stroke his neck. He turned his head and touched the back of my hand with his top lip, wiggling it from side to side ever so gently. I completely lost my heart to him. I stroked his neck with my other hand, scratching it where he had rubbed it against the tree. He wiggled his lip harder on my other hand in response, and I sensed his enjoyment.

When I could feel that his itch had been well and truly scratched, I set about unpacking my back-sack until I had found the parcel of herbal preparations and unguents my mother had collected from Lowtown's Herbalist before I left. They were intended for use on humans, but I could think of no reason why they wouldn't work on a horse. My horse, I decided with a smile as I emptied a measure of herbs into my food bowl, added some water from my flask as per the instructions on the packet, and waited until I could smell that the herbs' properties had infused the water.

My horse flinched as I cleaned his cut, but he didn't move. His trust in me was as absolute as my trust in myself had always been non-existent. When I was satisfied that I had cleaned away all of the dirt and nastiness, I applied healing unguent from a small jar, placed a dressing over the top and wrapped a short bandage around the bulb of his heel and the top of his hoof, securing it with a safety pin.

You can't move around too much, I told him, *in fact it would be better if you didn't move at all until you really have to.*

We will rest, he agreed. He relaxed his left hind leg so that it rested on the front of his hoof, lifting the cut further away from the sand.

Do you need water? I can pour some into my bowl for you?

We will rest, he repeated and half closed his eyes.

I looked around us both. Trees and bushes dotted the grassy, sandy plains. What if they hid danger? Wild cats and dogs were rarely seen, but they were out there somewhere, what if somewhere were here?

There are no predators in the vicinity. I would know. I will keep watch. Rest, my horse told me.

My mind began to race in its quest to find all possible arguments to his statements.

Trust me as I trusted you, my horse instructed. *Rest.*

My arguments evaporated. I sat down at the foot of the giant larch and leant back against its trunk. No. I wouldn't rest very well like that. I shifted around the trunk a little so that I was directly in front of my horse's front legs. I curled up around them and rested my head on my back-sack. I trusted him as he had trusted me. My eyes closed without effort.

Chapter Seven

I sat up with a start. Where was I? I breathed in the scents of the night as a distant owl hooted in the darkness, but the sensations that normally soothed me did nothing to quench my panic. My stomach felt as if it were plunging around within my body, continually exchanging places with my heart. My head spun and I thought I was going to be sick. I had been asleep out here. A blessedly deep sleep, but one that could have led to my death; anything could have happened. Anything could still happen.

A low whicker sounded nearby, followed by the soft thud of footsteps. My horse. The events of the previous day came flooding back. I was Horse-Bonded. No, no, no, I couldn't be that; I was a wreck. I couldn't be out here in the middle of nowhere, I couldn't be away from my home, my work, from everything that was familiar. I couldn't go to The Gathering, which was no doubt where my horse would soon have us heading, I just couldn't. There would be other Horse-Bonded there, lots of them by all accounts. I wouldn't know what to say to them, I'd never fit in, I'd never be able to…

Hot breath warmed the side of my face and neck even as something else wove its way into my mind, taking hold of each and every thought, each and every tangled worry, and smoothing them all out so that they slipped past one another and then slipped away from me.

What is your condition in this moment? My horse's thought was as gentle as his warm breath that continued to soothe me.

I'm fine. The thought escaped me before I had a chance to argue with myself. I was incredulous. How could I be fine? My life was spiralling away from me, I was Horse-Bonded, I'd have to go to The Gath…

You are here. With me.

I calmed as he smoothed my fears away once more. *Well, yes, I guess I'm fine here while I'm here with you, but…*

So you are fine.

I couldn't argue because it was true. But it wouldn't be for much longer, not once we…

How are you in this moment?

I paused. *Um, I guess I'm still fine.*

How about now?

I stood up and brushed sand from my shorts. *Still fine.*

And now?

I'm okay. How many more times are you going to ask me?

As many times as proves necessary. How are you in this moment?

I sighed. *Fine.*

And now?

I'm okay. I'm really okay, can we stop this?

Do you remain so even now?

Flaming lanterns, yes, I'm fine. It isn't right now I'm worried about though, it's the future.

Yet when we reach the future it will be the present and when you are in the present you are…

'Fine,' I said out loud. I frowned, trying to find a hole in his reasoning. I found one and latched onto it. *I haven't always been fine though. How do I know I always will be?*

You have always been fine. You merely failed to notice because your mind was thinking about the future instead of feeling its way through the present which in truth is all there is.

I folded my arms in the darkness. *I wasn't fine when I was drowning.*

You were finer than at any other moment except one for you were focused exclusively on the present. The force of the river allowed you no time to be anywhere else. You stepped aside from your fear and allowed it to increase the speed of your thoughts and actions instead of ruling them. That is its proper use.

How do you know what happened? You weren't there, you just left me to it.

I have been with you always. I appeared to you when the time was right for your learning to begin and I have appeared again because it is time for it to continue.

I could feel that he was telling me the truth. *How is that possible?* I strained my eyes, but could still only make him out as a shape that was darker than the darkness that surrounded us both. *Who are you? You look like a small, beautiful horse, but that isn't all you are, it can't be.*

You must decide that for yourself.

If I had felt overwhelmed by him while he was tugging me, it was nothing compared with the all-consuming sense I had of him as he unfolded in my mind like a flower opening in the sunshine.

He was immense. How he managed to pack himself into such

a dainty body was beyond me. He knew everything and he was everywhere, yet I was his sole focus. I gasped. He had chosen his body because its small size and stature matched my own and would be less intimidating to me. Because it would be born when I needed him. Because he could help me and between us, we could help others. Everything about him was concerned with what he could do for others – but mostly what he could do for me.

You weren't trapped by the river by accident, I observed. *You jumped down there on purpose. You were only a few days old. You came into the world and within a few days, you risked your life so I would find the courage to be among horses, so I would have an opportunity to know what it is to feel strong. Capable.*

So that you would know who you are when love anchors you in the present.

'My other finest moment,' I whispered. 'You said my finest moment save for one was when I was drowning. I saved myself out of fear but I saved you out of love.'

Fear can assist survival. Love gives survival a purpose.

And your purpose is me, just as my purpose is you now. My heart had long since ceased its turbulence and now I thought it would burst out of my chest with everything I felt for the dark shape that stood in front of me. *You're Noble, that's who you are. This is how the other Horse-Bonded name their horses, isn't it? For what they see in them? Their names make sense now. Noble doesn't seem a big enough word for who I know you are, but it's the best I can come up with.*

It will serve us well. Noble shuffled away from me and almost immediately, I heard him begin to tear at grass and grind it with his teeth.

I was wide awake and also starving, I suddenly realised, so I felt around in my back-sack for a food parcel and began to eat alongside my horse. Every time my mind began to wander and worry about the future, I focused on the sound of Noble grazing, on the sense of him in my mind, on his dark outline against the lesser darkness of the grassland, and reminded myself that I was fine.

As soon as the sky began to lighten, I rushed to Noble's side and peered down at his bound heel. I was relieved to see that my bandage had remained in place throughout the afternoon and night since I had applied it, but not surprised; I had felt how carefully my horse moved around, limping on the toe of that foot so that he kept it as still as possible. I could sense through my bond with him that his heel no longer throbbed, and decided to remove the bandage and apply a barrier unguent that would hopefully keep out the worst of the dirt and sand until we found ourselves on firmer ground. I was just about to ask him if that was okay when I felt his assent that it was.

I grinned and told him, *I'm bonded to you and I LOVE IT.* He accepted my proclamation as a given, and I loved that too.

Once I had removed the bandage, I worked quickly to get the barrier unguent in place and applied it liberally.

That should do it, I told him. *You need to drink, and you've already scented water, so we'll get going, shall we?* I hoped it was just a pool or stream, and not a river. I felt Noble observing my thoughts and pulled myself up guiltily. *Okay, I get it, I'm in this moment, with you, and I'm fine.*

He lifted his head and watched me as I repacked my back-sack. *You are more than fine.*

I'm great, I agreed. *How far is it to The Gathering, by the way? This food weighs almost much as I do, so if I don't need it, I'll leave some here for whichever animals want it.*

We have some distance to travel. I passed our destination on my way to you.

I'd best lug it all along with me then. Why did you come all this way to meet me if you were near The Gathering? Why didn't you just tug me sooner and wait for me to come to you?

You ask from your present state of mind. Do you think you would have fared well had you been required to travel further by yourself in your previous state?

I was shocked as I thought back to how I had been a mere day ago. Mere hours ago, even, when I awoke. How had I so easily forgotten the anxiety that had plagued me ever since I could think?

The present is a powerful place in which to reside.

I guess. But I could have come to you, couldn't I? You were with me all the way until I found you. You made sure I left my home and then you pulled me to you so strongly, I didn't have time to panic.

You also did not sleep. In time you would have forgotten to eat and drink. Occupying the mind of another to that extent is helpful at times but unhelpful for too long. I will not do it again.

But what if I need you to? What if I panic when I get to The Gathering? Or on the way there? Or even once I've been there for a while?

How do you feel in this moment? His gaze bored into me as surely as his thought, reminding me of his mother.

I sighed and calmed down. *I feel fine. I am fine, I know it. Sorry.*

Then we shall begin our journey. He moved off slowly, then picked up his pace when I fell in beside him.

You're very like your mother, I told him. *She stared at me exactly the way you just did. You must miss her.*

I am with her as surely as I have always been with you.

How is that possible?

You believe you are your body, Noble told me. *It is one of the reasons you have been anxious to protect it despite the cost to your mind and soul. When you recognise more of yourself then everything will make sense. For now merely accept that you are where you need to be and with whom you need to be.*

You make life seem so simple.

I merely refrain from joining you in your belief that it is complicated.

I walked alongside him in silence, wanting to believe everything he had told me, and finding that I did, not because most of it made any sense to me, but because I could feel that he knew it to be true.

I was so busy trying to figure out how I could believe things that I didn't even understand, I almost fell into a narrow stream that flowed across our path. It ran shallow between steep banks, and as I teetered at its edge, trying to regain my balance and step back away from it, my heart raced. If I fell in, I would break my ankles, my legs, even, and there was no one out here to find and heal me as my parents and the Healers of Lowtown had done the last time calamity struck me. Noble wouldn't be able to help, I would starve to death. The birds would begin picking at my eyes long before I was dead, and when they began circling, they would attract countless animals who would tear me limb from limb.

My breaths came short and fast, and my legs tingled and weakened as I managed to stagger backward. Nausea convinced me I was about to throw up, and dizziness caused me to stagger into Noble as he stood with his front feet down in the stream, slaking his thirst. I put a hand to his flank to steady myself.

Where the rest of my body trembled and shook, it felt as though my hand suddenly belonged to my horse. I moved so that my arm lay along his side, and my body was in contact with his hind leg, from his hip down to his stifle. My breathing slowed and my eyes stopped darting about and focused on Noble as he gazed back at me.

He was completely unfazed by the fact that he was doing a handstand in a stream while I stood attached to his hindquarter and belly. His dark brown eyes looked into me as I was beginning to realise they probably always would. He blinked. *It would serve you to consider what it is that you gain from creating the type of realities that you favour. I would move.*

I stepped away from him as he launched his forequarters up onto the far bank of the stream and then hopped over it with his hind legs.

I didn't create anything, I was just worried about what might happen.

Noble began to graze the greener, lusher grass that grew down the sides of the bank. *And as a result you experienced the exact trauma you sought to avoid.*

I didn't want to panic like that, I couldn't help it. I need to be able to recognise danger so I can avoid it.

Do you regret your experience in the river?

Of course I do, I was terrified, I could have... I frowned. It wasn't true, not anymore. Not now I had relived it differently at Noble's prompting.

My horse stopped grazing and gazed at me. *When you are present the opportunity exists to experience danger as possibility.*

My heart plummeted. *Are you telling me you actually enjoy being in danger? Do you go looking for it?*

I welcome possibility and seek it regardless of the guise it takes.

My knees weakened and nausea announced itself again.

Learning To Soar. His thought attached itself to me in a way that left me in no doubt what it meant.

My eyes flicked back to him. *That's your name for me. That's how you see me? That's what my parents told me to do, they told me to fly, but I can't. I can barely walk.*

You have always fought the wind of life but now we are bonded you are learning to soar upon it. How do you feel in this moment?

Terrified.

Your focus is not in this moment but in a future that you so desperately want to be free of fear you have again created what you wish to avoid. Where are you in this moment?

In the middle of nowhere.

How are you?

I stared back at him as his eyes bored into me, and eventually sighed. *You win. I'm with you and I'm fine. Thirsty though. And tired, which is ridiculous because we've only been on the move for an hour or so.*

Which you chose to experience as traumatic. Trauma is tiring. I will eat and you will rest. Then you will continue learning to soar.

His thought was accompanied by such a strong sense of accomplishment, as if he knew I couldn't possibly fail, that suddenly, the idea didn't seem so bad.

Chapter Eight

*I*t took us nearly three weeks to reach The Gathering. We could have made it there more quickly had it not been for Noble grazing for long periods at a time and being in no particular hurry when he wasn't, but I was grateful for the time alone with my horse; I got to know him and to appreciate his strength and consistently calm outlook as well as his dark, dainty beauty. I was also grateful to have the time to mull over everything he had taught me, which was fortunate, as he communicated little and I had a very clear sense from him that for now, learning to soar involved doing exactly that.

I was dizzy with it all at times – not in the way that fear caused me to be, but at the implications of what everything he had told me could mean not only for me, but for humankind.

I came to realise that I was an echo of the people of The Old. Like all children of The New, I had learnt in school about the obsessive need of those of The Old for safety and comfort. Like me, their need for total control over their physical circumstances had only resulted in them becoming ever more fearful. Unlike me, however, they had become ever more paranoid and eventually obliterated one another, leaving behind only those who had followed their intuition and escaped the insanity of the tightly controlled cities – the founding members of the communities of The New – to ensure the survival of the human race.

Noble left me to contemplate the implications of my realisation without comment or interference, but I was aware of him monitoring my musings as he grazed and I rested, or we walked side by side across grassland, through woodland or as we negotiated countless hills, from small mounds to steep-sided peaks.

My food supplies dwindled and I was forced to get used to the fact that we never knew when we might come across water. We slept out in the open where I felt exposed and uncomfortable, and in the forest where I could sense increased alertness from Noble as the instincts of his species warned of his inability to escape predators at speed due to the trees. Through it all, the only time I continued to panic was on first waking.

As soon as I woke, I would be assaulted by my usual concerns about my ability to navigate the day ahead, and would leap to my feet and reach out to Noble if he dozed nearby, or run to him if he grazed further away than an arm's length. The second I was in physical contact with him, I would begin to calm down. I would stand with him until I had worked my way to telling myself, usually out loud, 'I'm fine.'

Why am I like this? I finally asked Noble. *I'm descended from those who knew that trying to protect themselves from all forms of discomfort was unhealthy, who followed their intuition and left the safety and comfort of the known for the potential danger of the unknown. They must have sensed the possibility in the situation, just like you're trying to help me to do, so why can't I? Why do I do what the people of The Old did and worry about what might happen, even though it only makes me feel worse? Everyone else of The New has inherited the tendency to follow their intuition above everything else – everyone but me.*

You are as capable of feeling your way forward as are your peers. More capable in truth. You are more sensitive and have in the past been quickly overwhelmed by everything you could sense from those around you from whom you subsequently withdrew. Your withdrawal afforded you relief from your discomfort and as a consequence you associated protecting yourself from stimuli as being beneficial and perpetuated the behaviour. It is a tendency that exists in all humans and has the potential to draw them back to the ways of The Old. You will learn to embrace life regardless of circumstances and in so doing you will gain experience that will be sorely needed by your peers.

Really? Who? I can't imagine anyone needing anything from me, except cloth, maybe.

You will recognise them when they appear in your present. We are almost at The Gathering.

We topped a hill and looked across paddocks of horses, crops and livestock that stretched away into the distance to where large buildings loomed against a backdrop of even taller hills than the one on which we stood. At the base of our hill was a wide stretch of grass that ran alongside a wide, deep, fast flowing river.

I gasped. Bubbles escaped my mouth as I tried to scream. I gasped again. Pain erupted in my hand… which was touching something warm and furry. My eyes flicked open.

How are you?

I took a deep breath and then many more whilst I tried to bring myself back into the present. Eventually, I was able to reply with a fair degree of conviction, *I'm okay.*

I followed Noble as he began to pick his way down the hillside.

And now?

I focused on Noble's dainty feet as he lifted each in turn before placing them back down among the tussocks of grass. *Fine.*

When we reached the base of the hill, my ears were filled with the roar of the water. My heart began to pound in my chest.

How are you?

I stopped walking. *I'm not fine at all. I can't do this, Noble, I can't. You didn't tell me there was a river near The Gathering. What if one of us falls in again?*

My horse moved in front of me, his muzzle soft against my neck as he rested it on my shoulder. *Then we shall have the opportunity to find out all over again how magnificent we are.*

Or I could lose you. I can't lose you, Noble. Promise me you'll never go near the river? Please?

Providing such reassurance would be unhelpful.

I disagree, it would help me greatly. Noble's head became gradually heavier on my shoulder until I was forced to try to support it with my hands, to no avail. His jaw bones dug into me. *Ouch, you're hurting me,* I told him, bending my knees and stepping out from underneath him. I rubbed my shoulder.

How are you?

Apart from having a sore shoulder, you mean? I'm fine. I frowned. The river was no less turbulent, no less noisy, and no less distant, but my panic had subsided.

Choose to be present. Noble tossed his head and then gazed at me. *You have proven to yourself that you can.*

You hurt me on purpose?

I gave you the opportunity to focus on the present. His thought was as calm, as steady, as truthful as always. *You may choose it again or you may choose that which does not serve you.*

It's not that simple.

You have just proven to yourself that it is.

You distracted me. I didn't choose to forget the river is there.

You allowed yourself to be distracted. That was a choice. Allow yourself once more. Noble made his presence in my mind a little stronger. *Think less. Feel more.*

I immersed myself in our bond. Noble was aware of so much more than I was by myself. Through him, I smelt the water as it raced past us. I heard the insects that buzzed over its surface, and each and every splash as waves merged with their source following impact with the riverbank or rocks. I saw the river through his eyes as we began to walk along its bank with him between me and the water. It was a dark grey-blue and moved with a singular force and purpose. It had a body, a voice, a scent – a life, even – of its own, and anything that got too close to it was sucked in and taken with it on its way. A branch glided past, having surrendered to its power, and I couldn't help but compare its harmonious journey to the thrashing, terrified one I had endured.

Consider how far it has travelled and how far it may yet travel, Noble volunteered pointedly. *Had it not fallen into the water it would merely have decayed where it landed.*

But now that it has fallen into the water, it could be thrown against a rock and smashed into a thousand pieces at any second...

...having experienced that which it never would have whilst rotting in place on the ground, Noble cut in.

But the result is the same.

The result is the same, agreed Noble. *A useful fact to remember.*

I put a hand to his neck as we walked, the river forgotten. *You're telling me that since we all die eventually, we might as well disregard life?*

I merely point out that since we will all depart our bodies at some stage there is much to be gained from surrendering to that which has the power to offer an enriched experience.

But it's scary.

Any more so than attempting to be safe? You have already proven to yourself that removing yourself from situations you consider precarious merely creates more opportunity to imagine situations in which you believe you will feel unsafe.

I considered and could find no argument, yet I couldn't bring myself to agree with my horse; the thought of just surrendering to the flow of life left me feeling more vulnerable than I ever had before, as if I would be welcoming anything and everything to come and terrify the hell out of me.

'You look like I remember feelin' when I first arrived here with Dili,' a deep voice boomed nearby.

I jumped so violently, I fell against Noble and had to push against him to right myself. I looked up and was amazed to find that Noble had guided me away from the river and down a grassy path that appeared to bisect the paddocks I had spotted from the hilltop.

'Sorry to have startled you,' the voice boomed again, 'I'm afraid hearin' human voices is somethin' you're goin' to have to get used to again now that you've been talkin' to your horse in your head for however long it's taken you both to get here.' A huge man with thick, black hair and a black beard stepped between the rails of a paddock and held an enormous hand out for me to shake. 'I'm Mason, and that's my Diligence over there. See her? The big, grey, beauty of a mare with her head down?'

I shook his hand and squinted into the sun, trying to make out the horse Mason was describing. I couldn't see her very clearly, but I didn't dare say. 'She's, um, she's beautiful.'

'You're a delicate little chap, aren't you? Small but exquisitely formed,' Mason said to Noble, holding his hand out to my horse.

Noble sniffed it and then licked it. 'Aaaah, you want the salt, don't you.' Mason turned to me and grinned. 'Been properly sweatin' out here, I have, groomin' Dili, she's a big girl and that sun's hot, isn't it?'

I could sense that Noble liked him, and found myself relaxing as wasn't normal for me when around people. 'It is. I'm, um, I'm Quinta and this is Noble.'

'It's great to meet you both, welcome to The Gatherin'. Like I said, you look like I remember feelin' when I first got here after Dili and I bonded, so I'll not bombard you with questions. You'll be wantin' to get Noble settled into a paddock with good grass, shelter and water, and then you'll be wantin' to find a room and get yourself cleaned up and settled in. Come on, this way.' He turned and walked away.

I stood where I was. Mason was going to separate me from Noble and I wasn't ready. Engrossed as I had been in my musings whilst walking along the riverbank, I hadn't had time to prepare myself for what I might face, I hadn't had time to consider how I would feel, what I would do. My stomach churned and my chest tightened, not allowing me to breathe other than in rapid, short, shallow breaths. I began to feel dizzy.

There was a shuffling next to me and I felt the warmth first of Noble's body and then of his mind. *How are you in this moment?*

Panicking, as you well know.

In this moment, Noble repeated.

I was standing with the most beautiful, loving horse in the world as he infused my body with his warmth, and my mind with his calm patience. I breathed in and out deeply. *Thank you, Noble, I am well.*

We will walk forward one step. He moved and then waited until I was once more beside him.

How are you in this moment?

I'm okay.

We will move forward one step at a time and with each we will reassess our situation.

When I had walked more than twenty steps whilst remaining in the present, Noble announced, *We will now assess our situation every two steps.*

When we came across Mason holding a gate open for Noble to enter what appeared to be the second closest paddock to the massive, grey stone buildings we had seen from the hilltop, Noble instructed me, *It is necessary for you to leave me here in body but in mind we will continue to practise occupying the present.*

I can't leave you here, I can't go anywhere without you, I won't know what to do or say, I'll make a fool of myself, I'll panic.

You need only remain in the present with me and from there do or say that which is completely honest.

But there are social conventions and expectations. I always worry I'll forget them and then I do forget them.

You are wise to do such. Conventions shift and change. Honesty is a constant.

But what if I offend everyone?

So long as you say exactly how and what you feel in any given moment then your words will be recognised as originating from your authentic self. That is a convention that is as powerful as it is both unconscious and universal. Learning To Soar do you trust me?

Of course I do.

Then follow my counsel. Remain with me in the present and be completely honest in all of your actions and communications. He walked through the gateway, leaving me alone with Mason.

'Um, I'm sorry that it, er, that it took me so long to get here,' I said, unable to prevent the shake in my voice.

Mason shut the gate and then stood in front of me, blocking

out the sun. 'Don't you be sorry about anythin'. I know how you feel. Everyone here does. You've been alone with your horse for, what, days? Weeks?'

'Um, nearly three weeks.'

Mason nodded. 'So then, you feel strange talkin' out loud, let alone leavin' Noble for the first time since you bonded and he turned your world upside down with everythin' he's told you that you don't understand, everythin' he's told you that you do understand, everythin' you sense from him, and everythin' you feel now you're bonded. And on top of that, you're tryin' to take in your new surroundin's and it's makin' you dizzy. Am I right?'

I nodded and tried to think what I should say in return.

Be honest. Noble's reminder permeated my mind, slowing it down as it began to thrash around and panic.

Be honest. 'Yes, you're right,' I said, watching Noble intently as he grazed, so that I didn't have to look at Mason. 'But I'm also not very good at being around people, and I'm worried I won't know what to say or do, and everyone will hate me, or they'll try harder to include me and then they'll hate me, or they'll notice I keep myself to myself and they'll take offence and hate me. Noble is adamant that we need to be here but I'm not sure how I'll fit in.'

'No one will hate you, Quinta, whatever you do or say.' Mason's voice was gentle. 'We're all here because we need to learn from our horses and from each other. That's it. You'll need to do your share of the chores that keep this place runnin', just like we all do, but if you need ones you can do on your own, you only have to ask and they'll be given to you. If you want to eat with us all in the dinin' room, you can, but if you want to eat in your room, you can do that instead. It's unlikely anyone will think to question you but if they do, their horses will pull them up sharpish, just as Noble does to you if you have thoughts that don't serve you.'

'That don't serve me? That's how Noble puts it,' I blurted out.

Mason chuckled. 'I think the horses probably all give similar advice. It isn't about right and wrong, see, but about what helps and what doesn't. It's so much simpler to see things the way the horses do.'

I nodded. 'I suppose it is.'

'Now, how do you feel about comin' with me to the accommodation block, so we can find an empty room for you to call your own while you're here? Or, you can stay here a bit longer if you want, and come and find me in my workshop when you're ready? I'm the Saddler in residence, anyone will point you in my direction.'

My heart began thumping more rapidly. I didn't want to leave Noble but I felt safe with Mason and didn't want to have to ask anyone where to find him.

I looked back at Noble. *Are you alright here on your own?*

I am always well and I will not be alone, he replied.

'Ah look, Integrity has a mind to join your Noble, isn't that nice?' Mason said as a grey mare sailed over the fence from an adjoining paddock, trotted up to Noble, whickering, and then stopped just short of him while he looked her up and down, his nostrils flaring as he took in her scent. He reached out to her with his nose and she sniffed it and squealed, then stamped a front foot. Noble tossed his head. Integrity moved closer and squealed again, not so forcefully this time. They both shied and cantered off together. When they came to a stop, Integrity sniffed Noble, nipped his neck and squealed once more. He didn't respond other than to toss his head again. He waited until she moved into place beside him and then reached up to bite her neck as she leant down to bite his in return. I could feel his pleasure.

'A bit of mutual groomin' will see him settled in no time,' Mason said.

I nodded slowly. 'He's happy. Please could you show me to the accommodation block?'

'Say no more, come this way.' He turned and walked towards a gap between a five storey, grey stone building on the right, and a slightly less imposing, yet still massive, building on the left, to which he pointed. 'The dinin' room runs the length of that buildin' there, on the side facin' the square. On its far side are the workshops, mine included, in case you need me for anythin'.'

We walked between the buildings and onto a large, cobbled square with a statue of a man and horse at its centre. There were lots of people standing around chatting while others wandered between the buildings, exchanging greetings with those they passed on the way. I swallowed hard.

Mason pointed to a door on the bottom floor of the building to our right. 'The tack room is in there, that's where you'll store Noble's saddle once I've had a chance to make it for him. It's been a while since I've made one as small as he'll need, I'll enjoy the challenge. Quinta? Everythin' okay?'

My heart was pounding and I had an urgent need for the bathroom. Mortified, I crossed my legs tightly, rendering me unable to move as thoughts slammed around in my mind. I would be expected to ride Noble. How had I not considered that before? I would have to be taught by someone I didn't know. I would be hopeless, I knew it, I would be too scared to even hear what they were telling me to do, let alone do it, and what if I hurt Noble, or fell off and hurt myself? I'd never be able to get back on again and then everyone would think badly of me. I'd never be a real member of the Horse-Bonded, I'd be unable to go out and visit villages to dispense Noble's counsel – a thought that terrified me anyway – so what was I even doing here? What was I thinking, that because I was bonded, I would suddenly turn into a person who just got on with life without a care in the world?

Not suddenly. Inevitably. Noble was still grooming with Integrity, but I could feel that he was as fully with me as he always was. I calmed slightly. *Learning to Soar we are here because it is akin to the river that swept you along with it and helped you to know yourself. Refer to our earlier conversation.*

Mason stayed by my side without question or comment as I stood, rooted to the spot while I did as Noble told me. *I'm the branch we saw in the river. I know you think I have to let myself be carried along with the flow like it was, but I don't know if I can.*

I have sufficient confidence for us both. You merely need to choose to reach for mine when your own eludes you. It will always be there. Always.

'Always,' I breathed with a certainty I could feel even though it wasn't mine.

'Better?' Mason said softly.

I looked up at him. 'Yes. Sorry. Thank you for waiting with me.'

His dark brown eyes were warm. 'Like I said, you never need be sorry about anythin'. You'll be feelin' strange bein' away from Noble, and you're bound to feel a bit panicky at times, that's why the newly arrived horses always go in the paddocks nearest the buildin's, so their newly bonded humans can get to them in a hurry when the need arises.'

'Really? Other people panic too? Even the Horse-Bonded?'

Mason smiled. 'Especially the Horse-Bonded. To begin with, anyway. Believe me when I tell you that Noble is everythin' you'll ever need. Whatever he tells you will be the right of it, and he'll never let you down. The longer you're bonded to him, the more you'll trust that's the case. In the meantime, believe me and all of the other Horse-Bonded who'll tell you exactly the same thing. That's what we're here for, Quinta, we're all in this together, you're not alone.'

I could have cried with relief, but managed not to. Instead, I whispered, 'Thank you.'

'Don't you mention it. Are you ready to carry on?'

'Yes, I think I am.'

We passed many people on the way to the accommodation block at the far side of the square, all of whom called out warm greetings to Mason and then to me when Mason explained who I was. I was relieved that he didn't linger though, and I hurried through the door of the four-storey building when he held it open for me.

'Any available rooms will have their doors wedged open, so when we find one, let me know if it takes your fancy. If not, we'll keep lookin',' Mason said.

We found an empty room on the second floor of the grey stone building, and by then, I was so desperate for the bathroom that I didn't even look inside the room before telling Mason I would take it. I dumped my back-sack on the floor just inside the door and followed him to the middle of the corridor where he pointed out the bathrooms. I immediately shot into one of them while he was still pointing out the cupboards nearby that were apparently full of towels, soap and bath salts.

'I'll come back for you in an hour or so, shall I, give you a chance to clean up and settle in, before takin' you to the dinin' hall for lunch?' Mason said through the bathroom door.

When I didn't answer straight away, he said, 'Or I can bring you a tray up here to your room?'

Noble increased his presence in my mind and I reached for his confidence, feeling it as if it were mine. I took a deep breath and called out, 'I'll be ready to come to lunch with you in an hour, thank you.'

'Don't mention it. See you later.' His footsteps faded away.

I returned to my room and saw for the first time that it was large and airy, with a bed, wardrobe and chest of drawers all made of a dark wood that matched the thick beam of the mantlepiece, on which was exquisitely carved a horse standing with pricked ears, looking out of the wood so intently it almost seemed alive with curiosity.

There was a fire laid ready in the hearth, at the side of which stood a basket of fuel bricks; the grey stone walls afforded a welcome coolness and relief from the heat outside and I supposed that as soon as the heat dropped, their coolness would quickly cease to be a benefit and a fire would be very much needed. I found the thoughtfulness of the person who had laid the fire as welcoming as the ready-made bed, and as welcoming as Mason and everyone and else had been.

I actually found myself daring to believe that I might enjoy my time at The Gathering.

Chapter Nine

My first day at the home of the Horse-Bonded wasn't as difficult as I had feared it would be. When I had bathed and was feeling both refreshed in my clean clothes and disgusted by my filthy ones, Noble's confidence and Mason's friendliness allowed me to follow the man across the square to the building he had pointed out earlier. It was built from the same grey stone as the others but had huge windows along its length that were almost the full height of the ground floor. We entered it through a large oak door that opened into a lobby with pegs for outdoor clothes, and then went through a much smaller doorway into the dining room that while full of people, seemed half empty as a result of it feeling part of the square due to the impressive windows I had observed from outside.

I wasn't comfortable among so many people, but I endured it, largely thanks to Mason engaging enthusiastically with all of those we met so that I didn't have to. I found an urgent need to go to Noble as soon as I had eaten a tasty lunch of onion soup with slices of freshly baked herb bread, and assured Mason I would be fine going to see him by myself.

'When you're ready, bring him to my workshop and I'll measure him up for his saddle,' Mason said. His eyes widened at the panic that must have shown on my face, and he added, 'Just when you're ready. It doesn't have to be today, whenever is as good a time as any.'

I'd never had a friend before and I began to see what I'd been missing. 'Thanks, Mason, you're very kind.'

He smiled. 'Just when you're ready,' he said again. 'There's no rush. I barely need my saddle, I hardly ever ride Dili.'

'You don't?' I said louder than I had intended. I stared at Mason, not daring to look to see if anyone had turned to look at me.

'Nope, I'm not very good at it, see. Dili doesn't seem to mind not being' ridden, and until she does, I don't see it as an issue.'

'So then, maybe Noble won't mind either.' My heart sank as I knew deep down that he would, that he would see it as me resisting the current of life instead of going along with its flow. 'Well, anyway,' I said to Mason, 'I'll be going.'

'I'll be in my workshop until dinnertime, so if you want company, that's where you'll find me.'

I surprised myself by how easy it was to smile at him as I nodded my goodbye. I hurried from the dining room looking downward so that no one could catch my eye, then on to the paddock that Noble was sharing with Integrity. I wondered if Noble would counsel me to behave differently, but he stayed quiet in my mind.

When I reached his paddock, I was disappointed to see that he and Integrity weren't alone. A tall, thin man with slightly greying hair and a pock-marked face was standing next to Integrity, brushing her neck. He caught sight of me, grinned and waved.

I lifted my hand and waved back at him awkwardly, unable to make my hand betray my heart. Was this how it would be from now on, that I wouldn't have a moment alone, not even when I was with Noble? I wanted to turn and run to my room, but my eyes found Noble some distance away from Integrity, standing in the shade of a large alder tree and resting a hind leg as he snoozed. I felt a fresh surge of desperation to be near him.

I climbed between the rails of the fence and walked towards my horse, taking a line that took me as far from Integrity and her Bond-Partner as possible whilst hoping that it appeared to be the natural line to take to Noble. I cursed inwardly as Integrity wandered over to me, bringing her Bond-Partner with her.

'You must be Quinta,' he said and held out his hand. 'I'm Newson, and this is Integrity, as I think you already know?'

I tried to smile at him as I shook his hand, then gazed up at Integrity peering down her nose at me. 'Yes, Mason told me her name when we saw her jump in here with Noble. She's big, isn't she? And… kind.' I had no idea how I knew that, but I did; I could see it in her eyes and I could feel it in my skin in a way I couldn't pinpoint.

Newson smiled. 'You're perceptive. She's as kind as they come, luckily for me; I'm not always the easiest person to be around. There are times when I wish for her sake that she'd chosen a more straightforward character as her Bond-Partner.'

'I've thought that about Noble too, I'm glad it's not just me,' I said, relief at his admission causing me to speak even as I shocked myself that I was doing it so naturally. 'I'm not easy to be around either, in fact, I'm a nightmare. I still don't know why Noble chose me.'

Integrity touched my forehead with her muzzle, and I was reminded of when my mother used to put her hand there to check whether I had a temperature, soothing me not only with her touch but with the air she always had about her that she would make everything okay.

'She makes everything alright. When you're struggling, she helps you through it and she's happy to,' I said and then blinked, my mouth and throat suddenly dry. 'I'm sorry, I don't know what came over me, I shouldn't have said that,' I croaked.

'Yes you should,' Newson said. 'It's something Integrity tells me often and I don't always allow myself to believe her. Thank you, Quinta. Sincerely. Now, I'm thinking you probably want some time alone with Noble, with it being your first day here and all, so I'll say goodbye, and maybe I'll see you later at dinner?'

I just stared at him, unable to comprehend that, like Mason, he was making things so easy for me. I shook my head and blinked. 'Er, yes, I think so. I mean, yes, probably.'

'But not definitely. I get it. Right now, you're feeling like the world is spinning,' Newson said with a wink. 'Just go with that until Noble helps it to slow back down, and then see how you feel. Whatever you're feeling, Quinta, it's unlikely to be anything that the rest of us here haven't felt before you. You're among friends who understand you and will help whenever you ask for it.'

'That's what Mason said.'

'Well, he was right. Try to remember it when you're finding everything strange, okay? Enjoy your time with Noble.' He turned and walked away. Integrity blew softly in my ear and then began to graze.

I lost all sense of time as I stood in the middle of the paddock with the sun beating down on the top of my head, going over and over everything that Mason and Newson had said to me. Try as I might, I couldn't find one instance where they had contradicted one another, or one thing on which I could fixate in order to worry.

Yet you fixate nevertheless. The past is as much of a

distraction from the present as is the future. You have yet to notice that your body is suffering.

Noble moved between me and the sun so that I was shaded, and it was only then that I noticed the blood pounding in my ears, the dizziness and the nausea that heralded the onset of sunstroke.

We will move towards the shade, Noble informed me. *Hold on to me or you will not reach it.*

I reached out with a trembling hand and took hold of a handful of his mane. I thought I would throw up as I began to stagger on shaking legs towards the tree. Even then, I worried what people passing by would think if they saw me – what they might already be thinking had they seen me standing motionless by myself in the sun like the complete and utter idiot I was. I couldn't just enjoy the fact that I'd managed to meet lots of people and hold conversations with two of them – neither of whom had seemed to consider me odd – I had to give myself sunstroke over it. How ridiculous was that?

Not ridiculous. Merely a pattern to which you hold because part of you yet believes it ensures your survival. While any part of you holds to that view you will have to actively put your focus where you have already proven to yourself it is more productive.

The present, I agreed as I stepped into the shade. *That way I might notice when I'm killing myself with worry over the past and future. The irony isn't lost on me.*

I sat down at the base of the alder tree and Noble stood beside me, rested a hind leg and closed his eyes. I closed mine too until my head stopped spinning and my nausea subsided. When I opened them, I noticed people waving to me as they passed by the paddock. I lifted a hand and waved back but began to shuffle on my bottom to the far side of the tree trunk where I would be invisible from the path; I felt vulnerable, and just because no one had entered the paddock to talk to me so far, it didn't mean they wouldn't. Then I stopped as Noble's contentment oozed into my mind from his own. He was fed, watered, shaded and he was with me. He was fine – and so was I. I was also as sleepy as he was. My eyes drooped.

When they opened again, the sight of Noble grazing around my feet made sense of the grinding noise that had brought me out of my doze. I smiled at him as he shook his head and swished his tail, dislodging the biters that were relentless in their efforts to draw his blood. I slapped at my neck as one bit me, then stood to swipe away those attacking my horse. It was only then that I realised I didn't feel anxious. For the first time in my life, I had woken up with a smile on my face, despite having fallen asleep in an unfamiliar place, in full view of everyone. What was happening to me?

You are learning to soar, Noble announced, then added, *I would have a saddle.*

You want me to ride you. I knew you would. Why? Dili doesn't mind whether Mason does or not.

Their situation is different from ours.

How?

They bonded for their reasons. We bonded for ours, Noble replied.

Which are?

Consider what you saw in me when you chose my name. It is not possible for you to recognise that which you do not already possess.

You're noble; you'll go to any length to help others. I'm not like that. My mind is so full of worry, I'm not even aware when others need help.

That is not true as you have already proven to yourself. When presented with a reason to be noble you become everything you saw in me. Up until now that reason has had to be drastic and traumatic. When you are more practised at maintaining your focus in each moment you will notice the less obvious opportunities to offer help. Your most recent conversation is an example. That which you saw in me will become all of you. It is a trait that will be much needed in times to come. Learning to ride will assist your effort to embrace each moment that passes. When your body can move with mine we will be able to travel efficiently so that we can offer help where it is needed.

In the villages. If I can ride, I'll be a proper member of the Horse-Bonded. I can really be that person?

You are already that person. You need merely clear all that blurs your ability to see it.

I sensed his patience, his confidence in me, his absolute knowledge that what he told me was true. Without giving myself time to talk myself out of it, I thought to him, *Come on then, we'll go and see Mason.*

As we left the paddock and made for Mason's workshop, I began to feel nervous about all of the people coming the other way. I moved closer to Noble so that no one could step between the two of us, and looked down at the short, rough grass on the path in front of me so that I didn't invite conversation. Everyone took the hint and before I knew it, I was walking alongside workshops with large windows that allowed light to flood in. I peered into each one until I saw the subject of my search bending over a bench positioned directly in front of his window. I knocked on the door to the Saddler's workshop, and Mason jumped. When he caught sight of Noble and me, he grinned and rushed to open the door.

'I didn't expect to see you two for a while, but I'm glad you're here, I'm lookin' forward to gettin' started. Come in, come in.' He moved to stand alongside the open door and stretched out his arm, beckoning us inside.

I looked at Noble and then back at him. 'What, both of us? In there?'

Mason chuckled. 'I've had far bigger horses in my workshop than your dainty lad. Come on, Noble, let's start work on gettin' you sorted.'

Noble strode in through the doorway as if it were a completely normal occurrence, turned and stood alongside the workbench. I was relieved to see that the biters didn't follow him in, and hurried in behind him, quickly shutting the door behind me to try to ensure it remained that way.

Mason bustled about my horse, placing different saddles on his back, and laying a measuring tape and different pieces of leather in different positions, from which he appeared to derive additional information. He chattered to Noble constantly and my horse's ears flickered back and forth, following Mason wherever he went.

I was curious about the man. I guessed that, like me, he was in his early thirties, but that was all we had in common. He was tall and heavily built where I was small and petite. Where I always tried to take up as little of anyone's time and space as possible, I had noticed at lunch that he was comfortable taking up far more of the room than that for which his physical size could account, by including everyone in the vicinity in his warmth and humour.

I thought back to Noble's assertion that Mason and his Bond-Partner had bonded for reasons of their own, and wondered what they were.

Consider what you saw in me when you chose my name. It is not possible for you to recognise that which you do not already possess. That was what my horse had told me when I asked him why he and I were bonded. I needed a reason to be noble. So, Mason needed a reason to be diligent? I watched him re-checking all of his measurements. He seemed diligent already, to me.

You are beginning to understand, Noble informed me.

You can't possibly think that I seem noble to other people, when I can barely look at them.

They will know why you chose my name. They will know of what you are capable. It will help.

'Right then, I think we're sorted. I'll have this ready for you in a few days' time,' Mason said, laying his measuring tape on the workbench and rubbing Noble's neck.

'There's no rush, honestly,' I said.

Mason grinned at me. 'There's no rush for you to use it, but allow me to immerse myself in somethin' that gives me so much pleasure?'

I nodded. A thought occurred to me. 'I'm a Weaver. When do I start work?'

Mason nodded behind himself in the direction of the dining room. 'It's Sunday today, so the new rota of chores will appear on the notice board in the dinin' room tonight. I took the liberty of lettin' the Overseer know you're here, so you'll be on the rota. Once you've seen when you'll be free of chores, you can go to the Weaver's workshop – that's three doors further down from this one – and offer your time there. It'll be much appreciated, I'm sure; when last I looked in on them, there were only two in residence.'

I nodded, relieved that there were only two with whose company I would need to learn to cope.

Mason handed me a cloth bag. 'I got these together for you.'

I peered into the bag and fished out a brush with a leather loop on its wooden back, just like the one I had seen Newson using on Integrity, then another with softer bristles. 'Wow, these are great, thanks, Mason.'

'There's a comb in there as well, for Noble's mane and tail, and a metal pick to get stones out of his feet. Newson will show you how to use it, I'm sure. Dinnertime is fast approachin', now, so if you want to let Noble back into his paddock and then come back here, we can go to dinner together, if you'd like?'

I nodded. 'I would actually like to do that.'

'You sound surprised.'

I smiled. 'Constantly, at the moment.'

He grinned back. 'Say no more.'

'See you later.' I opened the door and stepped through it, followed by Noble. As we made our way back to the square and then to the paddock, I found myself making eye contact and nodding my greeting to those who passed closest by. Maybe I could be a proper Horse-Bonded after all.

Chapter Ten

*M*y fledgling confidence was short lived. When I went into the dining room for dinner with Mason and stood next to him in front of the noticeboard, my heart began to thump wildly and my appetite fled. I had been rostered to work in the washroom with countless others, and on the first shift of the day too. I would have to be up well before the early summer dawn in order to spend time with Noble first, and even then, I wasn't sure I would cope with being around that many people.

'Um, I'm not hungry after all, I think I'll go to my room,' I muttered to Mason, and fled. I needed to get my things together, fetch Noble and leave, I decided as I tore across the square to the accommodation block.

No. You do not. You need to consider this an opportunity to practise that which you know will afford you a different perspective. How are you in this moment?

Freaking out, that's how I am, and don't tell me to stop, because I can't.

On the contrary.

I think I can cope and then I can't. You get me to see it differently and I think I can cope again, only to realise yet again that I can't. It's exhausting and overwhelming, Noble.

It is exhausting and overwhelming noble.

So you're repeating what I say now? Like children do? I entered the accommodation block and tore along the corridor of the ground floor to the stairwell.

Learning To Soar. Your thoughts are exhausting and overwhelming the part of you that is noble. Think less. Feel more. His thought rang with such urgency that I obeyed.

I felt my way through the meaning of his thought, and calmed down as understanding crept through me. I stopped at the stairwell and sat down on the bottom step. *I'm sorry.*

You require sustenance and rest.

My stomach rumbled. I stood up just as the door at the far end of the corridor banged open and Mason appeared, hurrying towards me with a tray.

'You'll be wantin' to have some time to yourself in your room and then get to bed, with you bein' on the early shift,' he said and held out the tray. 'Here you go, it's stew, salad and bread, nothin' fancy, I hope it's okay?'

I sighed with relief. 'Thank you, Mason, again.'

He lifted a hand in farewell as he hurried back along the corridor, then disappeared, the door banging behind him.

Wearily, I climbed the stairs to my floor. On reaching my room, I put the tray on my bed. I opened the window and sat on the windowsill for a while, listening to the birds and the hum of voices as people made their way to the dining room from all of the various buildings surrounding the square. The scents of summer flowers, freshly watered soil and horses floated in through the window, and combined with that of the stew cooling on my bed. Noble was with me all the while.

I moved with my horse from one moment to the next as I sank into the softness of the mattress and began to eat, revelling in the taste of the stew and the fresh summer vegetables that constituted the salad. Then I explored everything else I could see, hear, taste, touch and smell, just like I had used to do during my nighttime rambles at home. All of the exhaustion I had felt less than half an hour before melted away and I felt energised.

I picked up the grooming kit Mason had given me, and made my way to where I knew my horse now waited for me. He was with me through every step it took me to reach him, and in every stroke of the softer of the two brushes as I loosened dust from his coat and flicked it away until he gleamed in the evening sunshine. When he wandered away, his mind retreated as surely as his physical presence, releasing me from my need to be there.

I stayed with him as I walked slowly, happily, back to my room, smiling and greeting the few people I passed as if it were normal for me to be that way. I washed and then set the intention in my mind for when I wanted to wake up, as my parents had taught me to do when I first started school. I revelled in the softness of the mattress and the sweet-smelling sheets as I got into bed, and went to sleep to the sound of horses whinnying in the distance.

My eyes flicked open in the dark. Immediately, all I could think about was getting to Noble before the sun rose and my shift began. I lit the lantern on my bedside table and pulled on the clothes I'd been wearing before I went to bed.

It felt strange to be dressing without working my way through all of the different options and combinations of clothes in my wardrobe – admittedly not currently a wide choice since most of my clothes were in my back-sack ready to take to the washroom – and then being paralysed by indecision, and part of me felt the urge to slow down and follow the pattern that had ruled my behaviour for so long, but the urge to be with Noble was much stronger. I could feel him in the part of my mind he occupied, and knew that he was grazing contentedly in the relative cool of predawn.

I hoisted my back-sack onto one shoulder and carefully closed my bedroom door behind me so that the only sound was the click of the latch. It echoed down the corridor and I froze, terrified that I may have woken others. My heart seemed to have relocated to my ears, it was thumping so loudly, but no doors opened, no heads poked out to see what the disturbance was, and gradually my breathing slowed down to normal.

I hurried along the corridor on tiptoe, and continued that way down the stairs and along the bottom corridor. It wasn't until I had stepped out into the square and closed the outer door to the building that I relaxed.

I hurried across the square, my sense of Noble easily filling in the gaps left by my vision and drawing me to the gap between the dining room and tack room in no time. As I walked along the grassy path to my horse's paddock, the sweet scent of cut grass assailed my nose, entwined with the sweet, uplifting scent of honeysuckle and the earthy, slightly sweaty smell of horses. I smiled to myself and skipped the rest of the way to where I knew Noble waited for me, feeling like the child I had never allowed myself to be.

I made out two shapes standing side by side in the darkness and my heart leapt at the sight of the smaller one. I dumped my clothes at the side of the path, climbed between the fence rails and ran to my horse, who whickered. I flung my arms around his neck as I had only ever done to my parents, and hugged him.

Everything was alright with the world. How could it not be when I was with my horse, my Bond-Partner – my life now, I realised.

I missed you. I know you were with me all the time I was in my room, but I still missed you.

Noble nuzzled my shoulder. *There is comfort to be gained from the physical presence of others. Not solely mine.*

People still make me nervous though, and I have to work alongside a whole load of them this morning. I'll spend my whole shift worrying about what they think of me or that I've caused offence.

Or you could interact with them in the present where worry does not exist.

You know how hard that is for me.

I know how easy it is for you when you put your focus where it is needed. You discovered for yourself some time ago that every moment is full of sensations whether they be scents or sounds or sights or tastes or touches. Whether they be observations of your mind or promptings from your soul. Do not wait to be alone in the darkness to insist on experiencing every moment to its fullest.

But everyone will think I'm weird.

Already your focus wanders, Noble informed me. *Feel more. Think less.*

He began to graze again and I felt the intensity of the connection we had shared as we communicated, fade slightly, as if he had turned away from me even though he remained facing in my direction. I was being dismissed, just like when my mother had patted my back in the school playground as my teacher led me away from her.

Tears pricked my eyes but then Noble snorted loudly, clearing his nose of the dust and dirt he had inhaled as he disturbed grass near to the ground. He shook his head so that his mane flapped against his neck, swished his tail and then began to tear at the grass again. I was distracted by the sounds he made, by his scent that was yet laced with the honeysuckle carried on the light, warm breeze.

All of a sudden, the first few rays of sunlight burst over the distant hills, defining Noble and Integrity as surely as the darkness had shrouded them. My heart was filled with love for my horse – for his dark, delicate beauty, his patience, his having chosen me as his partner and pulled me along with him even as I fought his counsel, his drawing me to him when it was necessary and his pushing me away when I could manage on my own, as he was doing now.

Feel more, think less. I turned and made for the fence, picked up my laundry and made my way back to the square without a backward glance. I would do this. For him.

I focused on everything with which my five external senses and sixth internal sense filled my moments as they passed one by one. When I stepped onto the square, I noticed the blades of grass that were tough enough to grow between the cobble stones, and the herbs bold enough to join them and even produce tiny flowers, adding colour where there would only have been grey. The sun's rays bounced off the statue at the square's centre, revealing its original grey colour as well as the greens and yellows of the lichens that clung to parts of it. Doors banged as people emerged onto the square, some yawning, others wide awake and smiling and waving at those around them. I took in the colours and styles of clothes they wore. I smelt soap as a man with wet hair walked past, nodding his greeting to me.

Where I had stood rooted to the spot so many times in terror, now I stood still in fascination. Noble was right; it wasn't just the darkness that could be experienced this way, or the moments when he distracted my mind from worry, but every single waking moment.

'You're Quinta, aren't you? Did I pronounce that right? Like query as opposed to quay?' A voice said from behind me. It was soft, rich and laced with kindness.

I turned to see a woman wearing a bright green headscarf that emphasized the green of her eyes, which had crinkles at their corners as she smiled at me. Her eyebrows were raised as she waited for my response. She smelt of freshly laundered clothes despite carrying a sack full of what appeared to be soiled towels.

'Yes I am, and yes you did,' I said and surprised myself by holding out my hand, which she shook.

'I'm Hannah, and I'm rostered to work the same shift as you in the washroom this week. I saw your name on the list. I can show you the ropes. Shall we?' She nodded towards the building that housed the tack room.

I smiled. 'Yes. Thank you.'

I fell in beside her as she said, 'It's going to be another hot day, isn't it, I'm glad we've got the early shift, it'll be sweltering in the washroom later. I saw your boy on my way to my Joy's paddock yesterday, and I have to admit, I wondered what you'd be like. You're perfectly matched, you and he, aren't you? Both small and beautifully formed.'

She was utterly genuine, I could feel it in my skin as well as hear it in her voice. I frowned. That was the second time in two days I had known something in my skin without even knowing what I meant by that.

Feel more. Think less. Noble's counsel burst into my mind and I realised that it wasn't just an instruction, but an observation – a consequence. I actually felt more when I thought less.

'I'm so sorry, I hope I haven't offended you?'

I realised I was still frowning, and smiled. 'Not at all. In fact, you just helped me make sense of something Noble's been telling me. Thank you. And for the compliment.'

'That's a relief. I open my mouth when I shouldn't sometimes, then I beat myself up for having caused offence even though my Joy always tells me that if I speak from my heart, my worries are groundless.'

'You worry too?' I said.

'All the time. Don't we all?' Hannah replied. 'Well, Joy doesn't, I know that. It's a lot simpler, seeing things the way the horses do, isn't it?'

'Simpler when I can actually do it,' I said. 'The rest of the time, it's excruciatingly difficult. Maybe when I've got myself a bit more together, it'll be easier.'

'You seem pretty together to me,' Hannah said as she held open a door at the far end of the building and beckoned me to go in before her. 'You have a calmness about you. The same air of calm that surrounds Noble, in fact.'

I spun to face her. 'I do?'

She grinned. 'It's always hard to see how quickly you're changing when you're newly bonded, because it's just one more shock on top of all of the other shocks that follow being tugged; leaving your family and everything you know, hearing your horse in your head and realising that your view of the world was just that and not even close to the truth of it, and then landing here, where you feel like you have to behave like a functioning human being when actually, you just want to run for the hills. If the experiences of all who have gone before you are anything to go by though, Noble has already had far more of an effect on you than you realise.'

I looked into her kind eyes as her soft voice and reassuring words settled within me, and I believed everything she said. I couldn't speak and I didn't know what to do with myself.

Hannah put her sack on the lowest of the grey stone steps that wound up and away from where we stood. 'I think you need a hug.' She drew me close and held me tightly as I hugged her back and cried for no reason upon which I could settle. When my sobs had lessened to the odd sharp intake of breath, she held me apart from herself and said, 'You've needed to do that for a while, I think.' She wiped my tears away with the end of her sleeve. 'If you need to do it again, come and find me, on the condition that if I need a good sob myself, you'll be there for me?'

I smiled and then giggled. 'Of course.'

She nodded. 'Great, it's a deal. Now, are you ready?'

I nodded and began to climb the stairs. 'I'm sorry, I've made us late.'

'There's no such thing as late here, it's more a case of either adhering to or taking a small step around the guidelines. You'll get to know how much work constitutes a shift, and you can always do less in one shift and more in another if you want or need to. Head out of the stairwell to your right, the washroom is on the first floor. That's it.'

I walked into a room that spread the width and length of the building. The far half of it was taken up with washing lines that hung across the room, attached at both ends to hooks in the grey stone walls between large, open windows that allowed a breeze to blow across them.

Men and women of all ages stood at the triple-sized sinks that lined the walls of the nearer half of the room, washing clothes, towels, kitchen cloths and bed linen whilst chatting, laughing, singing, and in the case of two younger men, flicking foam at one another.

Sacks of washing were piled by the door – some were back-sacks with names written on them, while others were large, cloth sacks like the one Hannah carried, with sheets and towels spilling out of them.

'Dump your back-sack here at the back of the pile, then take one from the front,' Hannah instructed me as she threw her sack on top of some others. 'There's space for both of us at the sink over there.'

By the time my four-hour shift was over, my hands were wrinkled and my arms, neck and back ached from wringing out sheets with Hannah, then standing on tiptoe in order to hang them on the lines. I had surprised myself by enjoying both the work and Hannah's company, and that of those who worked around us, most of whom chatted with their own work partners and those closest to them, so I didn't have too many conversations with which to cope.

I walked with Hannah to the dining room for breakfast with a spring in my step, pleased with myself for having survived that which would previously have been one of my worst nightmares, but also feeling positive about life in general now that I was beginning to believe what the Horse-Bonded I had met so far had all told me; my Bond-Partner was always right. If he told me how to cope with something, then it would work. If he left me to my own devices, then it was because I was doing okay. If he counselled me to do something then the reason would become clear even if it wasn't at the time.

I was beginning to feel safe, not because I was distancing myself from the world, but because I felt that if I stumbled, Noble would catch me and right me again.

I ate breakfast with Hannah and some of the others who had been on our shift. I kept quiet, only answering when spoken to so that I could devote myself to doing as Noble had told me and allow my senses to overpower my thoughts so that each of my moments was too full to allow me to be self-conscious or to worry about my situation. When I'd eaten a hearty meal of scrambled eggs on toast, I said my goodbyes and made my way to the workshops, remembering Mason's direction that the Weaver's workshop was three doors down from his.

He looked up from his bench and waved as I walked past his window, then pointed to some black leather he was stitching, and grinned.

I swallowed, shaken at the reminder that he was working on Noble's saddle and I would have to ride soon. No. I refused to ruin my morning when I was doing so well. I focused on the smell of leather that wafted out of Mason's workshop door, on the delight in his eyes as he went back to the work he clearly loved, on the sound of Noble whinnying to me from the paddocks, and on the hedge that ran between the workshops and the paddocks. Bees were buzzing in and out of it, always on the move as they searched for nectar and pollen, yet not appearing to be in any particular hurry but rather living each and every moment as it came. I envied them for how naturally it appeared for them to be that way. They were obviously much wiser than I.

They know no other way, Noble informed me. *It is easy to do something when one is incapable of doing anything else.*

You're just trying to make me feel better.

I merely highlight that we all have different challenges. Different reasons for existing. None of them are more or less relevant or important than any other.

Your reason for existing, your challenge, seems to be me?

Both your and my reason for existing is to assist in the advancement of humankind. Your current challenges and experiences will allow you to play your part. Were you born resilient to the risk of feeling vulnerable then you would be in no position to both recognise and overcome it. You would be in no position to assist those who will require the benefit of your experience when humanity reaches the crossroads it is approaching.

'Are you alright, Quinta?' Mason's voice interrupted my thoughts. I realised I was standing with my back to his workshop, still staring at the hedge.

I spun around. 'I think so. Noble's just landed another load of stuff on me that I think I follow and yet don't.'

Mason chuckled. 'Then I'll leave you to it. You know where I am if you need a chat, but my advice would be to just mull it over while you're doin' somethin' else. You're on your way to the Weavers' workshop?'

I nodded.

'There you go. Work a loom for a while and things will become a bit clearer, I guarantee it.'

I smiled and waved him goodbye, then counted doors until I heard the familiar clacking sound of a loom being operated.

I knocked on the open door to the Weavers' workshop and then stepped tentatively inside. A man was just inside the door, operating as large a loom as I had ever seen, and a woman was folding cloth at a bench that ran along the back wall. They both stopped work to take stock of their visitor, then the man stood up and offered his hand as the woman hurried over.

'You fit the description of The Gathering's newest arrival,' the man said. 'Quinta?' When I nodded, he continued, 'I'm Ted and this is Celia. You have no idea how relieved we are to see you, we were ecstatic when we heard that you're a Weaver. Can you start right away?'

I smiled. 'Of course. That loom is a bit big for me though, do you have a smaller one?'

Celia smiled as she shook my hand. 'Just over there, look. The orders it can fulfil are pinned to the notice board just above it. If you're happy to get going with those, I can start dying the enormous pile of cloth I've just depressed myself by creating.'

I looked past another two looms, one nearly as large as that which Ted was expertly using, and another of a slightly larger size than the one Celia had assigned to me. 'Sure, I'll get started.'

I was too far away from both Ted and Celia to hold a conversation while I worked, for which I was grateful, not – for once – because I feared I would say the wrong thing or be drawn into a friendship I didn't want, but because I had so much to think about. Not that I really did think about it, for I was fast becoming addicted to focusing on that which I could feel; I felt my way around everything Noble had told me, examining the sense of his thoughts, rather than trying to make them into thoughts of my own.

Eventually, long after I had refused Ted's invitation to go to lunch with him and Celia, I felt that I understood.

Once I've managed to stop terrifying myself with everything that could happen, I'll be able to help other people who are fearful because I'll understand how they feel and I'll know what I need to do to help them? I asked Noble, and immediately felt his assent.

There will come a time when the fear patterns of The Old will resurface in order to undergo further clearing. You will be in a position to assist those who have the potential to shift humankind from the path it could choose onto the one that will be far more productive.

Why me? I can't be the only one ever to have overcome being fearful.

You are not. But you are the only one who is bonded to me.

Chapter Eleven

*I*t was dinnertime before I had anything to eat. Ted and Celia had both offered to fetch a belated lunch for me from the kitchens when it became clear that I had no intention of leaving my loom, but I had declined their offers. Having felt my way around Noble's counsel and glimpsed what could be achieved by feeling in place of thinking, I was preoccupied with filling every moment of my afternoon with feeling my way around my work and as such, experiencing it in a way I never had before – the smell of the wool, the different sounds made by the different parts of the loom, and, more interestingly, the different sensations I experienced through my hands and fingertips as I worked.

When I had weaved before, my mind was so busy dreaming up new scenarios from which I might need to protect myself, I had out of necessity operated my loom from muscle memory, paying only as much attention to it as necessary to ensure I adhered to the pattern and didn't trap my fingers. Now, I felt everything.

I felt the softness of the weft threads as I wound them into the shuttle ready to be passed between the thicker, tensioned warp threads. I smoothed my fingers over the smooth wood of the shuttle as I passed it back and forth, weaving the weft into the warp, and compared it with the slightly rougher wood of the reed as I pushed the newly woven weft against the body of fabric I had woven so far. I noticed the minutely different pressures required to press the pedals that lifted the frames attached to the heddles through which individual warp threads passed, so that the shuttle could pass between different combinations of warp threads according to the pattern and potential purpose of the cloth.

I felt as if I were at one with the loom, feeling the operation of its parts as easily as those of my own body so that I operated it more smoothly, more efficiently – more enjoyably – than ever before.

By the time the bell rang for dinner and I finally stopped work, I had worked a longer shift than I had ever worked in my life and my body was tired as a result of my day's efforts, but I felt more vital than I could ever remember having felt before... no, that wasn't true, I corrected myself as I hurried to the dining hall, my stomach griping uncomfortably; I had felt like that when I rescued Noble.

Instantly, my mind leapt to relive both that event and that which had followed. I withdrew from my memories and hurled myself into the part of my mind occupied by my horse, and felt instant relief – and Noble's approval.

In embracing our bond you step further away from the pattern that does not serve you. Learning To Soar you are doing very well.

I could have hugged myself but settled for smiling, so that when Mason caught sight of me as he opened the dining room door ahead of me and turned to go in, he thought my smile was for him. He stood to the side and gestured for me to go in ahead of him.

'Thanks for the advice, Mason, it worked,' I said as we wiped the dust from our boots on the huge, thickly bristled mat in the lobby.

'T'always does in my experience,' Mason said as we continued on into the cavernous dining hall. 'Sometimes it takes longer to get there than others, but we always get there in the end. Whatever it was you were chewin' on, you look mighty happy about it. Hungry though, by the sound of it.'

I flushed red at the loud rumble my stomach had just emitted, but focused on the sounds of crockery and cutlery clinking together and the laughter coming from those seated at the nearest table, before I could think any more about it. 'I missed lunch.'

'So, it was a big deal then, huh?'

'I guess so,' I said as we approached the food-laden tables at the far end of the hall. 'I've always been a worrier, you see.' I looked up and down the length of the tables, trying to decide what to have, and then began to spoon some shepherd's pie and green vegetables onto my plate as Mason helped himself to some slices of meat from a nearby platter.

'Well, that's pretty normal, isn't it?' he said. 'I mean, we all have worries, we're human, after all.'

I waited with him while he loaded his plate with vegetables, telling him, 'There's nothing normal about the extreme I used to take it to. That I'll still take it to if I don't watch myself in every single second I'm awake.'

I breathed in the rich smell of gravy emanating from my pie and found that I could separate out the smell of the accompanying green beans with which it was laced, as well as the scents of honeysuckle and cut grass. I grinned to myself as I realised that I had combined my awareness of my surroundings with Noble's of his. I scented water nearby and knew he was near the paddock gate where the water barrel was situated. I tasted the sugar his teeth liberated from the grass he was chewing, and heard voices encouraging one another to finish turning the hay they had cut the previous day, before the best of the food had been stripped from the tables at which I currently stood. I blinked as a huge hand waved up and down directly in front of my face.

I looked up at Mason as he said, 'Ah, you're back with us. We'll go and sit down, shall we?'

I flushed again as I saw the queue of people waiting for us to move along the food tables so they could reach their choices out of all the dishes on display. 'Yes. Sorry.' I hurried on ahead of him and sat at the nearest empty table.

'No need to be,' Mason said as he took the chair beside mine. 'We all drift off with our horses from time to time. There's a slightly vacant facial expression that tends to accompany the phenomenon, you'll come to recognise it in others when they're doin' it. It'll be fleetin' in those who have been bonded a long time, but with those who haven't been bonded long, it's a lot more obvious. You don't need to worry what anyone is thinkin' about you when you do it, we're all in the same boat. But you were sayin' you have a bit of a tendency to take worryin' to a different level?'

I nodded as I revelled in the taste explosion that was the shepherd's pie. 'Before Noble tugged me, I could barely leave my parents' house and workshop for fear of everything that might happen.'

Mason raised his eyebrows and whistled softly. 'Noble's name makes even more sense than it did before. You're a brave lass, Quinta.'

'I am? I mean, no I'm not. The only thing I've ever done that was remotely brave was to help Noble avoid drowning when he was a few days old, and I had nightmares over it for the four years after that until he tugged me.'

Mason frowned, his vegetable-laden fork halfway to his

mouth. 'You rescued your Bond-Partner from drownin' when he was a foal? Years before he tugged you? Seriously? Ignore that, of course you're serious.'

I buried myself in the smell and taste of my pie, and in Noble's contentment as he grazed, then began to tell Mason all about it, focusing on all of the sensations I could remember; the sounds of the horses' hooves pounding the dry earth; their whinnies and whickers; their scent and that of the river; the feel of Noble's fur and the soft riverbed as my toes dug into it; the sudden disappearance of Noble's warm little body; the silence as the water took my hearing from me; the solidity of the rock with which I collided; the roughness of the branch in my hand as I pulled myself back into a world where the sun's rays warmed my skin, the grassy riverbank filled my vision and the water gurgled and splashed its way past me.

When I had finished, I was as stunned as Mason appeared to be; I had felt no fear whatsoever whilst reliving the memory. The whole event had merely been a string of sensation-filled moments, just like those I was learning to intentionally experience now. I even remembered the pain of my broken bones as being less severe when I attached no thoughts to it. Could I really just sail through life, taking whatever threw itself at me without feeling any fear whatsoever?

It is inevitable yet unrealistic at this stage, Noble advised me.

'Well, I've never before heard the like,' Mason said before I could question my horse. 'Usually, the first time someone bein' tugged knows anythin' about their Bond-Partner is when they meet them for the first time, but you'd already met yours four years earlier? I wonder why?' Then he slapped one of his meaty hands on the table, making it judder and causing those sitting further along it to jump. He held his hand up to them. 'Sorry, sorry.' He turned to me. 'I'm an idiot. Apologies, Quinta. It's not for me to wonder what you and your Bond-Partner are about. Your Noble will have done what he did for good reason, there's no doubt about that, and that's between you and him.'

'He did it to give me a reason to be noble,' I said. 'So I could prove to myself that I can be who he's told me I can be, otherwise I'd never have believed it. I guess he had to do it when he was tiny; I was only just about strong enough to support him then, if he'd done something like that when he tugged me, I'd have failed miserably.'

Mason shook his head slowly. 'Horses constantly surprise me. All I can say is, I'm glad I managed to finish your saddle this afternoon, because whether you want to ride yet or not, I'd hate to be the one holdin' you and Noble back from whatever it is you need to be about.'

'Assisting the advancement of humankind, apparently,' I said, then at the sight of his startled face, grinned ruefully and added, 'I kid you not.'

Mason blinked. 'Then we shouldn't tarry. Get the rest of your dinner down, then we'll go back to my workshop, fetch the saddle and try it on Noble so he can choose from the saddle pads I've had the Tailors make for him.'

I was just about to argue that the following day would be soon enough for that, when Noble increased his presence in my mind. I sighed. 'Sure, why not. Thanks.'

I was glad that most people were either still at dinner or hurrying towards the dining room as Mason and I made our way to Noble's paddock. He carried the black saddle he had crafted for my horse, while I was barely able to see over the top of the huge pile of saddle pads he'd had made specially to fit under the smaller than normal saddle. He explained the difference between them all as we walked – some were made of sheepskin, others from pieces of cloth stitched around different types and thicknesses of padding, and there was one that appeared to be made of incredibly soft leather – and made clear his intention to try each and every one under Noble's saddle so that my horse could let me know which gave the best combination of cushioning, stability and comfort.

I marvelled at the amount of trouble to which Mason had gone for my horse, his passion for his work and, when he put Noble's saddle down on the top fence rail of the paddock, the intricate craftsmanship he had employed in creating it. The stitches were black, tiny and almost invisible apart from those that comprised an image on the back of the seat of the saddle, which were silver.

My mouth dropped as I looked more closely at the image and recognised myself standing next to Noble. To anyone else, the figures would probably just appear to be any horse and person, but the delicate, tapered head of the horse was unmistakeably Noble's, and the way the person stood on one leg with one foot on top of the other, as I so often did, was Mason's way of personally depicting me. His talent was breathtaking.

'I don't know what to say,' I said, 'other than it's beautiful. Really. It's a work of art, Mason. I can't sit on it, I can't get it wet and dirty as it surely will if I ride in it.'

He grinned. 'My enjoyment in my work comes as much from knowin' my saddles are helpin' to enrich a partnership, even if it's only in a very small way, as from creatin' them in the first place. Don't you worry about it, Quinta, you just get every bit of enjoyment from it you can.'

I didn't like to tell him I was struggling to view riding as a form of enjoyment when it appeared to be such a precarious thing to do, and Noble saved me from having to reply by cantering over to us with a whinny.

'Hello, my beauty, come to help us out?' Mason said as Noble gathered himself together and halted gracefully in front of us.

I could feel my horse's anticipation and focused on that, the scent of him that I had come to love so much, and the sound of him sniffing his saddle and then each of the pads in turn as Mason separated them out and lay them along the fence.

Mason climbed between the rails and offered the saddle to Noble for him to sniff again, telling him, 'I'll just pop this on your back by itself, if you have a mind to stand still for me? Then we'll try it with the different pads.' Noble tossed his head and then was still. 'Thanks, lad.'

I climbed onto the top rail by Noble's head and rubbed his forehead as Mason went about his work. Each time he tried a different pad with the saddle, he looked to me and when I nodded that I had sensed how Noble felt about it, he removed it and tried the next. Once he had tried them all, I pointed to the two of which Noble had most enjoyed the feel – a thin, sheepskin pad and one of the thicker cloth ones.

Mason nodded and untied what I had thought was a wide leather belt from around his waist. 'With Noble's permission, I'll girth him up with the sheepskin pad and we'll see how it feels with your weight in the saddle, then we'll try the same with the other pad. When we have his choice, I'll have the Tailors make a few more of the same, so you have spares.'

My heart clenched so hard, I thought it would stop altogether. 'Ride? Now?' I whispered, unable to squeeze any more of my voice out. 'Can't we just take the two pads Noble's chosen and see which he prefers in due course?'

Mason scratched his chin. 'I suppose we could, but then you won't have any spares made in advance of needin' them. It would be better if you could have a little sit on the saddle now. I'm not askin' you to actually ride or anythin', I wouldn't dream of askin' you to do that, I'm no ridin' instructor, no, not at all, you need to be under Mistral's instruction for that. This is just to see what Noble thinks of the feel of the saddle and pad once they have your weight compressin' them, as small an effect as that'll be, with you bein' so diddy and all.'

My heart pounded and I began to feel lightheaded. This was all going too fast. I didn't feel as if I had a choice, everything was spinning out of control.

Noble shifted closer to me as I sat frozen on the top rail of the fence, and rested his chin on my thigh, his eyes dark and warm as they gazed up at mine. *There is much to be gained from surrendering to that which has the power to offer an enriched experience,* he reminded me.

I swallowed and stroked his nose with a shaking hand. *Like the branch going with the flow of the river. I get it, but understanding doesn't mean I don't find it scary. If I sit on your back, do you promise to stand still and not move?*

It is likely. Movement is not required.

I know, but do you promise anyway?

I will not make assurances to which I am uncertain I will adhere.

But why not? It's not much to ask, is it, that you keep still so I don't fall off?

Would you have me remain stationary were light to flash from the sky? Were slitherers to exit the long grass with the aim of poisoning me? Were the largest biters to draw blood from me?

No, of course not.

Then live each moment with me. Attach no meaning to anything that happens other than to live it and learn from it. With me. His last thought echoed around in my mind and expanded to fill it, then slowly shrank back to the part of my mind he occupied, leaving a trail I could easily follow; an invitation, but an invitation only.

Could you fill my mind back up so I can stay in the moment with you, so I'm only aware of you? I asked him.

That would not serve you.

But I don't trust myself not to panic.

You may immerse yourself in our bond at any time but you must choose to do so as you have before. You must step aside from your pattern else it will always have a hold upon you. His invitation remained.

I took it. The moment my mind was with his, my heart and breathing rates slowed down.

Remain with me. Experience every moment with me regardless of what the moment brings.

Regardless. I panicked and withdrew from him. Regardless? I rubbed my face and breathed deeply. I had to do this, for him, for me. I was the branch in the river, being carried along, going with the flow. I pictured it gliding past me, the current carrying it around the rocks and ever onward… and joined the flow of Noble's mind as he waited patiently. *Okay, I'm ready.*

I nodded to Mason, who grinned and immediately began to attach the wide, leather strip to the buckles on one side of the saddle.

I hear the chink of the buckles, and your breathing. It's very slow, Noble, so slow and calming. I can feel your breath too. It's warm and a little damp. I reached out to stroke Noble's neck. *You're sweating under your mane and your coat is sticky.* I ran my fingers through his mane, wondering at how its texture was so different from that of his coat – so coarse and strong and yet so silky.

Mason moved to Noble's other side and reached below him for the leather strap. 'Looks like I guessed right with the length of the girth, that's a relief,' he said and there was another chink of buckles as he attached it.

Noble's ear flicked back towards the sound, magnifying my perception of it and I focused on it, noting that it was composed of far more individual sounds than I had noticed before; there was the spinning of the cylinder on the bar of the buckle as the leather strap rolled over it, the thud as the spoke fell into and out of holes in the strap until it came to rest in the one Mason selected, and the chink as the adjacent buckle knocked against it.

Birdsong filled my senses and I found that the same was true as with the buckles; where before I had listened to the birds, now, whilst I was living the moment even more fully with Noble, I could make out each and every bird. I half convinced myself I could even tell when they were taking their tiny breaths.

'Okay, Quinta, you're all set. You can just stand on the fence and swing a leg over Noble's back, he's close enough,' Mason said.

The sounds became fainter as I withdrew slightly from my bond with my horse and slid back into my worry pattern.

Live every moment. With me. His reminder was faint and from his corner of my mind. I had to choose it – choose him – for he wouldn't come after me.

Live every moment with him. I compared the richness of experience, of life, when I lived it his way, with that when I lived it my way. I chose him. I lifted my leg over his back and sat down in the saddle.

I was flooded with a myriad of sensations as my legs touched the flaps of the saddle and his warm belly; as my seat bones sank into the softness of the saddle and felt the small movements of Noble's body breathing below me, his skin shuddering and his tail swishing to dislodge biters; as the scent of his sweat became stronger; as our energies entwined. If I had felt at one with my loom earlier on, it was nothing compared with the feeling of connection that came from sitting astride my horse. Everything I could sense from his mind became clearer, as if it were my mind. I felt as if I myself were standing on four feet, as if I were scenting everything of which his nose was capable, rather than picking it up through him, as if I were directing my attention to the sensation of weight on my back and how it altered the feeling of the saddle and pad on my back.

'Okay, step off again, Quinta, and we'll try the other pad,' Mason said.

I did as he said, and found to my delight that I still felt the same level of connection with Noble even as I sat back down on the fence rail. By the time Mason had removed the saddle, however, the enhanced sense of connection was starting to fade. I reached for it, trying to find it again, but it slipped away from me. I jumped off the fence and reached for the girth even as Mason was still attaching it on Noble's other side. As soon as I grasped it, I fumbled with the buckles and began to slide one of the girth straps through, almost wincing at the screech of the roller as I pulled the girth strap against it.

'Keen, eh?' Mason said. 'That's great. Don't pull it tight to begin with, that's it, attach it loosely, thread the other strap through and then tighten them both one by one so that it's not too much of a shock for Noble's body.'

As soon as I felt that the saddle was stable, I climbed the fence and was back in the saddle. Immediately, the heightened level of sensation, the connection, the exhilaration of sitting on my horse's back returned. We preferred this pad. We would move.

We turned away from the fence and walked around the outside of the paddock until we were back with Mason, who was standing with Integrity, scratching her withers and grinning from ear to ear. He had already gathered the other pads together into a pile. 'I'll ask the Tailors to make you another couple just like that one, then, shall I?' he said. 'You're a sight for sore eyes, you two, just don't be lettin' Mistral know you began without him, he isn't the Master Of Ridin' here for nothin' you know.'

I jumped to the ground and hugged Noble, then did the same to Mason. 'I did it, I rode Noble! It looks so scary when everyone else does it, it's so high up and there's nothing to hold on to, and the horse can move anywhere at any time, so much faster than we're used to being able to, but none of that matters when you're up there, does it? It's amazing.' I turned back to Noble. *You're amazing. Thank you for your patience, thank you for being you, thank you for everything.*

He turned and looked right into me. *Remember this feeling and how you achieved it. The body vibrates more slowly than the mind and as a result changes its patterns at a slower rate. Unless you are vigilant it will draw your mind back to the arrangements and repetitions in which it has been settled for so long. Remember.*

I don't see how I could possibly forget. I'm so looking forward to our first riding lesson with Mistral, I'll ask Mason how to find him, and get it organised for as soon as possible.

As if reading my mind, Mason said, 'Shall I let Mistral know you're all set with your saddle, and you're ready to begin your lessons?' When I spun around to him in surprise, he took a step backward and said, 'Sorry, did I assume too much? I'll only do it if you want me to.'

I grinned. 'I'd love you to, thanks, Mason. So then, I just wait for him to let me know when it'll be, do I?'

Mason nodded. 'Sometime tomorrow, I should think, Mistral is usually all for gettin' going as quickly as possible.' He took my saddle and pad from me, placed them atop the pile of pads, and said, 'I'll take this lot back to my workshop, and I'll drop your saddle and pad in to the tack room on the way. That alright? I'll choose a rack on the lowest level so you can reach them tomorrow.'

'Only if you're sure? I can carry something?'

He shook his head. 'You stay on here with your boy for a bit. Enjoy yourself. You've worked hard today, and if you can't reward yourself with some Bond-Partner time, then what's the point of it all?'

I called out, 'Thank you,' to his retreating back, fetched Noble's grooming kit from where I'd hung it in the field shelter the previous evening, then set about grooming him, feeling excited.

I should have listened to my horse. I should have been vigilant with my mind so that my body couldn't drag it back down from the high of riding. By the time I realised, it was too late.

Chapter Twelve

*W*hen I went down to breakfast the following morning, I was already wondering what the hell I'd been thinking, allowing Mason to send Mistral my way. I wasn't ready for a riding lesson, how could I be? I'd only been here a few days, didn't I have enough to cope with, without taking on something that I would find so challenging? If I fell off and hurt myself, I wouldn't be able to work either in the washroom or at my loom; I would be letting people down and I was absolutely not going to do that. Riding would have to wait. I would look for Mason in the dining hall and let him know that I would go and find Mistral when I was ready. Maybe next week or the week after. It was too hot at the moment, anyway. Noble was so dark, he felt the heat more than lighter coloured horses. Maybe it would be even better to leave riding him until the real heat of summer had passed.

Remember. Noble's invitation to join him in his calm confidence was firm but gentle.

Immediately, I remembered my high of the evening before and

part of me relaxed and looked forward to creating that again. But then the rest of me began to argue; what had happened was all well and good, but it didn't mean I'd find that state of mind again, did it? I'd had to go through a whole process in order to just sit on Noble's back, and the very thought of having to work my way through it all over again was exhausting.

Feel more. Think less, Noble interrupted. *Feel your way forward and go with the flow of energy. Which way creates possibilities? Which way closes them off leaving you stagnant?*

His thought was soft and gentle yet thrummed with energy and confidence, its cadence snapping me out of my worrying and inviting me to find its answer. Instinctively, I reached for Mason and then for Mistral, finding myself groping along filaments of energy that flowed both to and between them. When I reached them and the three of us were connected, it felt as if the filaments flowing away from me suddenly split into dozens more, all of which immediately grew longer and then themselves split, so that a whole network of filaments streamed away from me, all beckoning me to follow them. Then, I put myself between Mason and Mistral, blocking them from one another, and the filaments emanating from me all shrank back into themselves until only the two linking me to Mason and Mistral remained. I spun around and around in my own private circle, within which everything stayed the same.

I didn't want more of how my life had always been. I wanted to change – I was drawn to change, I realised as I remembered how much of it I had achieved already. I wanted it, but on my terms. I tried to pull Mason and Mistral towards me, into my circle.

By attempting to include them in your pattern you will hinder them on their own paths through life as well as holding you back from following yours. You feel the energy that both composes and surrounds you. Go with its flow one moment at a time. You know you can.

I had stopped in the stairwell on my way down from the washroom, my foot hovering above the second to bottom step. I let it drop and put my weight on it. One moment at a time. I could do that.

I crossed the square to the dining hall, focusing on the sound of my footsteps, the individual voices that composed the chatter and shouting both close by me and far away, and the creak of the door to the dining room opening and closing time after time. When I reached it, I pulled it open slowly, not just because it was a solid, heavy door for me to manoeuvre but because I wanted to hear the component squeaks and groans that made up the creak I'd heard from further away.

Suddenly, the door opened the rest of the way more quickly. 'I've got it, go on in,' a male voice said from behind me. I could feel its attributes. It wasn't kind as such but more matter of fact, as if no time would be spared for pleasantries but it would always deliver help and the truth.

I knew whose it was and smiled as I turned and looked up at Newson. 'Thank you. And thanks for collecting the dung from our horses' paddock yesterday, it was a relief not to have it to do last night.'

Newson followed me through the doorway. 'You threw yourself into helping the other Weavers catch up with their orders by all accounts, it was the least I could do.'

My throat tightened. Did everyone know everything I did around here? Were they all talking about me behind my back?

Newson continued, 'Ted and Celia were full of praise for you at dinner last night, they're mighty relieved you're here and they asked if I'd help you with the paddock chores since my horse is in with yours.'

I let out a deep breath, relieved that was all it was.

'Is everything alright?' Newson asked.

I nodded. 'Kind of. I'm still just finding it all a bit overwhelming at times.'

'You'll feel better once you start riding Noble. It's necessary that we all ride so we can travel to more villages more quickly, but it's about a lot more than that; riding our Bond-Partners brings out who we are inside. Once we know that, we can work at being better. It's a humbling process but a very worthwhile one.'

I selected a couple of pieces of toast and then began to spoon scrambled eggs onto my plate. 'Do you mind if I ask how long you've been bonded?'

'Not at all,' Newson replied. 'I'm forty-four and Integrity tugged me when I was thirty.' He whistled. 'Fourteen years! I had no idea until I just thought about it, it seems more like four. The time flies by so fast when there's always so much to do and learn.'

I nodded. 'Time's funny like that, isn't it. Noble keeps reminding me to live every single moment, and I'm finding that some moments last seconds, some last minutes and some last hours. Maybe someday I'll experience a moment that lasts days or even weeks.'

'Everything's possible where horses are involved,' Newson said. 'Ahh, there's Mason waving at us.' I couldn't see over the heads of everyone sitting down at the tables nearby, so Newson pointed. 'Over there. I'll join you both once I've managed to fight my way to the fried onions.'

Everything is possible, I thought to myself as much as to Noble. I saw again in my mind's eye the filaments of possibility that continued to grow and split, then grow even further away from me if I didn't prevent Mason from letting Mistral know I was ready to have riding lessons, but it didn't mean it was easy sitting near Mason throughout breakfast without succumbing to my constant urges to ask him to refrain from approaching Mistral on my behalf. Every time my heart began to pound, my throat tightened or my legs tingled, I had to work hard to focus on everything else that assaulted my senses, so that the moments of my life were filled with them alone and my mouth remained firmly shut.

As I walked from the dining hall to the Weavers' workshop, I checked in with the filaments of possibility and was both relieved and nervous to find that they still spread out from me in all directions.

It was a relief to sit at my loom and have its familiarity, sensations and rhythms all helping me to stay in the moment as I worked. Every now and then, I would remember why it was so important that I remain focused, and I would grind my teeth at the feeling that my life wasn't under my control; that I was being swept away by a river even stronger and more terrifying than that to which I had already been subjected. Every time, I would focus on the branch I had seen gliding along on the current beyond The Gathering's paddocks, and allow its serenity to draw me back into the flow of operating the loom.

When the bell rang for lunch, I was all for working straight through again, unwilling to leave the sanctuary offered by my loom for all of the unknowns from which I would have to distract myself once I left the workshop. Ted and Celia were insistent that I eat, however, as was Noble.

Your body requires both movement and nourishment if it is to release old patterns and embrace new ones, I was informed during my attempt to refuse my fellow workers' invitation to join them for lunch. It was delivered as an instruction rather than an attempt to persuade me, and I found myself getting to my feet without further protest.

Almost as soon as I had sat down at a table with a bowl of

salad, two gnarled hands gripped the back of the chair opposite me. I looked up into fierce, blue eyes beneath grey, bushy eyebrows as the man said, 'Quinta, it's a pleasure to meet you, I'm Mistral.'

I was shocked by the smoothness and kindness of his voice, so at odds with the glare of his eyes that I hesitated to reach for the hand he held across the table to me.

He began to withdraw it. 'Forgive me, you're eating and I've disturbed you.'

I got to my feet so quickly that my chair overbalanced and landed on its back with a crash. Heat flooded my face as I held my hand out to Mistral. 'Um, no, not at all, sorry, you just surp... um, never mind, hello.'

Mistral smiled and his eyes softened even as his wizened face wrinkled further. He shook my hand and said, 'I'm expecting you and your Bond-Partner at my riding paddock in an hour's time, so please eat lightly and give yourself time to begin digesting your food, so that all of your attention is available for your horse and the instruction I will give you.' He nodded. 'Until then.' He marched off, leaving me standing in horror as the filaments of energy that flowed around and through me seemed to thicken and pulse in a slow, steady rhythm that wouldn't let go of me, wouldn't allow me to call him back and say I couldn't make it to my lesson after all.

'Here you go,' Ted righted my chair.

I sank down onto it, my appetite gone. I couldn't stop this, there was nothing I could do, I would have to ride, whether I'd had time to prepare myself or not. Unless I was suddenly taken ill? That would do it, no one could argue that I should ride if I were ill. But then I remembered Mistral's eyes and voice and I knew who he was and what he was about; I could feel it in my skin as I had with Integrity. He was knowledgeable about far more than just riding. He knew about horses and he knew about people. He knew about me. I thought I knew the answer to the question that arose in my mind, but I had to ask it.

I turned to Ted and whispered, 'What's Mistral's Bond-Partner called?'

'She's long gone, I'm afraid, but her name was Prudence.'

I nodded as my heart sank. *He's as shrewd as he appears. I'll never be able to fool him.*

His observations and judgements are sound, agreed Noble. *He is an ideal instructor. Nourish your body and then come to me.*

I focused on the sense of him in my mind as I forced down everything on the plate in front of me, then, after promising Ted and Celia I would return to the workshop following my riding lesson – and hoping upon hope I would be physically able to fulfil my promise – I collected my saddle and pad from the tack room and hurried to Noble's paddock, where he waited for me at the gate.

His dark coat gleamed in the sun, whose rays highlighted strands of red and brown in his otherwise black mane, that I hadn't noticed before. He was so dainty and neat, standing there with his front feet together and hind feet together, and when he let out a soft whicker of welcome, my heart melted. All of the tension drained from my body and I breathed in slowly and deeply, relieved that the tightness in my chest had eased. How bad could anything be if Noble were with me?

I would be groomed.

I'll get right on it.

I put the saddle and pad on the fence, fetched my grooming kit from the field shelter, and set to brushing his face, then his body and legs. I was fascinated by the dust particles that hung in the air after every stroke, each of them glistening in the sunlight as they danced on the breeze. I was mesmerised by the whine of hair against the bristles of the brush as I brushed out his mane and tail, and by the sparkles that seemed to dance along each hair with each stroke.

The saddle creaked as I placed it atop its pad on Noble's back, making sure it was in the exact spot in which Mason had positioned it. When I bent to grab the girth hanging down on the far side of Noble's belly, I slapped a biter away from him and gasped as my hand seemed to move in slow motion – and yet still managed to connect with the blood-sucking insect.

When one is truly present each moment is as long or as short as one requires it to be, Noble advised me.

I nodded. *I've noticed that. It's surreal.*

It is as real as anything else. When you choose it as your experience you need never feel hurried.

But what if I have somewhere I need to be? Like now? I stood up, holding the end of his girth.

Noble turned and blinked at me. *You are always where you need to be.*

As with everything else he had told me, I knew to my core that it must be true. I had never felt so completely safe as I did in that moment, despite what I was about to do. I held onto the feeling so that the moment it occupied extended until my feet had taken me to the paddock to which Celia had directed me following Mistral's announcement at lunch.

There, however, I froze before even reaching the paddock gate. There must have been more than thirty people sitting on the fence, waiting for Mistral to begin his afternoon's instruction.

I can't do this, Noble. I thought I could, but I can't. No amount of being in the moment is going to block out all those people.

You won't be doing it. We will.

So why does it feel so scary? Even though I'm with you?

We position ourselves on the outer limit of that which you find comfortable for that is where the possibility for change is greatest. Were we to step back then it would be even harder to move forward. Were we to take too large a step forward then you would fail and your body would have a stronger argument for remaining stagnant. So we are here. Where we need to be.

'Well, don't just stand there, pull your other stirrup down its leather, and then we'll get you on board,' Mistral said, making me jump as he pulled the stirrup on his side down its leather with a slap.

'Um, do all of these people have to watch?' I whispered, not quite looking at him as I followed his instruction.

Mistral's eyes bored into me over Noble's neck. 'They don't have to, they're choosing to. This is a place of free choice, after all, isn't it?'

My bottom lip began to tremble and I bit it, trying not to cry.

Mistral stepped closer to Noble and lowered his voice so that only I could hear him. 'You're one of the Horse-Bonded now, Quinta, you'll have eyes on you wherever you go. It's best to begin getting used to that from the outset. We've all been beginner riders and I'm sure we can all remember feeling nervous during our first few lessons. If anyone here has forgotten, you can be very sure that I will remind them.'

'You won't make us go too fast, will you?' I said.

Mistral chuckled. 'I won't make you do anything you don't want to do, but I normally have a job stopping newly bonded riders from trying to gallop before they can walk.'

'None of them have been me though,' I whispered as Mistral strode away. He unlatched the paddock gate and held it open for Noble and me.

'Good on you, Quinta, we're right behind you.' I turned to see that Mason was one of those leaning on the fence by the gate, and

Newson was two along from him. Both waved and grinned and I felt a little less like throwing up.

'Right then, there's no time to waste,' Mistral said, bending down beside me with cupped hands. 'Bend your left leg at the knee, and jump on three.' I swallowed so that my heart wouldn't jump out of my throat, and almost choked. By the time I had finished coughing, Mistral was standing straight beside me. He immediately bent down again. 'Ready?'

I felt anything but, however I couldn't delay the inevitable any longer. I could barely see for the dizziness that overcame me, but I bent my leg obediently and jumped in the same instant that Mistral lifted me.

As soon as I landed in the saddle, I felt all wrong. Where the previous evening, I had felt an enhanced connection with Noble, today I felt as if I were perched atop him, separate from him – vulnerable.

We are where we need to be, Noble reminded me.

I didn't find his thought even remotely reassuring, and my heart thumped even harder as I realised that he hadn't meant it to be. I panicked and looked to Mason and Newson for reassurance, which they both gave with a wink in Mason's case and a brief nod in Newson's. Mason's wink was quickly replaced by a slight frown, however. Had he seen the panic on my face, or had he seen something else I should be worried about?

'Your stirrups are the right length, Mason estimated correctly as usual,' Mistral said, and placed my left foot in its stirrup. 'Find your other stirrup and then we'll make a start.'

I swallowed and reached for Noble in my mind, desperate for the calm confidence I knew I would find there. I couldn't find him. It was as if wherever my mind tried to go, it hit walls that only closed in the more I panicked. Despite being on my horse's back, I felt a million miles away from him. Alone. Terrified. I wanted to get off, but I didn't know how and my throat was so tight, I couldn't get the words out to ask Mistral.

I fumbled around with my right foot, trying to put it through the stirrup in the frantic hope I would feel safer, but the metal hoop seemed to be alive as it evaded me. I began to lean to the right in my ever more frenetic attempts to find it, then almost passed out as I slipped in the saddle. I grabbed hold of Noble's mane in my effort to stay on his back, feeling as if the hard-packed, grassy paddock were rising up to meet me and then dropping back down again, enticing me down onto its hard-packed surface so that it could shatter my body.

A hand grabbed my shirt at the waist and pulled hard until I was upright again. 'There's no rush, you can take your time with anything I ask you to do,' Mistral said. He let go of me and then appeared by my right foot and helped it into its stirrup. 'There, now you're all set. All I'm going to do in this session is to introduce you to the feeling of Noble's body moving beneath you, and get you relaxing or holding the relevant parts of your body that will allow you to balance and move with him without impeding his movement. We'll take it nice and steady, so you can just relax, listen to what I'm telling you, and enjoy riding your horse for the first time. Okay?'

I was too busy trying to stop my eyes from flicking all over the place as they wanted to in order to make sense of the dizziness I was now experiencing, and holding my bladder so I wouldn't wet myself, to answer.

Mistral clearly took my lack of response as either agreement or anticipation for further instructions, and said, 'Gently close your ankles to Noble's sides and keep them there until he moves forward into a walk. Like this.' His hand closed around the top of my boot and pushed it against Noble's belly.

Noble immediately walked forward. The breath I had been

holding came out as a gasp and I thought I would faint with terror as everything moved beneath me, giving me no reference point upon which to balance.

Mistral walked beside me. 'You're leaning forward, which is unbalancing Noble and is actually quite a precarious position for you. Relax into your seat and sit up straight.'

I couldn't do it. I wanted to get as close to curling up as I possibly could. The thought of sitting up and being even further away from the ground held me in position, my hands gripping Noble's mane so tightly, they were white. I shook my head. I couldn't do this. I would never be able to do it. I knew Noble wanted me to, but he was being no help whatsoever. Why had he abandoned me in my thoughts? Why wasn't he helping me when I was so scared? I tried to reach for him in my mind again, but bounced back in on myself, the walls feeling even tighter around me now that I had continually failed to breach them.

'Quinta, you're holding your breath and in doing that, you're holding your whole body rigid. Relax your diaphragm and breathe out, then breathe in and out slowly. Relax and sit up straight,' Mistral said, his voice soft, kind and patient. It made no difference, I was completely frozen into position. Mistral whispered, 'You know you can trust your Bond-Partner, don't you? Even if you don't trust me yet?'

But I couldn't, could I? He had abandoned me when I needed him the most, just like he had when the river had taken me. I couldn't trust anyone. Noble walked slowly around the paddock, giving the impression that he was oblivious to my trauma and discomfort.

'Okay, I would normally ask you to stop moving your body in concert with Noble's in order to ask him to slow down and stop, but since you aren't moving and he barely is, I think you can just close your knees against him, and that will do it,' Mistral said.

Finally, an instruction that made me feel less precarious. I grabbed hold of the saddle with my knees, and Noble halted immediately. I let out the breath I had been holding and felt even dizzier.

'Can you relax onto your seat in the saddle and sit up now that Noble is stationary?' Mistral said.

I shook my head.

Mistral looked behind himself for a moment, then back up at me. 'Hang in there for a second, help is on its way.' Footsteps sounded nearby and Mistral turned and said, 'One of you on either side, please.'

Mason appeared by Noble's right shoulder and Newson by his left.

Mistral said, 'Quinta, would you permit your friends to each take a hold of one of your legs? I need you to feel secure enough to do as I ask.'

I nodded, relieved beyond measure for anything that would help me to feel less precarious. Strong hands grasped my legs just above my knees and I breathed out again, then instantly held the next inward breath to stop myself from crying.

'Okay, now these two could hold someone three times your size in place, so you're completely, utterly secure, Quinta,' Mistral said. 'Just relax back off the front of your pelvis and sit down as if you were sitting on a chair with a comfy seat but a straight back. That's it, lovely, well done. Now just sit there for a little bit. Breathe.'

My surroundings came back into focus as my dizziness began to fade, and I realised that no one was moving. Those sitting or leaning on the fence were all watching in silence, some with their mouths slightly open. I was flooded with shame as I realised how right Newson had been when he told me that riding horses brought out who we really were. I had just broadcast in the loudest way possible to all of my onlookers, what a nervy, cowardly excuse for a human being I really was.

I swallowed, relieved to find that my mouth was producing saliva again. 'I need to get off,' I said. 'I can't do this, I have to get off.'

'You absolutely can do this, you just need to take it in very small steps,' Mistral said. 'You'll have seen others riding their horses as if they were born to it, well let me tell you, Quinta, very few of us found it easy to begin with. It's just a case of finding what you're comfortable with and then slowly building on that. All I want you to do in the coming days is to saddle Noble and sit on his back for a minute longer than the previous day. When you're feeling more comfortable with sitting on him, let me know and we'll get back to your lessons. Okay?'

I nodded. I would have agreed to anything in order for him to tell me how to get off without falling off.

'Right then, take your feet out of your stirrups, lean forward a little more than you are now, and swing your right leg over Noble's back.'

My eyes widened. Take my feet out of my stirrups?

'I won't let go of you until you tell me to,' Mason whispered and tightened his hold on my right leg. Newson did the same, so I slid my feet backward out of the stirrups and leant forward.

'I'm ready,' I managed to say in a squeaky voice.

As soon as my friends released me, I swung my leg over the saddle as Mistral had instructed, and slid down Noble's side to the floor. I leant my forehead against the saddle so that no one could see the tears streaming down my face.

A hand rubbed my back gently and when I eventually stepped away from Noble, only Mason remained with us both. Newson was over by the fence, speaking to the last of my spectators as he gestured with his hands for them to disperse.

'Mistral has moved his lessons to a couple of paddocks down, so you have all the time you need,' Mason said gently.

'I've never been so frightened,' I whispered. 'And Noble was no help, he left me alone in my head and wouldn't tell me what to do.'

Had your fear not blocked me from your mind then I would have reminded you to employ the same practice as you have previously when negotiating that which challenges you. Noble's thought was as calm and confident as always, and carried no hint of disapproval or displeasure.

I stood back from him. *I blocked you?* I reached out to him and in the absence of the walls that had closed in on me, found him exactly where he always was. Relief flooded through me and I hugged his neck. *I blocked you. Thank goodness, I missed you so much, I was completely lost without you. So when I have to ride you again, you'll be with me? You'll help me?*

I am always with you. You need no help other than that which He Who Is Prudence offers. You have already learnt how to negotiate your way through your life. Everything that will ever challenge you is merely another opportunity to practise remaining present. To practise adhering to the path that feels difficult yet creates possibility instead of reverting to the path that feels safe due to its familiarity yet spirals inward to stagnation.

But what if doing all of that feels too difficult? It was all very well throwing caution to the wind and throwing myself in harm's way when your life was at stake, but this is different.

It only appears that way. The situation in which we met merely appeared urgent due to the short length of the moment it occupied. The situation humankind will soon face will occupy a longer moment and so will seem less urgent but the decisions must be made from the same place as when you helped me out of the water.

The same place? You mean I need to make my decisions out of love?

I sensed Noble's agreement. *This is an opportunity for you to gain experience in moving past fear in all of its guises so that you will be capable of allowing love to anchor you in the present when it matters most. When humankind depends on it.*

Suddenly, everything appeared simpler and more complicated at the same time. I knew what I had to do, I just didn't think I'd be able to do it.

Chapter Thirteen

*O*nce Newson had cleared the fence of people, he waved to me and then went about his day. Mason remained with me until, in his words, I was back to my normal self – I dreaded to think what he considered that was – then made me promise I would seek him out if I needed to chat, and hurried back to his workshop.

Noble and I made our way along the strangely empty path back to his paddock; I got the distinct feeling that Newson had cleared that for us too, but then berated myself for being paranoid. Regardless, I was grateful not to have to face anyone.

Rejection is one of fear's guises, Noble advised me as his small hooves thudded on the pathway beside my booted feet.

Marvellous. Just one of the many forms it comes in to trap me, block me from you and ensure I make an idiot of myself. How many forms does it take, exactly? Just so I know?

You must learn to recognise the energy of fear so that you will know it for what it is regardless of the form it takes.

I sighed. *So my life is just going to be composed of lots of episodes that are going to make me scared and miserable until I've learnt all there is to know about fear? I suppose I just need to try to keep going until I've got through them all and then at some point, I can finally be happy?*

You will never be happy with that mindset for it is self-perpetuating. Noble focused his thoughts so that they seemed sharper, more pointed. *Every time you reach the 'when' for which you were aiming you will stop focusing on it. Your mind will be so used to aiming for it that it will create another 'when' for which to aim. You will be holding your happiness away from you instead of embracing it in every moment.*

Everything always comes back to that, doesn't it? Living and embracing every moment?

From your experience of doing such can you think of a better way to be?

I guess not. No, I know not. But when I think of doing it, it just seems like such an effort.

Think less. Feel more.

I sighed. *It always comes back to that too. I just find it hard to remember everything you've told me when I really need to.*

That is why we must practise. Riding will help.

Can't I just practise doing it in the rest of my life for now? It's not as if I have that sorted. Do we have to pile riding on top of everything else when it scares me so much?

As always it is your choice whether to take the path that opens more possibilities or the one that spirals in on itself.

I nodded my understanding but felt relieved at the thought that I wouldn't have to make that choice again today; I'd be back at my loom soon, where I felt confident.

I opened the paddock gate for Noble to walk through and then undid his girth, pulled the saddle from his back, and rested it on the fence. I fetched my grooming kit and spent a long moment grooming him until I had brushed all of the sweat and dust from his coat. I spotted dapples outlined on his flanks that I hadn't noticed before.

I have not been this free of dust before, Noble noted with approval.

I smiled, glad beyond measure that at least I had done something right. I rubbed his neck and then as he wandered off to graze with Integrity in the shade of the alder tree, I gathered my grooming brushes together into their bag and hung it back in the field shelter.

I hurried to my workshop, my eyes down to discourage comment from anyone passing the other way, and spent the rest of the afternoon ploughing through my orders whilst revelling in the sanctuary of all the sensations afforded me by my loom. I was proud of myself that by the time the dinner bell rang, I felt that I could stay present enough in each moment to be able to endure eating in the dining hall. Nevertheless, I took a quick detour to Noble's paddock and allowed the sight of him to further cement the sense of him in my mind for which I had reached and then immersed myself the second I finished work at my loom.

I wandered to the dining room full of Noble's calm confidence, and smiled at those whose eyes met mine as I entered. Everyone smiled back and a few waved before returning to conversations with those at their tables. The sights, sounds and smells filled my awareness and before I knew it, I was seated with a bowlful of stew and a bread roll. I ate slowly, savouring each and every mouthful. When Mason sat down opposite me with concern in his eyes, I smiled at him.

He nodded and tucked into his own meal. We ate in silence, although every now and then, Mason would look as if he was going to say something, pause with a slightly glazed expression and then shrug and go back to his meal. I smiled in the knowledge that Diligence was counselling him; I could see it in his face and feel it in my skin, almost as if she were there with us. She was helping me as surely as was my own Bond-Partner.

'May I meet Diligence, please, Mason?' I said suddenly. 'I've seen her and I feel as if I know her, but I've never actually met her.'

Mason flinched at my unexpected interruption of our companionable silence, then a broad smile broke out over his face. 'Of course, she'll enjoy that, she knows all about you.' He stopped suddenly and flushed. 'Not in a bad way, just in a way that means she helps me to not say the wrong thing, until just now, obviously.'

I smiled. 'I know. I felt it in my skin when she was communicating with you just then.'

He blinked. 'You felt it in your skin? How do you mean?'

I shrugged. 'I don't know how to explain it. It's like trying to describe how you can feel the wind blowing. You can just feel it. When I met Integrity, I felt her kindness in my skin, and I just felt that Dili's trying to help me, in the same way.'

'And you have it exactly right. You're a sensitive one, aren't you,' Mason said, his dark eyes holding mine. 'We'll finish up here and then go and see Dili, shall we?'

I nodded and didn't speak again. When I had finished my stew and mopped all of the gravy from my bowl with my bread, I sat back and waited for Mason to finish. I stood up when he did, and we walked towards the paddocks in silence. As we passed Noble's paddock, I sensed that he was snoozing in the shade of his field shelter, away from the flies. We carried on walking almost as far as Mistral's teaching paddock, until the huge, dark grey mare whom I knew to be Dili whickered to us over a paddock gate. I looked up at Mason to see that his face had lit up.

'Quinta, meet my Diligence,' he said, holding a hand out towards his horse, 'my Bond-Partner and the love of my life.'

The mare towered above me but as she reached down to sniff my face, my skin tingled with her nurturing gentleness. I stroked the downy hair that surrounded her nostrils and she blew gently over me, coating me in her protection in a moment that seemed to last for eternity.

When she finally moved to greet her Bond-Partner, I had a fleeting moment of wishing she were my Bond-Partner instead of Noble.

Immediately, Mason said, 'Dili wants you to know that your Bond-Partner is all you need and more.'

I felt chastened. *Noble, I'm so sorry. Forgive me?*

He was unaffected by either my feelings for Dili or my apology, and felt no need to reply. I was where I needed to be, that was all, I realised, just as he had taught me. He was indeed all I needed and more.

'I know it,' I said. 'I just feel so safe with Dili.'

'She has that way about her, doesn't she?' Mason said.

'So why don't you ride her, if you don't mind me asking? I know you said you're not very good at it, but surely you feel safe to practise with her?'

Mason chuckled. 'I don't mind you askin' at all. Sure, I could ride more and try to improve, but whenever I wonder whether Dili would like me to, I get the sense she's waiting for somethin', so I put it to one side. There are certain people she likes me to take notice of, yourself included, and she and I watch out in case any of you might need anythin' from us both, so here we are. My Dili always has it right, just as your Noble does,' he added. 'We're always here for you, Quinta, me and Dili. Okay?'

Dili moved back to me and blew in my ear again. I stroked her nose with the back of my finger. 'Thank you,' I whispered. 'Thank you both.'

I walked back towards the buildings with Mason, then left him to go on alone as I climbed over Noble's gate and followed my sense of him to where he was still snoozing in his field shelter. He whickered as I entered and found him lying down. I sat in the straw by his head and crossed my legs. He lowered his head into my lap and sighed deeply. I would be okay tomorrow, I decided. All I had to do was to sit on Noble's back and then get off. I'd loved it when I'd done it with only Mason there, I'd love it again without all those people watching me. I would feel my way to doing it, and I would be fine.

Predictably, when I woke the following morning, I was far from fine. I had relived my riding lesson over and over in my dreams, each one progressively more torturous than the previous one until I dreamt that I couldn't dismount for the jeering and taunting coming from my spectators, and just sat on Noble's back, screaming.

I sat up and opened my eyes in the darkness of predawn, with sweat pouring from me. Had I been screaming out loud as well as in my nightmare? Had I woken everyone in the accommodation block? Had I made even more of a fool of myself? I shook myself. I couldn't stay here, I was due for my shift in the washroom soon. I had to get up and get dressed so I could get down to the paddocks to see Noble first.

I lit my lantern, leapt out of bed and flung open my wardrobe door. I couldn't decide what to wear. Each shirt I looked at would go with any of my shorts. No, I realised, I should wear leggings despite the heat, because I would be riding later. Panic stabbed at my heart as the nightmares I had only just escaped burst back into my mind. I breathed in and out deeply, trying to get a hold of myself, trying to focus on the moment in hand and choose which clothes to wear. The shirts. Which would go with which leggings? I leafed through my leggings but then had forgotten which shirts were there. My arms and legs began to tingle and I felt an urgent need for the bathroom. I raced down the corridor and just made it in time, then raced back to my room. I would be late. I had to hurry up, or I would be late. I stood in front of the wardrobe again – and was no further forward.

'No, no, no, no, no,' I wailed to myself. I couldn't revert to how I was before Noble tugged me, I couldn't go back to that, I just couldn't.

I dragged a shirt from a hanger with a shaking hand, then pulled a pair of leggings from another hanger. I dressed quickly, then undressed again, ran to wash, then ran back to my room and redressed. I looked around my room. Had I forgotten to do anything else? I couldn't remember. I stood, rooted to the spot. Had I brushed my hair? Had I cleaned my teeth? Did I have the right clothes on for the day? My mind began to race through everything I would be doing that day, and then rechecked the clothes I was wearing, over and over.

I was still standing there when the sky lightened. I was due in the washroom right now, I'd run out of time to see Noble. Okay. It would be okay. I'd check in with him in my mind. Where was he? Cold dread worked its way through my body as I realised I had blocked him out of my mind and couldn't find a way to let him back in. I was on my own. I sat down on my bed, then lay on my side and curled my knees up to my chin.

I jumped at a loud bang somewhere below me and then again at a crashing and clattering that got louder and louder. I closed my eyes tightly, waiting for the building to collapse and almost hoping it would, so that there would be an end to my situation.

A whinny joined the crashing and clattering and my eyes flicked open. *Noble?*

He whinnied again as the clattering got louder and then suddenly there was silence.

I jumped as someone knocked loudly on my door. 'Quinta?' Newson shouted breathlessly. 'Quinta, are you in there? Are you alright? Noble's out here. Please don't make him break the door down, he's already left one hanging in its frame.'

A low whicker brought me back to my senses. I ran to the door and opened it to find Newson bending over with a hand on the doorframe, panting hard. Standing next to him was my horse. My beautiful, incredible horse was heaving almost as hard as Newson, and dripping sweat all over the stone floor.

'Noble, how did you get up here? What are you doing here?' I whispered as I flung my arms around his neck.

He filled my senses. Heat radiated from him. His sweat was sharp as it reached my nose. His short, harsh breaths blocked out the sleepy voices of those poking their heads out of their rooms to enquire what was going on. He was there because I had blocked him out of my mind. He was there to bring me back to myself. He was there for me as he always had been and always would be. My heart filled and then overflowed with love.

You have returned to the present, he observed. *To me.* He nuzzled my cheek and then turned and wandered back down the corridor as if it were an activity he performed regularly. A man frowned and rubbed his eyes as if convinced he must still be asleep, and a woman yawned as she held a hand out for Noble to sniff and nuzzle briefly on his way past.

'It's all over now,' Newson gasped to them and the others

looking between him, me and Noble. 'Noble was needed here and now he isn't, sorry for the disturbance.'

Heads nodded and disappeared, and doors closed. The corridor was quiet.

'Are you alright?' I asked Newson.

'I'm fine now I've got my breath back. You look awful though. What happened? I was filling up the water barrel in the paddock when Noble came flying out of the field shelter and started galloping around. He skidded to a stop in front of the gate and then galloped round and skidded to a stop when he reached it again, quite obviously wanting to get out, so I opened it and then followed him here. When I say followed, I mean followed his trail; the people standing in the square, staring towards the accommodation block and the entrance door hanging from its hinges gave away his destination. I only caught up with him because he kept slipping in the stairwell. Honestly, he could have broken his neck.'

'He wouldn't have thought about that. He's Noble,' I said.

Newson's grey eyes sharpened and he nodded. 'I see that. Can I help at all?'

I smiled. 'You already did. Thanks for letting Noble out. He knew I needed him and he reached me thanks to you.'

Newson nodded slowly. 'Is this likely to be a regular occurrence, or shall I ask one of the Carpenters to fix the door downstairs?'

I looked down at the floor. 'I don't know. I'm sorry. I hope it won't happen again, but I don't know. I have a long way to go before I can be sure of anything.'

Newson put a hand on my shoulder. 'We all do. Don't worry about anything, I'll get the door sorted, and if it needs sorting again in the future, I'll organise that too, okay?'

I tried to smile. 'Thank you. I'd better get going, I'm already late for my shift.'

'You're in the washroom, aren't you? Why don't I let them know they'll be one short this morning? They'll understand.'

I shook my head. 'No, I can't stay here and think about things, I need to practise everything Noble's taught me. Thanks, Newson, I'll catch up with you later?'

He looked searchingly into my eyes, then gave a brief nod. 'If you're sure. Take care, Quinta, okay?'

'I will. Thanks.' I shut my bedroom door, rushed to my window and pulled back the curtains, then made my bed and brushed my hair back and secured it in a tail.

I hurried along the corridor, hoping no one would hear my footsteps and come out to talk to me, then out past the entrance door which was indeed hanging off its hinges. I reached out to Noble to check he was uninjured even though I was sure I would have known if he were, and found him drinking from his water barrel, sanguine as ever. I searched his mind and witnessed his mad dash to my room. I was relieved that it was only his tail catching on the door handle that had caused it to be dislodged from one of its hinges, with no negative consequences to my horse other than the loss of the clump of tail hair still curled around the door handle.

I rushed to the washroom and took my place beside Hannah.

'There you are,' she said. 'Is everything okay? You look pale.'

'I'm sorry I'm late, I'm fine thanks, Noble just had to, er, get me moving, but I'm here now and ready to work. Is that sheet ready for wringing out?' I held my hands out to accept one end of it.

'It is. Thanks. Are you sure you don't want to go back to bed? You really don't look well.'

I didn't feel it, but I knew that retreating to my room to hide wouldn't help. I shook my head and managed to smile, then began to twist my end of the sheet one way while Hannah twisted hers the other.

I lived through my day from moment to moment, just as I was supposed to. When I'd finished in the washroom, I fetched my breakfast and took it to eat in Noble's paddock while he grazed nearby. He didn't offer me counsel and I didn't ask for any. I spent the morning in the workshop, fetched myself some lunch which I also ate with Noble, then returned to the workshop where I worked until dinnertime. I assured Newson I was okay when he looked in on me during the morning, and grinned and waved at Mason when he poked his head around the workshop door during the afternoon and bellowed a greeting over the noise of my, Ted's and Celia's looms. All the while, I remained immersed in the sanctuary offered by my loom, Noble, or both.

When Mason found me sitting, eating my dinner in Noble's field shelter where my horse once more stood out of the heat and flies, he crouched down in front of me, his bulk making him seem no smaller to me than when he was upright. 'Shall I fetch Dili?' he asked me. 'She'll come if you need her.'

I smiled. 'Thanks, but no, I have all I need right here.' I nodded towards Noble.

'Okay, well, shall I fetch your saddle then? Do you want to have a little sit on Noble, like Mistral said, while I'm here?'

The thought of riding shook me out of my place with my horse and I shuddered. I grasped for Noble in my mind, desperate not to lose him again, and sighed with relief when I found him. I shook my head. 'I haven't had a very easy day and I'm really tired. Thanks for your offer, but maybe tomorrow?' I held my breath for a second, wondering whether Noble would intervene and remind me to go with the flow, but to my relief, he remained silent. I would ride him the following day, I promised both him and myself.

I didn't make it back to my bedroom that night. Every time I got to my feet with the intention of returning my dinnerplate and cutlery to the dining room and then retiring to bed, I was jolted out of the sanctuary of the moment by terror that I would wake in the morning to find myself back in my old pattern of being immobilised by anxiety. I would immerse myself in my senses' interpretation of the summer evening, or in Noble's relaxed slumber – whichever I managed to reach first – and remain there until I felt strong enough to try again, but the result was always the same and eventually I fell asleep in the straw.

When my eyes flicked open in the dark, I wondered for a moment where I was. I smelt the earthy and slightly dusty straw and heard a grinding sound that made me smile. I was with Noble. I reached for him in my mind and sensed him munching hay from a rack attached to the far wall of the shelter. I was calm and in the moment. All was well with the world.

I got to my feet, hugged my horse and then made my way back to my room, leaving my dinnerplate on the cobbles by the dining hall door on the way past. I bathed and donned fresh clothes, then got to the washroom just as the birds announced the dawn. Glad to be there first, I began filling both the sink Hannah and I tended to share, and those either side ready for those who would be working alongside us.

'Well, hello there,' Hannah's voice echoed from the doorway. 'Feeling better?'

I grinned. 'Yes, thanks.' I meant it.

Chapter Fourteen

*I*n the eyes of most at The Gathering, I was adjusting well to being one of the Horse-Bonded. I even managed to persuade myself of it at times. I never missed a shift of chores; whichever time I was rostered to work and whichever task I was allotted for a given week, I was present, cheerful and steadily made more friends. I spent the rest of my time either weaving, eating, hanging out with or grooming Noble, or – unbeknownst to anyone else – sleeping in his field shelter so that I could be near him at night, and more importantly, when I awoke.

I had a fresh reason every day why I couldn't ride. I was either too tired, had too many orders to fulfil with there still being only three Weavers at The Gathering when four would have been the full complement, I'd hurt various parts of my body on my loom, it was too hot for Noble with him being dark in colour, it was too wet when we had the storms that finally broke the oppressive heat, and then the ground was too slippery. The list was never-ending and exhausting to keep up. I told myself that each and every excuse was true and everyone believed me except for Mistral –

who questioned me every few days as to how I was getting on even though I knew he knew – and those who knew me better than the rest.

Neither Mason nor Newson questioned my excuses, but not a day went past without one of them offering to be with me while I sat on Noble for a few minutes. Noble himself remained quiet on the subject but his calm confidence that I would work my way through my fear was like a stone in my boot that constantly prodded at my foot and which I couldn't shake out, never allowing me to forget that about which I was trying so hard to avoid thinking.

I told myself that it was acceptable to avoid that which I found so difficult because I was working so hard on being in the moment, and any thought of riding shook me out of my increasing ability to focus on that which was in front of me in any given instant; the longer I avoided riding, the longer I would be able to maintain my newfound state of mind. But the longer I avoided riding and all thoughts of it, the more drained I felt.

Evasion of that which is difficult takes much energy, Noble informed me one evening as I was grooming him. I was with him in every stroke of the brush against his dark coat, in every pull of the comb through his long, black tail, and with every flick of the hoof pick as I eased out small stones and hardpacked dirt from the cleft between the frog and sole of each foot in turn. But I wasn't as strong in my strokes, as determined in my combing, or as efficient with the hoof pick as normal, and as a result, Noble didn't look quite as neat and shiny as he usually did when I'd groomed him.

I stepped back and looked at him, shocked not only by his thought – the closest he had come to berating me for not riding since our lesson with Mistral – but by the fact that his appearance corresponded with both the piece of cloth over which I'd been cursing earlier that day in my workshop, and how I felt; we were all fraying at the edges.

Your inner self cannot help but manifest in that which you believe to be external to yourself since they are one and the same, Noble told me.

What do you mean?

You believe you are separate from everything around you and so that is largely what you experience. But when you try to hide part of yourself in one way it merely bursts out in another. I can help you to work through the aspect of yourself that you avoid. You know I can.

But you refuse to reassure me that you'll look after me if I ride you, you won't promise that you won't do anything that will cause me to fall off.

I refuse to shield you from your fear. Were I to do that then I would merely be reinforcing your beliefs that you are unsafe and incapable of coping with whatever arises in front of you. You have already proven to yourself that neither of those beliefs are true. You must continue to prove the same until you can recognise the truth in every moment.

It's too hard. I'm too scared.

The more energy you put into avoiding it the more difficult it will seem. I felt the truth in Noble's statement and knew he was right. I couldn't go on like this. Noble put his chin on my shoulder and blew softly in my ear. *I am always with you. You know this. Immerse yourself in our bond for there you will always find the truth of who you are.*

I knew it was true and it seemed such a simple solution when he reminded me to do it. So why couldn't I remember for myself to reach for him as he so often encouraged me to do? Noble didn't volunteer an opinion and I realised I didn't need him to, for I knew the answer; fear. It was insidious. It hid in my body and mind, grasping hold of me before I realised what had happened, blocking me from Noble, scaring me into turning in on myself so that I was a prisoner in my own mind. All I had to do was step aside from it and reach for Noble – it was so simple and yet I found it so difficult.

The greater the challenge the greater the possibility, Noble reminded me.

'I'm sorry to intrude, I waited as long as I could, but I just need to give Integrity a groom before it gets too dark to see.' Newson's voice wafted softly across the paddock from the gate, carrying his apology as obviously as did his words.

I jumped and stepped closer to Noble, putting my arm under his neck and resting my hand on the other side of it so that I could maintain my connection with him now that my mind was distracted. 'It's fine, I'm sorry to have held you up.'

Newson lifted a hand and shook his head slightly. 'No problem at all, I could see you two were having a chat. By the way, while I'm here, I can help you if you'd like to sit on Noble for a minute or two?'

Where normally I bristled and retreated into my awareness of the surrounding sights, smells and sounds so as not to panic whenever he or Mason made that suggestion, I hugged Noble tighter and put everything of myself into keeping my mind with his. I nodded. 'Thank you, that would be great, and then I can help you to groom Integrity afterwards?'

Newson grinned, his smile lighting up his usually serious face. 'Of course. Do you already have your saddle here?' He looked back at the fence and then towards the field shelter.

I shook my head, knowing what I needed to do. 'Could you just help me to get on without it? If I leave Noble to go and fetch it, I don't think I'll be able to do this. I need to do it now.'

Newson nodded. 'No problem. Come on then, bend your knee

and I'll give you a leg up.' He bent down by Noble's shoulder and cupped his hands.

Before I could give myself a chance to think, I was sitting on Noble's back. His calm confidence thrummed through me as certainly as the warmth of both his body and mind. There was nothing we couldn't do. I closed my heels against Noble's sides as Mistral had told me to, and Noble walked forward. Still with him in my mind, my body moved easily with his as if we were part of one another.

It was dark when Noble finally stopped walking. Newson was exactly where we had left him, a broad grin allowing the moonlight to highlight his teeth.

He rushed to Noble's side. 'Do you remember how to dismount? Lean forward and swing your leg over Noble's back, then bend your legs as you land. That's it. Quinta, well done, so very well done. You followed his movement perfectly, and without a saddle too.'

I was elated. Blood coursed through my veins, but where normally the sensation was accompanied by a thumping heart, rapid, shallow breaths and a desperate need for the bathroom, this time it was accompanied by pure, unadulterated elation.

'I did it, I can't believe it,' I said. 'All I had to do was keep my mind with Noble's so I couldn't worry, and the riding bit was easy. But, Newson, I'm sorry, you wanted to groom Integrity while you could still see her properly, and instead you stayed there to keep an eye on me. Come on, I'll help you now.'

Newson chuckled. 'You sort your own Bond-Partner out, he'll be all sweaty where you've been sitting. Integrity is more content at your achievement than she would have been at the grooming I had planned for her, don't you worry. I'll give her a quick flick off and be down early to groom her properly before I'm due out in the fields to help with the harvest. That's if I won't disturb you?'

I sighed, thankfully still on too much of a high to feel mortified. 'How long have you known?'

Newson chuckled again. 'It isn't just you who can sense everything their horse can, you know.'

I laughed along with him. 'Integrity. Of course. I'm an idiot.'

'You're newly bonded, a condition that has made idiots of us all, believe me, and continues to do so where most of us are concerned. Are you planning to sleep out here with Noble for much longer? It'll be getting cold at night soon.'

'That may be, but I don't trust myself not to panic when I wake up if I'm not near him, and I don't want him to have to come up to my room and snap me out of it like he did a few months back.'

'I guess the field shelter will hold its warmth for a little while yet, and you could bring some blankets down here. Okay, well I'll get a move on with Integrity and then leave you to get some sleep.'

I was still washing Noble down by the water barrel when the gate creaked and then clicked shut.

'Night, Newson, and thanks,' I whispered into the still night.

'Don't mention it,' came his whisper as his footsteps faded into the night.

'So, are you goin' to ask Mistral for more lessons, now that you're happy to sit on Noble again?' Mason asked me with a wink as I sat down opposite him with a plate of toast and marmalade the following morning.

I grinned. 'News travels fast, I thought Newson was a Metal-Singer, not a Herald. And no, I'm not. I know I need Mistral's help, but at the moment, I need to find a way to be able to ride

Noble at will, not just when I happen to find myself in the right state of mind – and by that, I mean by being in Noble's.'

Mason chortled. 'I think you sell yourself short, I refuse to believe there's anythin' wrong with your mind.'

'It tangles itself into a mess of fear and worry if I'm not careful, you've seen it for yourself,' I replied.

'What I've seen, Quinta, is a very brave lady doin' her utmost to conquer her fears,' Mason said quietly. 'Now, you let me or Newson know whenever you're ready to sit on Noble, whatever the time of day or night, and one or both of us will be there to help you. Will you promise me?'

'I can't ask you to do that, either of you, you're both as busy as everyone else here.'

Mason sat back against his chair. 'You're workin' towards being everythin' you named your horse for. Allow Newson and me to do the same?' His dark eyes held mine, the crinkles at their corners softening his words.

'But I may need to do it there and then, like last night. If I have to come and find you, I might have lost the concentration I need to be able to do it.'

Mason winked. 'You let Integrity and Diligence look after that side of things. There's nothing Noble knows that they don't, and Newson and I are well used to downing tools when they decide our time could be put to better use.'

I smiled. 'Thanks, Mason. Really. Thanks.'

He nodded as he returned my smile.

Summer gave way to autumn, which passed in all its glory and gave way in turn to winter before I felt ready to approach Mistral for more riding lessons.

I had sat on Noble every single day, however long it took for me to be firmly enough with him in his confidence that I could either accept a leg up from whichever of my two closest friends arrived to help me, or increasingly, I could stay with him in my mind as I walked to the tack room to fetch my saddle, tack him up and then mount myself from the ground while Mason or Newson held the other stirrup.

As soon as I was on Noble's back, staying with him in body and mind was no effort whatsoever. Every time, I wondered why it had taken so much effort to get myself in the right place mentally to be able to ride him, when once I was on board, it was like returning home and I felt like there was nothing we couldn't do.

As the days, weeks and months passed, I became more and more able to get myself together to ride at a time of my choosing instead of having to focus and refocus over and over until I was calm enough, whatever time of the day that might have been. I was still sleeping in the field shelter, however, an activity from which Mason and Newson repeatedly tried to coax me away.

'There's always a deep straw bed in there, as you both know, and I have blankets. If Noble knows I'm cold, he comes and lies down near me so I can snuggle up to him,' I whispered to them both one lunchtime. 'I won't risk him hurting himself by having to come and get me out of my room again.'

'Or everyone knowing why he had to?' Newson whispered back. 'We're all on your side, Quinta, you know that. You can trust us. All of us.'

My voice trembled as I said, 'But I don't trust myself. I can't go back to being who I was, I just can't. First thing in the morning, when I've just woken up, has always been the worst part of the day for me and it's still the time that my mind can get away from me. If Noble's nearby, it doesn't happen. The cold is a small price to pay for that, believe me.'

Mason looked at Newson and said, 'We do. I just wish there was a way around it. Maybe once you're having lessons and it's all going well, you'll feel differently?'

I shrugged. 'My first one is this afternoon, so I guess we'll find out, won't we?'

Chapter Fifteen

*D*espite my increased ability to reach for Noble when I felt anxious instead of allowing my fear to block him out, a small part of my mind managed to escape his calm confidence as I saddled him ready for our lesson. I felt nervous about riding in front of people again and hoped upon hope that I wouldn't let myself and my horse down by freezing or falling off.

I managed to mount him myself from the fence, with no assistance from either of my loyal friends. As soon as I sat down in the saddle, I felt as if Noble expanded around and then above me until he completely enveloped me. He and I were all that mattered. I felt his heartbeat, as slow and steady as mine was wild and erratic. I felt his breaths, as long and deep as mine were rapid and shallow. And I felt him, as prepared to give everything of himself to help me as I was selfish in my attempts to protect myself. The part of my mind responsible for my body not quite being in concert with my horse's snapped back to the rest of me and I immersed myself in our bond.

The ride to Mistral's preferred teaching paddock was a short

one, since now that I was no longer considered newly bonded –
and the paddock nearest the buildings needed to be rested and its
field shelter readied for any other newly bonded horses who might
arrive – Noble and Integrity had recently moved to a new paddock
about halfway between the buildings and the river. I fully
experienced every single sensation that each and every moment
had to offer on the way.

Noble's dainty footsteps seemed deafening as he thudded his
way along the grassy path, for I felt them as surely as I heard
them. A sharp winter wind buffeted its way past us both, freezing
my face as it carried the scent of a bonfire from where one
blazed in a paddock near the river. Distant as the inferno was, its
flames burned so tall and so brightly that it seemed as if they
were right in front of me. I heard their spits and crackles through
Noble's ears, as well as the thundering and gushing of the river
beyond.

When we reached the gate of the paddock for which we had
been aiming, I focused on the chatter and laughter of those few
people hardy enough to brave the winter wind in order to watch
Mistral teaching. I heard them as a single combined sound and
then as the different component voices – high and low, soft and
rough, chattering and laughing. They were sounds, just like all of
the others, and in need of no judgement or opinion as to their
nature or what they might be discussing.

'Quinta, Noble, welcome,' Mistral said, waving as he strode
over to us. He looked up at the enormous canopy that had been
erected above the paddock several weeks before and said, 'The
canvas will protect us from rain, sleet or snow but I'm afraid it
makes a bit of a noise when it's windy. I'll try to make my voice
reach you wherever you are, but if you can't hear me, raise your
arm and I'll try again, okay?'

I focused on the sound of his voice as well as on each and

every word before I allowed my mind to comprehend their combined meaning. I nodded.

'Okay, so then could you ask Noble to walk a large circle around me by turning your body as you would if you were walking on your own two feet? That's it, see how he matches your body's direction? You're moving very well with him, Quinta, your time since I last saw you has been very well spent. I think we can move you both up to a trot.'

It was easy. I followed every single instruction Mistral gave me without really being aware that was what I was doing; I just allowed his words to filter into my momentary experience and become part of everything else there so that Noble and I responded without thought.

When Mistral called for us both to stop, I barely heard his words of congratulation, I just smiled because it felt like the correct response to his voice. I jumped off Noble and loosened his girth whilst listening to Mistral explaining that we would move on to work in canter the following day. I thanked him and wandered back to Noble's paddock feeling exhilarated, yet as if what I had just experienced could only be described by one word – and one which Noble had used several times. Inevitable. As if I had arrived somewhere I already knew even though I had only just discovered it.

The following week passed me by in a blur of happiness. I loved doing my chores – I enjoyed contributing to the running of the place I was coming to cherish, whilst befriending those rostered alongside me – almost as much as I revelled in my weaving; I was finding that as my riding improved, I was becoming bolder and more keen to explore working with far more intricate patterns when I wove, whilst working at a rate nearly double that which I had been able to achieve in my parents' workshop. Neither of those activities, however, came close to giving me the joy I felt whenever I was on Noble's back.

I enjoyed Mistral's praise and appreciation of my rapidly improving riding, but it was the feeling of becoming ever closer to my horse in both body and mind that really made my heart sing. It was as if with every improvement I made to my posture, balance and timing, it became easier to keep my mind with Noble's, to see the world as he did, to realise, as he had told me I would, that I was both capable and safe, no matter what we were asked to do.

Six nights after our lessons restarted, I felt strong enough to return to sleeping in my bedroom at nighttime. I had a hot bath as I did every evening, and then, feeling slightly strange to be wearing a nightshirt instead of the many layers of clothing I had grown used to donning in order to go out to sleep in the field shelter, I got into bed.

A fire blazed in the hearth, giving the grey stone walls of my bedroom a cosy glow, and the two quilts I pulled up over me were thick and heavy, and smelt of summer flowers. My pillows were soft and as my head sank into them, I wondered how on earth I had endured sleeping in a bed of straw in the freezing cold for so long. Then I remembered.

Because you were there, I thought to Noble as I drifted off to sleep.

I opened my eyes and immediately tried to wrinkle my nose. I couldn't feel it. I smiled to myself as I revelled in my body's warmth under the covers, a stark contrast to the cold that numbed my face. Even so, I was able to separate out the faint smell of ash from the fire that had long since burnt out, from those of my recently washed hair, the quilts that weighed me down, and my leather boots that stood on paper in front of the hearth. In contrast to all of the scents in which I immersed myself, there was no sound. None at all. I pulled my quilts around myself and dragged them with me to the window, where the grey light of a winter dawn was peering through a gap in the thick, green curtains.

I pulled a curtain to one side and gasped. The square below was cloaked in several feet of snow.

I reached for Noble and found him in a standing doze in his field shelter whilst Integrity lay sound asleep at his feet. He could hear the river in the distance but apart from that, all was as quiet as where I was.

As if to make a liar of me, a door thudded and two heavily-clothed people jumped and staggered their way through the snow, across the square to the dining room. I supposed they were rostered for the first shift in the kitchens. I was glad I had been given the afternoon shift, where I and fifteen or so others would help the head cook to prepare the food for the evening meal. I would do a morning's work in the workshop, have lunch and then a lesson with Mistral, then I would spend the afternoon in the warm kitchens.

There was nothing that could come up with which I wouldn't be able to cope. I hugged myself.

I washed and dressed, then fought my way through the snow towards the paddocks, dragging a four-wheeled barrow rammed full of hay for Noble and Integrity. Newson was already at their paddock, pouring fresh water into the water barrel from containers sitting in his own wheelbarrow. Both horses whickered when they saw me, and Newson hurried to take a handle of my barrow.

'I was just about to go back for their hay,' he said as we dragged it to the paddock gate. 'We'll be having to make two or three trips a day like this now that they can't reach the grass. Don't you just love winter?'

'Do you know, I've never really thought about it, but I actually do,' I replied as we packed some of the hay into racks hanging from the fence. 'Everything that's usually colourful is suddenly white, the air's sharp where it was soft, the ground isn't where it normally is, there's silence where there was noise and the only smells are those of hay and horses. It's like nature is taking a break, and it feels… peaceful.'

'It just feels cold and inhospitable to me,' Newson said. 'We'll need to put the rest of this in the field shelter in case they want to get out of the weather.' He pushed the gate open through the snow and then picked up a handle of the barrow. We dragged it into the paddock, leaving the gate open behind us, and then through deep, untrodden snow towards the field shelter. It was hard work and by the time we got there, we were both panting. 'Still finding it peaceful?' Newson said with a grin.

I picked up a handful of snow and flicked it at him. His eyes widened and then glinted mischievously. I just managed to leap to the side of the wheelbarrow and duck down before a snowball flew over my head.

'Can anyone join in?' called a voice from the pathway.

Before I knew it, Newson and I were engaged in an all-out snowball fight with thirteen others, while Noble and Integrity stood calmly munching hay at their racks with only the occasional glance in our direction. Newson threw snowballs at everyone else to try to make himself the primary target while I quickly pulled the hay from the barrow before it got snow mixed in with it, and heaped it in piles along an inside wall of the field shelter. When I had finished, I joined him in hurling snowballs from behind the shelter afforded us by the barrow until everyone else – each of whom had received a snowball in the face at one point or another due to Newson's excellent aim – converged on us, pounding us with snow until, laughing, we cried for mercy.

We were a sodden lot who piled, red-faced and dripping, into the lobby of the dining hall for breakfast. None of us had time to sit and eat, so we all squelched our way to the food table to gather food we could carry with us to whichever tasks awaited us. We were the butt of teasing and joking from those in dry clothes who were seated and eating in a manner which, according to them, befitted the Horse-Bonded, to which we responded in kind.

I was still chuckling when I reached my workshop.

'What happened to you?' Ted said as he opened the door to let me in.

I waved my thanks with a wet-gloved hand holding what was now soggy toast, and swallowed my mouthful. 'Snowball fight. I inadvertently started it and a whole load of others finished it. It was the best fun.'

'But you're soaking wet, don't you want to go and get changed?'

I grinned as I shook my head. 'It looks worse than it is, I'll soon get warm once I'm working.'

He smiled at me and held my gaze as he said, 'I'm happy for you, Quinta.'

I smiled back, knowing that he wasn't talking about my clothes.

Lunchtime was a noisy affair due to an animated discussion involving most of those who were there, about staging a rematch of the morning's snowball fight on a far larger scale. I was still chuckling at the ensuing banter as I left the dining hall and slid my way across the now hard-packed snow to the tack room, having been assured by Mistral that his teaching paddock had been sufficiently protected from the snowfall by its canopy for his day's lessons to be able to go ahead.

I lightly brushed Noble's thick winter coat so as to flick any bits of dirt or dust away from where his saddle would sit, without removing the grease that was helping to keep him warm. Then I saddled and girthed him, and walked ahead of him to Mistral's paddock, not wanting my horse to have to cope with my weight whilst negotiating the path of compacted snow and ice.

I frowned as we neared our destination. The canvas canopy above the paddock was sagging with the weight of the snow atop it and I wondered whether the ropes tethering it to the huge poles at intervals around the paddock, would hold. I climbed the paddock fence and checked out the weave of the cream-coloured canvas. It had been very well made and I judged that it should be strong enough to cope with the snow sitting atop it. I knew nothing about making ropes, however, so I decided to trust those who did.

Learning To Soar you have come far, Noble announced.

I hugged him and hopped onto his back from the fence. Mistral opened the gate for us and stood aside to allow us through.

'It's a little darker under here than normal, but at least it's dry,' Mistral said. 'The ground is frozen solid though, so we'll just work at walk and trot. I want to address the fact that your lower back is still a little tight at times, which prevents you from sitting into your pelvis properly at pivotal moments. It might not seem much of an issue, but I can assure you that the difference to both your stability and Noble's balance will be great if you can make the change I want you to make.'

As always when Mistral taught me, once he pointed out a part of my body that I needed to utilise differently from how I had done to that point, I became fascinated with trying to isolate the part in question – whether it be my head, shoulders, arms, legs, ankles, feet, chest bone or any other bone, even an individual muscle sometimes – and engage it with Noble's body as Mistral suggested.

I thought I had it. I felt that I had isolated the muscles I needed to relax and those I needed to contract so that instead of sitting slightly on the front of my pelvis, I relaxed back into it. It was so much more comfortable sitting in the saddle that way and I felt so much more stable, as if nothing could shake me out of position – but then I lost it again and had to isolate the muscles in question and adjust their use all over again.

Noble was as interested in my efforts as ever, and as involved; his body instantly backed up my own observations as to my improved position in the saddle, by loosening and flowing even more than he normally did, and then reverting to a slightly more stilted movement when I tensed those muscles that pulled me onto the front of my pelvis again.

Sorry, I'll practise this when I'm sitting at my loom, at the dining table – everywhere I can – so I can be better at it by tomorrow, I told him.

The pattern in which your body holds itself is merely a reflection of that to which your mind yet holds. You can feel how minor is the necessary adjustment and you know you can make it. Take heart from that in the days to come.

Like I told you, I'll just work on changing it. I'll be better by tomorrow and even better the next day. There we are, I've got it again...

My thought was interrupted by a loud splitting noise as the wooden post just ahead of us – as thick as my waist and four times my height – to which a portion of the canopy was attached, seemed to bend into the paddock in slow motion. Then everything happened at once.

The top third of the post came crashing down, bringing a portion of the fence, a length of rope, a section of the canopy and a whole load of snow with it. Honed in on my lower back as I had so intensely been, I felt the pattern with which it was so familiar re-establishing itself, pitching me slightly onto the front of my pelvis just as Noble did the only thing he could to save us from being buried by the avalanche in front of us, and spun around on his hindquarters before leaping out of the way.

I was already out of the saddle by the time he landed on the hard ground and when he slipped on the worn grass and his left shoulder disappeared from in front of me, I had no chance of recovery. The air was knocked out of me as I landed on my left shoulder and hip. The pain that shot through both was nothing compared to that which followed as Noble landed on his side on top of me. I felt a brief moment of agony before all sensation faded away and everything went black.

Chapter Sixteen

A soft voice sounded by my ear. 'Quinta? Can you hear me? Try to open your eyes if you can.'

Hannah. I smiled a smile that didn't reach my eyes or even my mouth, for I felt strangely disconnected from both. Was I dreaming? Maybe, but Hannah's voice didn't sound the way voices tended to sound in dreams, where they could belong to anyone yet the dreamer always knew who they were.

'I thought she was coming back, I was sure I saw her eyelids flicker,' Hannah said. 'Mason, pass me that flannel, please? Her eyes have clogged up again. Maybe she was trying to open them but couldn't.'

I tried to tell her I hadn't been trying to do anything, but I couldn't seem to get any words out. My forehead suddenly felt cool as a very slight weight pressed down upon it and then moved to each of my eyes in turn. I wanted to open them, but I couldn't find the wherewithal.

Noble. Where was Noble?

I am with you as always.

In my dream?

In all of your dreams both waking and sleeping.

Which type is this?

You are awake but barely. Your mind hides from that which it knows it must face. The last step in clearing a pattern of behaviour is often the smallest yet the most difficult for once you take it you will never return to whom you once were.

I don't want to be who I was. I want to be confident and capable of taking on anything, like you.

Your body now knows the adjustment it must make so that you can be everything you know you can be. It will prod at your mind as much as will your soul until you take the small step necessary to make the adjustment part of you. The process will not be comfortable but remember that you can do it. You have already done it. You need merely do it when you are experiencing that which you perceive to be an extreme challenge for it to become part of you. Learning To Soar open your eyes.

There was a surge of energy through our bond, and my eyes flicked open.

'Oh, thank goodness,' Hannah said, her face filling my vision. Then she yelled, 'ADAM, THUMA, GET YOURSELVES IN HERE, SHE'S AWAKE.'

'Curse the clouds, Hannah, she'll shrink back into her coma from the noise,' Mason said. His face appeared next to hers. 'Thank the light you're back with us, Quinta. The Healers said it would just take a little time, but you've been lyin' there so white and still. Anyway, welcome back, ah, here's Adam.'

I frowned. Did I know an Adam? I didn't think I did.

Hannah's and Mason's faces disappeared and were replaced by that of a man with thick, almost completely white, shoulder length hair and a ruddy complexion. His green eyes twinkled as if he were delighted to see me, though I couldn't remember ever having met him.

'Hello, Quinta, I'm Adam, and I've been tending you in my capacity as one of the Herbalists in residence here. Would you like some water?'

I wasn't sure. Did I want water? Or just to go back to sleep? Sleep seemed easier. I closed my eyes but opened them again as I realised I was indeed thirsty and also had pain in my lower back. I tried to shift, but couldn't seem to move.

'Would you like to sit up?' Adam said.

I tried to nod, and must have managed some movement, as Adam turned to Mason. 'Would you mind going around to Quinta's other side? Hannah, if Mason and I lift Quinta, would you be so kind as to put some pillows behind her so she has some support to sit upright?'

There was a flurry of movement and my upper body was raised gently but firmly by a strong hand behind each of my shoulder blades. When the hands disappeared, I nestled back slightly into the softness of a stack of pillows.

A woman with short, black hair and closely set eyes strode into the room and stood at the foot of my bed. She stared at me for a few seconds and her eyes came to rest just below my waist. She began to hum, and as her tone changed to a softer, more soothing tone, the pain in my back eased and then disappeared.

She nodded to herself and murmured, 'Just a bit of residual muscle tension.' Then she looked at my face for the first time, and smiled. 'We haven't met, but I'm Thuma, one of the Tissue-Singers here at The Gathering, and you're one tough woman to have survived a fall like that. You're in great shape now, you just need to get your strength back, so I'll shoot off to the kitchens and fetch you some soup, unless there's something else you'd prefer?'

I managed to shake my head.

She smiled. 'Okay then, I'll be back in a tick.' She whisked from the room.

'A fall.' I tried to say the words but my throat was so dry, they wouldn't come out.

Adam held a glass to my lips and I sipped at the deliciously cool water within. 'That's it,' he said. 'Just slowly while your body remembers what to do with it.'

He spoke as if my body had a life of its own, just like Noble did. Noble! I turned my head away from the glass, spilling water down the front of my nightshirt.

'I had a fall. From Noble,' I whispered as everything came flooding back to me. 'How is he?' I shook my head as soon as I had uttered the question, for I knew. He was with me in my mind, just as he always was, and he was fine. More than fine, actually. He was enjoying a roll in the snow. 'Snow,' I recalled. 'The weight of it broke one of the canopy posts. Noble and I were having such a good lesson and then everything went wrong so quickly.'

Adam nodded. 'Mistral has been popping in whenever he's had a spare moment. He'll be overjoyed to know you're awake.'

I looked around. 'Where am I? This isn't my room.'

Mason chuckled. 'No, it isn't. You're in one of the rooms usually occupied by the Healers, since they're on the ground floor. We wondered whether Noble might be of a mind to come and see you as he did when you were in your own room, and we thought there was less chance of damage to him or, er, the buildin's if you were down here.'

I smiled. 'And did he come and see me?'

'Nope, your Noble has been actin' like there's nothin' untoward. It's given me heart, if truth be known.'

I nodded, unsure whether to be pleased or hurt that my horse had been so unaffected by what had happened to me. 'Was I that badly injured?'

Hannah took my hand and squeezed it. 'By all accounts, if it hadn't been for so many Healers being involved in a snowball fight just a few paddocks along from Mistral's, you would have died. You had four Bone-Singers and three Tissue-Singers beside you within minutes, and it took all of their strength and most of yours before the worst of your injuries were no longer life-threatening. Noble may not be the largest of horses, but he could have crushed Mason here, let alone your little body, Quinta. He was up and off you as soon as he could get a purchase on the ground, but he couldn't reverse the damage that had been done.'

'But happily, our excellent Healers did, and here you are,' Adam said cheerfully. 'You have a few surface wounds that still need my attention, but other than that, you're as good as new. Now, while you're waiting for your soup, would you like some herbal tea? I took the liberty of combining some herbs that I felt would suit your body's requirements once you woke, and the result has been heating up over the fire while we've been chatting. It's just about ready now, if you fancy some?'

My stomach was churning and my heart felt as if it were jumping up my throat at the thought of what had happened to me, but I caught the scent of whatever it was Adam was brewing, and instantly, I craved some. I managed a nod and was rewarded by a beaming smile.

Adam hurried off and then returned with a mug of such a vibrantly green tea, the sight of it would have been vomit inducing were it not for the myriad of scents I could now pick out, each of which enticed me to drink it.

'It's not so hot that it'll burn, so drink as much of it as you need,' Adam said.

I couldn't decide whether it was his voice or the ridiculously inviting tea that made me feel better even before I had drunk any. I took a sip and then another. The tea was delicious; sweet and slightly spicy at the same time. Warmth spread throughout my body, easing the churning in my stomach and slowing my heart rate, making me feel as if I was okay. As if everything was okay. Before I knew it, I had almost finished it.

'Wow,' I said. 'I've never had anything like this before. Our village Herbalists were amazing, I mean, their preparations always did their job but they always smelt and tasted foul.'

Mason chuckled. 'Adam's the best Herbalist there's ever been, by all accounts. If you were going to have an incident, you couldn't have timed it better than an hour before Adam and Peace arrived back here for the winter.'

My heart began to pound again at the thought. I took another sip of tea and said to Adam, 'Peace is your Bond-Partner?' I needed no reply. Of course Peace was his Bond-partner; a quiet calm swirled around within me from the tea he had prepared, every bit as much as it seemed to ooze from him and settle in my skin. 'What a lovely name. And so right for you both.' I flushed. 'Sorry, I didn't mean to say that.'

Adam grinned. 'The things one doesn't mean to say are so often the things that need to be said. Thank you, Quinta, your words have helped me more than you can possibly know.'

The confusion on both Hannah's and Mason's faces told me that they had no more clue what Adam was talking about than did I.

Thuma breezed into the room, distracting any of us from wondering further. 'Here we are, Turi's best leek and potato soup, with a little bread and butter on the side.' She put a tray on my lap. 'Eat it slowly so your stomach doesn't object, and then see how you feel. If you need to sleep, your friends will leave you to do just that.' She glared at Mason and Hannah until they both nodded. 'But if you'd like more food, give me a shout and I'll get you some. My rooms are just across the hall. Okay?'

'Okay, thank you very much.'

'You're welcome. I'll pop in to check on you in between my appointments. See you later.' She whirled out of the room, which I noticed for the first time was equipped and arranged very like my own, but had a door adjoining it to another room.

Adam followed my gaze. 'We Healers have our treatment rooms within easy reach, so that we can be available at short notice. It's unusual for that to be necessary, but when it is, we're glad of the arrangement. My rooms are just down the corridor, but I'll hear you if you need me, so please do call out if necessary.'

'Um, would it be possible to have another mug of your herbal tea before you go?'

A broad smile lit up Adam's eyes so that they twinkled even more brightly. 'Of course.' He took my mug, refilled it and gave it back. 'There's still half a panful left. I'll leave the pan on the hearth so it keeps warm and you can help yourself whenever you like. Now, don't forget, call out if you need me.'

'I will. Thank you.'

Hannah waited until Adam had left the room and then said, 'That tea must taste a whole lot better than it looks. I've never seen anything so disgusting.'

'It tastes every bit as amazing as it smells though,' I said.

Hannah looked at Mason, who shrugged and said, 'It just smells like herbal tea to me.' Hannah nodded her agreement.

I frowned, wondering if maybe I had suffered a head injury that had altered my perception.

On the contrary. You perceive with the same accuracy of which you have always been capable, Noble informed me. *Trust yourself.*

I nodded and drank the second mug of tea. Its warmth spread throughout my body, just as before. I tucked into the food Thuma had brought me while Hannah bustled around the room with a broom and then a mop, cleaning a floor that didn't need cleaning as far as I could see, and Mason sat snoozing in an armchair in front of the blazing fire. I felt my eyes beginning to droop and hastened to finish my bread and soup.

'I'll just take that before you nod off into it,' Hannah said. I was aware of the tray sliding across my lap, and then gentle hands guiding me to lean back further into my pillows.

It was five days before Adam judged that a flesh wound on my thigh and some shallow but large abrasions on my hip, back and shoulder were all healing well enough, and I was strong enough, to both return to my own room and to weaving in the workshop. I was to be given a further week off from doing any chores, and Thuma firmly instructed me that I was to rest as much as I felt I needed to whilst re-entering normality.

As I got dressed in the clothes Hannah had fetched for me from my bedroom, I felt a sense of loss. Keen as I was to return to the life at The Gathering that I had grown to love – and, I allowed myself to admit, to prove to myself that I could join it as the exact same person I was before the accident – I knew I was going to miss having Adam close by.

It had seemed that whenever I was struggling to fully experience the present moment, whenever my mind strayed back to what had happened and to Hannah's description of my injuries and the fact that I had nearly died, whenever my stomach churned and I felt nauseous and dizzy, Adam would appear with some of his amazing tea. He would sit in the chair by the fire and chat to me as if he had all the time in the world, despite the fact I had come to realise both from hearing snippets of conversation and from the volume of footfall outside my door, that he was in huge and constant demand for his skill in herbalism.

　He asked me all about my life, about Noble and how I'd been getting on at The Gathering, and I told him everything as if it were the most natural thing in the world to do. He was such a soothing, comforting presence that I felt as if nothing bad could happen while he was around, yet there was a slight air of sadness about him, as if he couldn't find for himself that which oozed from him and settled within me. It didn't make sense, but I could feel in my skin that I was right. I wanted to help him and be helped by him all at the same time, without having a clue of what either of those things would entail.

A soft knock on the door sounded as I was lacing my boots. Following my invitation to enter, Adam stepped into the room. 'Ah, you're ready. I thought you might be wanting your first port of call to be Noble's paddock, so I'm here to offer you an arm. The snow's melting, and it's mighty slippery out there.'

I smiled. 'You thought right. That would be lovely, thank you, if you're sure you have time?'

Adam held my cloak up and wrapped it around my shoulders. 'I always have time.'

I was glad of his arm as we picked our way across the layer of ice and slush that still hid the cobbles of the square, and I was also glad to be able to help him on the single occasion his feet almost went from under him.

'Thank you, thank you,' he said breathlessly as I stood with my feet apart, just about balancing us both as he tried to regain his footing. 'Look at me, silly old man, I'm no use to you when I can't keep my own feet, am I?'

'It shouldn't always be about everyone else, Adam. Sometimes it needs to be about you.' The words were out of my mouth before I could recall them, yet I found that I didn't want to.

He regained his balance and looked deeply into my eyes. 'The two are one and the same. But I think you already know that?' The twinkle in his eyes was still there but there was an intensity about it that held me so securely in that moment, I forgot where we were.

I nodded. 'I guess so. I think that's what Noble's trying to help me to understand.'

Adam smiled. 'I'm looking forward to meeting him. We'll carry on, shall we, before we freeze in our boots.'

We slipped and slid our way along the path between the paddocks. I was so intent on staying on my feet that we were almost upon Noble by the time I spotted him watching our approach. My heart leapt at the sight of him... and then pain lanced throughout my body as echoes of all the injuries I had suffered when my horse crushed me announced themselves one by one. I screamed and dropped to my knees in the slush, the cold searing at my legs and making the pain in them even worse.

'Quinta, try not to worry, you'll be okay, I think we just need to get you to Noble,' Adam said calmly. 'Ah, here comes Newson, he'll help. I know it hurts, but hang in there, it'll be over soon. Newson, would you be so kind as to link hands with me under Quinta's legs? We'll need to carry her to Noble. It's a shame the fence is a little too high for him to jump over and come to us, but there we are. That's it, now, Quinta, Newson and I have got you, just keep screaming until you feel you can stop.'

I was lifted out of the slush that I could have sworn was eating into my skin, and screamed even harder as the arms beneath my knees and behind my back sliced into my skin like knives. What was happening to me? Had the sight of Noble somehow unravelled the healing performed on me by the Bone-Singers and Tissue-Singers? Was I going to die out here in the freezing cold while my horse, the perpetrator of my injuries, calmly looked on?

'Quinta, I'm just going to lift up your hand,' Adam said in my ear. A hand enclosed mine and moved it until it touched something soft and warm.

The silence was deafening and I realised I had stopped screaming. Noble came into focus in front of me as Adam continued to hold my hand to my horse's cheek.

My horse stretched over the fence as far as he could and wiggled his upper lip on my forehead so that my attention shot there and away from the agony in the remainder of my body… which instantly disappeared and was replaced by warmth that originated in my forehead.

I looked down at my legs, which apart from being encased in wet leggings, were whole and uninjured, as was the rest of me. In my peripheral vision, I caught sight of Adam nodding to Newson, and I was lowered to the ground. I stood on my feet feeling absolutely fine and very stupid.

'I'm going mad,' I said, my voice trembling.

Adam and Newson both gazed at Noble in silence, clearly feeling no need to reassure me when my Bond-Partner was present.

You merely processed consciously that which was held by your subconscious while you were unconscious, Noble informed me. He stood in the snow with his small front hooves neatly together, his thick, winter coat as dark as everything else was white, his eyes bright.

Merely? There was no 'merely' about it, that was excruciating, I retorted.

Yet necessary. Now we may proceed.

That's it? No concern for me? No apology for nearly crushing me to death? No sympathy for what just happened? We're just going to 'proceed'? As if nothing has happened?

We will proceed because of that which happened. It was a necessary part of our experience.

How do I know it won't happen again, in the interest of 'proceeding'?

You do not. That is why it was necessary. Noble turned his head and watched Integrity as she rolled, grunting, in a newly exposed patch of mud, as if he had just answered the most mundane of queries rather than having just announced that he could kill me at any moment.

He turned quickly back to me, his movement holding my attention as surely as the intensity of his thought. *Where were you when the incident was in the process of occurring?*

In the paddock, with you.

Where was your mind?

With yours. Immediately, I understood, even though I didn't really want to. *I was in the present, with you.*

And how were you?

I thought back to the incident and frowned. *I was fine.*

And how are you now that you have cleared that which was necessary?

Cold, wet, and terrified at the thought of it all happening again, even though I was fine when it happened. I told you, I'm going mad.

You are merely experiencing fear in another of its guises. Try to identify it.

I thought it through. I hadn't been frightened when I was thrown or even as I lay on the ground in agony; while it was all actually happening, I had coped with being out of control and with being in pain. So, what was it that scared me so much? What was it that I was trying to avoid?

A voice from deep inside me whispered the answer. I couldn't believe it could be that simple, but I knew it was true. I'd been drinking Adam's tea by the gallon in order to dampen down my inclination to go over and over what had happened, but in those moments when I was alone and without anyone to help me to stay calm, I'd failed. I'd gone over and over it, attaching fear to it that I hadn't felt at the time, until it was being frightened itself that I was trying to avoid.

I'm frightened of feeling frightened, I admitted. *And it's worse than being frightened of anything else.*

There is nothing so frightening as fear itself, Noble agreed. *Yet it has a natural remedy. You felt it when you touched me. You felt it when you first saw me. You feel it when you partake of nourishment imbued with it. You have access to as much of it as you need but you must choose it in each moment.*

Love.

Love, Noble agreed. *Act out of love and fear cannot take hold.*

Being noble means that fear can't affect me? It made sense and yet it seemed too simple.

It is simple in principle yet that does not mean it will always be easy. In time you will be presented with the ultimate opportunity to demonstrate that it is possible to choose love over fear. The fate of humankind will depend on it since the one for whom we wait will require your example and guidance.

Wait a minute, is that what this has all been about? Did you crush me and almost kill me on purpose, in order to add to my experience of fear? To ram it home to me that the thing I'm most afraid of is fear itself?

You ask if there was intent yet my kind do not include such as part of our existence. We merely respond to that which surrounds us. You found the adjustment in your body that allowed your mind to begin the final clearing of your pattern and as such drew into your experience a situation that will further enable the process. I was merely a part of that.

So what happens now?

That is up to you. Noble turned and walked away from us all.

Chapter Seventeen

$\mathcal{I}$ stood at the fence, watching Noble roll in the muddy spot recently vacated by Integrity, and thought through everything he had told me. I remembered sitting into my pelvis when I last rode him, and feeling stable, calm, solid, as if nothing could affect me. I remembered that I hadn't been able to maintain that position when the post had split under the weight of the snow-covered canopy; the instant something unexpected had happened, I had lost my stability and subsequently my balance. I needed to work my way through the terror I had attached to the thought of riding Noble since my accident-that-was-no-accident, by choosing to feel love in its place, and attain that position again. When I could stay there regardless of what happened around me, I would never be fearful again.

It was so simple; we had been going from strength to strength when I had been riding my horse before, I already knew the adjustment my body needed to make in order to solidify that which I knew in my mind, and I also knew that whatever happened, I could endure it fearlessly… but the fact remained that I had nearly died, and I just couldn't seem to get past it.

'Quinta, you're shivering,' Newson said. 'I can see to Noble and Integrity if you want to go and change out of those wet leggings?'

I jumped, startled out of my reverie. 'Um, yes, I suppose I should. Sorry, I just got caught up with trying to figure out what to do next. Noble says it's up to me.'

Newson chuckled. 'Don't you just love it when they say that? Good luck with your musings, but maybe do them in the warm?'

I nodded and turned to walk back towards the buildings. Adam offered me his arm and I took it.

'It's really rather difficult at times, isn't it,' he said, 'trying to be the person you know you can be when there's so much in the way.'

'You struggle too.' I didn't phrase it as a question because it wasn't one.

'At some times more than others. I'm better when I'm out and about, visiting villages and helping where I can. Maybe that would be helpful for you too?'

I swallowed hard. 'I'm terrified at the thought of riding though. I'd love to go and visit villages, but it's like you said; there's so much in the way.'

'So, don't ride. Peace is in his thirties now and although he insists he can still carry me, I don't ask it of him unless it's absolutely necessary, so you, Noble, Peace and I can walk together. I'll be leaving in a few weeks' time, which should give you plenty of time to regain your strength. We won't be travelling at any sort of speed or to any set time frame, so your body won't be under any pressure.'

'But you've only been back a week or so.'

'I'm only ever here for the worst of the winter. The Weather-

Singers have confirmed my suspicion that Spring is on its way early this year, and Peace assures me he's rested enough. Ah, here he is, you'll experience the proof of his assurances for yourself.'

Adam reached a hand up to the neck of an enormous, largely white horse with a few brown patches on his body, a black head with a white blaze down his nose, and long, white hair hanging from his legs. White hair surrounded his eyes and there was a white streak in his black forelock. He was leaning over the paddock fence, stretching his enormous head to where I stood beside Adam in the middle of the path. He turned his head on one side and wiggled his upper lip, making me smile.

I lifted my free hand for him to sniff, and when he withdrew his head, I stepped closer. Immediately, he grabbed a mouthful of my cloak and pulled at it, dragging me to the fence. Then he pulled off my hat by its bobble, swung it around and hurled it into the paddock on the opposite side of the pathway, which happened to be occupied by Mason's horse, Diligence, and three others. His unexpected behaviour lifted me out of my worries, and I laughed out loud. He put his muzzle on my shoulder and rocked his head backwards and forwards so that I felt I was being shaken, and would have lost my footing had Adam not tightened his hold on my arm and held me firm.

'Now, now, Peace, Quinta's as light as a feather, go gently, now,' he said with a chuckle. 'Do you see what I mean, Quinta? There's no keeping Peace down. He was so tired when we arrived here, but a week on and look at him, fighting fit and ready to go again.'

Peace rested his head on my shoulder and snorted the contents of his nose into my ear. I laughed even harder. When I finally stopped, the big horse nuzzled my cheek and then my mouth, then my other cheek, then stepped back and watched me with dark, soulful eyes as if he were the epitome of calm wisdom and far removed from the perpetrator of his previous antics.

'Oh, Adam, he's wonderful,' I breathed. I reached a hand up to Peace's nose and gently stroked the white hair of his blaze, telling him, 'Thank you for cheering me up. I wish Noble would do that for me.' I looked over at Dili, who was watching me in return. My skin rippled with her nurturing warmth as surely as if I were standing right next to her. 'Or even just reassured me, like Dili does.'

'If I may ask,' Adam said, 'were Noble like either Peace or Diligence, do you think you would have achieved all that you have?'

I continued to stroke Peace's nose and he sighed and half closed his eyes. I pictured Noble in my mind's eye – small, delicate and precise in everything he did, whether it be his physical movement, the timing and content of his thoughts to me, even what had appeared to be his mad dash up to my room at the precise moment I had needed him. I sighed. 'No, I guess not. I just feel as if he leaves me on my own a lot when other horses might give me reassurance. Or a much-needed lift.' I nodded towards Peace.

Adam stroked Peace's neck thoughtfully. 'There were many times after Peace and I first bonded when I wished he'd chosen anyone but me as his Bond-Partner. He pulled me out of the life I'd created for myself and then pushed me when I didn't want to be pushed, opened me up to feelings I didn't want to feel, and provoked me into showing the very worst of myself. Treasure your Bond-Partner, Quinta, because he's the only one in your life with the wisdom and strength to be exactly who you need him to be.'

I thought back to when I had left my parents, and my mother had told me of her concern that they had done me no favours by protecting me from myself in the way Noble constantly refused to do. I looked back to Dili and realised that where I would have felt safer with her, I would have hidden in my bond with her every bit as I had hidden behind my parents. Peace nudged me and I grinned. 'I get it,' I whispered to him as I continued to stroke his nose. 'Having Noble in my face like you are wouldn't have helped either, would it? I need pushing and then to be left alone to practise doing what I need to do, because I'm the only one who can do it.'

I reached for Noble and immersed myself in our bond. *I'm sorry. Again. Thank you.*

He was as aware of my thought as he was of everything else about me, but as when I had doubted him before, he didn't respond. He needed my gratitude and apology as little as, in truth, I needed his reassurance, for it was right there in the corner of my mind whenever I needed it.

Noble, I'd like to go out to visit the villages with Adam and Peace. How do you feel about us doing that?

It will be a positive way to proceed.

I turned back to Adam. 'I think you might be wrong on one point; I'm not sure Noble's the only one in my life with the wisdom and strength to be who I need him to be. Thanks, Adam, Noble and I would love to come with you and Peace when you leave.'

He smiled and winked. 'Marvellous. The villagers we'll visit will be thrilled to meet you both. I have a few patients who'll need to finish their courses of treatment with me, and then I'll be ready to leave here. It just so happens that Mildred returned from her travels yesterday – she's a Weaver, like yourself – and has already begun work, so with you on board as well, the Weavers should be well up to date with their orders by the time we leave. Shall we say two weeks from today?'

'That sounds perfect.' Relief flooded me not only at the thought of leaving behind the pressure I would be under to ride Noble that would accompany remaining at The Gathering, but at the thought of being in the constant company of Adam and Peace. Then I remembered the swiftness with which Noble had agreed to go, and my heart sank slightly. If he thought it would be a good idea, then it wasn't likely to be because it was the easy thing to do at all.

Two weeks passed quickly if not particularly easily. I threw myself into catching up with the orders of cloth that had continued to come in whilst I was recovering from my injuries, and with Mildred's help, all of the workshops' orders were fulfilled with two days to spare before I left. I also returned to my share of chores, originally being assigned one that allowed me to sit down, until I asked to be changed onto a more manual one with the aim of building more strength before I left. Whilst I enjoyed my work, the company of my friends, and the feeling that my body was recovering well, I found myself spending less time with Noble than I had before our accident.

It wasn't that I didn't love him, that I didn't value his counsel, or that I no longer enjoyed being with him, but more that I felt his presence in my mind as a constant pressure that was only amplified when I was with him in person. He never mentioned what happened, advised me to get over myself and ride him, or even counselled me to do anything other than I was doing – he just waited.

I went to see him first thing in the morning, as I always had before our accident. I groomed him, I did my share of paddock chores, I checked on him at lunchtime and before I went to bed, all as before. Yet I hurried through my time with him and was relieved to be on my way back to the buildings even though I carried him with me in my mind. I couldn't bear to admit that my greatest love was now my greatest fear, so I ploughed back into living each and every moment in its entirety so that there was no room to think anything.

No one asked when I was going to return to riding, not even Mason or Newson, until Mistral stopped by the table at which the three of us were sitting, eating lunch on the day before I was due to leave. My stomach churned at the sight of him, and my head spun as I tried to think what I should say.

'I hear you're off on your travels with Adam tomorrow, Quinta,' he said. 'Before you go, would you like to have a quick practice of what you and Noble were about before that blasted pole snapped and brought the whole flaming canopy down on top of you?' He winked, completely unaware that his words had caused me to feel everything I had spent the best part of two weeks trying to avoid feeling, using all of the practices Noble had taught me.

I swallowed. 'Um, I'm still not feeling strong enough. I'm hoping that once we're on our way, I'll get to the point where I can carry on where we left off. I know what I have to do, I felt it and I felt how it allowed Noble and me to balance better, so I'll work on it as soon as I can.' The words tumbled out of me so quickly, I gasped and then started coughing.

Newson passed me a glass of water and I sipped at it gratefully.

Mistral nodded slowly, his eyes never leaving mine. 'You do seem a little frail still.' His voice was as soft as always but it held no sympathy and his gaze was as sharp as ever. He knew I was lying to him. 'It's a fine balance, isn't it, pushing yourself just hard enough that your strength improves, without pushing yourself so hard that you take a backward step.'

I felt a glimmer of hope at the suggestion that he might be prepared to indulge me. I nodded, not trusting myself to speak.

Mistral nodded. 'In that case, I'll leave you to your lunch. If I don't see you before you go, enjoy your trip, and I'll look forward to seeing how far you've progressed with that fabulous little horse of yours when you get back here.'

I managed a smile. 'Thanks, Mistral, for all your help. I really appreciate it and so does Noble.'

He gave a curt nod. 'It's what I'm here for.' His boots clicked on the stone floor of the dining hall as he strode away.

Mason caught my eye. 'You know, you can't go wrong in Adam's and Peace's company. You'll get past this, Quinta. Do you have everythin' you need for your travels, or can I help you gather anythin' else?'

I smiled at him. 'Thank you, I think I'm fine. Those saddlebags you made for me are brilliant, I can get all of my food, cooking stuff and bedding in them so I'll only have to carry my clothes in my back-sack.'

Mason nodded. 'And you've packed the spare girth and stirrup leathers?'

'Yes I have, thank you for those too.' I looked fondly between him and Newson. 'I don't know how long a trip Adam has planned, but however long it is, I'm going to miss you two, and Hannah, and all of the others. I never really had friends before I arrived here, and I had no idea what I was missing.'

Newson smiled one of his rare smiles. 'We gathered as much. With that in mind, we'd like you to take this with you.' He held out his hand, in which nestled something small and shiny. 'Mason designed it and I sang it into its current form from some of the nails that were holding a fence rail in place in the paddock Noble stayed in with Integrity when you first arrived. Since you'll be travelling with Adam, we figured you'd be gone for some time, so we thought that this would be a good way of ensuring you take our good wishes with you.'

I picked up the clasp of a delicate metal chain from which swung two pendants, both images of horses' heads.

I gasped at the detail that allowed me to immediately recognise both of them. 'Integrity and Diligence! This is absolutely beautiful! Integrity's sharp features and slender nose, Dili's wide forehead and you've even managed to capture the softness of her eyes – oh, thank you, both of you, so much, it'll be lovely to feel I'm taking them both, and you both with me.' I raced around to their side of the table and hugged them in turn. 'Would one of you do it up for me, please?'

'I'll never be able to do it with my big, clumsy fingers,' Mason said. 'Over to you, Newson.'

When Newson had fastened the clasp around my neck, I stood and looked at them both. I pointed at Mason. 'You shouldn't put yourself down. Just because you want to be perfect at everything, it doesn't mean you have to be.' I pointed at Newson. 'And you should smile more. Just because you want to do the right thing all the time, it doesn't mean you have to be so serious.'

They both looked shocked and then grins spread over both of their faces.

Newson pointed back at me. 'And you should give yourself a break. Just because you want to be able to put helping others before everything that frightens you, doesn't mean you shouldn't stop every now and then to remember that you've always done that, even when you didn't realise that was what you were doing.'

I looked between them both, waiting for them to laugh at the joke I didn't get. When they didn't, I said, 'I don't understand.'

Mason grinned. 'Yeah, you do, if you think about it. Enjoy

your last afternoon here, Quinta. Take my advice and have a long, hot bath because it's the last you'll get the time for until you get back here.'

I took his advice, and by the time I'd had a bath, dinner, lit the fire in my bedroom, re-checked I had packed everything I would need, and settled into bed for an early night, I was feeling excited for what lay ahead.

It felt strange to be saddling Noble the following morning, even if it were only so that I could attach my bulging saddlebags to the saddle in order for Noble to share my load as he had agreed to. I hoped Mistral wouldn't suddenly pop up and suggest a last minute lesson now that we were all set, but thankfully, the footsteps that sploshed towards our paddock in the dull, winter morning light, belonged to Adam and Peace. They were attired in the same way as Noble and I, with the stocky, white and brown horse saddled and carrying saddlebags, and Adam carrying a bulging back-sack.

'Well, it's a relief to see the end of the slush, but I'll be glad to leave this mud behind,' Adam called out cheerfully. 'Are you all set?'

I waved to him. 'Yep, I'll just do a quick check to make sure nothing can rub Noble, and we'll be there.

You need not revisit that to which you paid close attention at the time, Noble informed me.

I took a deep breath at his reminder to remain where I had managed to be from the moment I woke, until the point of worrying that Mistral might appear.

Okay, I'm back with you. Thank you. Are you ready?
Always.

Nausea announced itself suddenly as his honesty couldn't help but prod at me, reminding me yet again of that which I was being so careful to avoid. I patted Integrity goodbye as she munched hay from a nearby rack, then focused on picking my way around the mud that surrounded the gateway of the paddock whilst listening to Noble squelching straight through the middle of it – which only prodded at me harder as the difference between our approaches to life manifested themselves even more obviously.

'It's just a case of putting one foot in front of the other until the going gets easier, isn't it?' Adam said, his eyes twinkling as he held the gate open for my Bond-Partner and me.

I nodded, suspecting strongly that he wasn't just talking about the mud, and feeling glad all over again that he and Peace were taking Noble and me with them.

Chapter Eighteen

I took Adam's observation as advice, so reminiscent was it of that which Noble tended to give me, and focused on putting one foot in front of the other as I picked my way down the muddy pathway towards the river with Noble just behind me and Adam walking at Peace's side behind Noble.

When the river's thrashing and gurgling reached my ears, I focused even harder on the ground in front of me as well as on the sights and sounds in my immediate vicinity that hinted winter was giving way to spring; the snowdrops at the very edges of the pathways dropping their petals, the birds singing with increased vibrancy and optimism, and the softening of the wind's bite.

When I reached the end of the path, I could avoid looking at the river no longer. It was much fuller in its banks than when I had last walked alongside it in the summer, and far more turbulent. Twigs and branches flew past in front of me, allowing themselves to be carried by the flow of the river every bit as easily and readily as I was resisting the flow of my life, and only adding to the pressure exerted on my mind by Noble's continued patience.

I put a hand to his neck and rubbed it as I began to cry. *I'm letting you down. I'm letting myself down. I know it but I can't get past it,* I told him.

You can. You have already taken the first steps. When the mountain appears too steep to climb it is often wise to walk around its base and look for another way up, he replied.

I was flooded with relief and then trepidation as I remembered how readily he had agreed to leave The Gathering.

Return your focus to the present. Think less. Feel more, Noble told me.

I nodded and wiped my face before turning to Adam. 'Sorry, I just had a bit of a panic. Rivers scare me and inspire me at the same time. I can't decide which is worse.'

Adam smiled. 'You'll have some time to consider your conundrum, we'll be walking alongside it for a good while, I'm afraid.'

Peace stamped one of his front feet and squealed. Noble jumped off all four feet and landed back down next to me, then spun around to watch Peace as the white and brown horse pawed the ground, the long, white hair of his front leg swinging around it like a cloak. Noble's nostrils flared and he stretched his neck upward, making himself look taller. Then he and Peace both leapt into a canter and tore off along the riverbank.

Adam laughed and I joined in as I sensed Noble's joy at Peace's company and the opportunity to really stretch his legs as he strived to keep up with his larger but more heavily built companion. *Feel more, think less,* I reminded myself. It was a good way to be.

'We'll keep up as best we can, shall we?' Adam said.

Our morning was spent doing exactly that. Peace and Noble stayed well ahead of us, playing and galloping into the distance before stopping to graze the fibrous, tussocky grass of the hills we were traversing, until we caught up, then setting off again. It was a side of Noble I had never seen before, and I relaxed as his enjoyment overtook his quiet patience in prominence in my mind.

When we came across some flat-topped boulders upon which we could sit, Adam and I stopped for lunch. Adam lit a fire and my spirits soon lifted further at the sight and smell of his hideously green tea heating in a pot hanging over the fire on a tripod, while we persuaded Peace and Noble to come back so that we could liberate some sandwiches from our saddlebags. They grazed nearby while Adam and I ate and he drank from his water pouch whilst ensuring my mug was constantly full of tea.

'Don't you ever drink it yourself?' I asked, lifting my mug to indicate the subject of my question.

Adam grinned. 'Sometimes, but I find I get more out of making it for other people, so don't you feel it's a chore for me to keep forcing it upon you, because it really isn't.'

I smiled back. 'You're hardly forcing it on me. What's in it, exactly?'

'Just some very ordinary herbs and a little positive intention. Giving others what I need myself reminds me that I already have it, you see.' Adam held my gaze for a long moment, then grinned as the twinkle returned to his eyes. 'So Peace tells me, anyway, when he's not being the world's biggest, most lovable buffoon.' His words rang with his love for his horse.

'How long have you been bonded?'

'Thirty odd years now. I think it's fair to say that I'm a lifelong project.' The same sadness I had glimpsed in him before appeared behind the twinkle in his eyes.

'It's hard to think that you can still have anything to learn from Peace when you practically radiate what you saw in him when you named him,' I observed, feeling as I always did that anything I said to Adam would be okay.

'Once again, I owe you my thanks for pointing that out, it helps me to hear it.' Adam said, his sincerity laced with sadness. Then he brightened. 'But I imagine I'm not the first to point out that you also radiate a confidence you don't seem aware you possess?'

I nodded and sighed. 'It has been mentioned. I think I'm so busy trying to experience every moment to its fullest so my mind doesn't wander to unhelpful places, I appear to be calm and together when actually I'm just preoccupied with scrambling to stay afloat.'

Adam chuckled. 'You're no different from the rest of us, Quinta, although I rather think there is more at stake in your case than in most.'

I frowned at him. How could he possibly know that? 'I'd heard your name before I arrived at The Gathering, with your talent in herbalism being known far and wide as it is, but there's far more to you than that, isn't there? I can feel it in my skin.'

'How very fascinating. What do you mean, exactly?'

'It's like my skin tightens when I need to realise something and then when I do, it feels comfortable again, as if the truth has settled there.'

Adam nodded. 'You hear the voice of your soul through your skin. I hear mine through my stomach, like there's something there that won't settle until I realise I know what it knows.'

'The voice of my soul?'

Adam nodded. 'That's what Peace calls it. I used to call it intuition but I like Peace's description better. And the voice of my soul tells me that you're learning what you're learning because of who it will lead you to be and who you will be able to help in the future as a result.'

'And you're doing the same, for the same reason,' I breathed.

Adam grinned ruefully. 'If only it were that innocent in my

case. There's far more to my particular journey, but regardless, I'd like to hope that its end point will converge with that of your own and we may both be the people our horses foresaw when they chose us. For now, it's one footstep at a time, one minute at a time, one hour at a time, one day at a time, one village at a time, and when we arrive at our destination, we'll be glad and grateful that those two,' he nodded at Peace and Noble, 'were with us every step of the way.'

'You've been living that way for a long time,' I observed with newfound respect and sympathy arising in equal measures. 'Do you ever find yourself wishing you could just take one giant footstep and be where you need to be?'

Adam began to dismantle the tripod he had erected over the fire. 'I used to. But with hindsight and having had the extreme honour of sharing a bond with Peace for so long, I couldn't possibly wish for that now.'

I kicked the fire about to spread its embers and ashes, then poured water over it from my flask. Full of warmth and courage as a result of having drunk several mugs of Adam's tea, I stepped carefully down the river bank and refilled both my flask and Adam's.

We repacked our saddlebags and chuckled as Peace and Noble took that as their cue to resume their game.

By the evening, we were all tired but happy. The late winter sun had shone down on us all day, giving a hint of the warmth that was to come, and had lit up the river so that its waves glittered delicately and its ripples shone as strips of light that appeared and disappeared as if playing hide and seek. I couldn't walk too close to the water, but I began to find the sound of it rushing relentlessly on its way less of a barrage, less of a threat, less of a reminder that it and life in general rushed on regardless of whatever stood in its way, and more of a constant; something that just happened, something that could be relied upon when everything else – the weather, what would happen, who we would meet, what would be said – was in flux.

When we reached a stand of trees, Adam said, 'Marvellous, this will do us very well. There's plenty of grazing for Peace and Noble, plenty of wood for us to keep a fire going, and the trees will shelter us should the wind get up.' He grinned. 'Isn't it wonderful when everything falls into place?'

I nodded. 'Absolutely. What will we do when it doesn't though? It was summer when I travelled to The Gathering with Noble, so I didn't have to worry too much about the weather.'

'You don't have to worry about it now. Whatever happens, we'll just keep going until it gets easier, and then we'll sit back and enjoy ourselves for a bit, as we're going to do now. It can be hard going at times but as you may have already gathered, one can never be downhearted for long with Peace around.'

I grinned as I dumped Noble's saddlebags on the ground and began to unbuckle his girth. 'I've gathered.'

I pulled my horse's saddle from his back and then brushed him where it had sat. *Thank you for carrying my stuff, I'm sorry if it got in your way when you were leaping around with Peace. It was good to see you that way. I bring you down, I know it and I'm sorry.*

I would be nowhere else. With no one else. As always, I could feel that he was telling me the truth.

Oh, Noble, I wish we could be like Peace and Adam are with one another. Like Mason and Dili, and Newson and Integrity. I can feel you in my mind and I've never been as close to anyone as I have to you, but my fear of riding you is holding us apart, I can feel it even though I know that's not really possible. I'm letting you down.

You are merely experiencing the form of fear that is the most difficult to overcome but overcome it you will if you continue to feel your way. All is progressing well.

I should have felt better, but when Noble wandered off, I stood watching Peace nuzzling Adam's back while my friend checked his horse's feet, and still found myself wishing that Noble and I were as close as everyone else seemed to be to their Bond-Partners. Then I remembered my conversation with Adam; Noble was being everything I needed him to be. I watched my horse grazing in the twilight and my heart softened.

We travelled onward for four days, waking with the dawn – on two occasions snuggled up to our horses when there were no trees nearby for fuel or shelter – and then washing and breakfasting before continuing on our way. We never hurried and we stopped frequently so that the horses could graze, yet I was still amazed at Adam's and Peace's resilience and endurance. Adam was around sixty, I judged, and Peace over thirty, yet both behaved as if they were at least twenty years younger.

When smoke rose in the distance, confirming that the village Adam had told me we were approaching was indeed close by, I said, 'You and Peace are amazing, but you must be glad that Peace will have a chance to rest?'

He chuckled. 'He won't rest much, you wait and see. We're well known here, so Peace will have a crowd to entertain and he'll want nothing less.'

I began to feel nervous at the thought of being besieged as a result of being in Peace's company; whenever the Horse-Bonded and their horses had arrived in my home village, they had immediately been offered lodgings by whoever saw them first, and then given space to rest before being approached for their counsel.

Think less. Feel your way, Noble reminded me.

I nodded firmly and reached out in front of me with all of my five physical senses as well as my sixth – the voice of my soul as Adam and Peace called it – so that when the village of Beechfield came into view, its grey stone cottages with their attached paddocks and cobbled streets so reminiscent of those of my home village, I was fully present in each and every moment, absorbing everything around me so that it was part of me.

I smiled when shouts and cheers were followed by the people emitting them racing out of their cottages and down the street towards us. Noble and I stopped to let Adam and Peace go on slightly ahead so that they could greet those who clearly knew them well, and were, as Adam had foretold, desperate for Peace's attention.

I put a hand on Noble's withers and stood with him, watching in amusement as Peace pulled hats from heads and flung them around, dribbled down cloaks, squealed and snorted to the delight of those surrounding him. No one appeared to notice my horse and me, so excited were they to see Adam and Peace, which suited me just fine.

I noticed that a few people were standing back from the crowd; a young girl, just into her teenage years, I thought, stood by herself, fidgeting from one foot to the other, and an elderly couple, holding one another's hands tightly, were on the fringe of the crowd a little further round.

A curtain moved at the window of a nearby cottage, affording me a glimpse of a woman with bright blond hair before the curtain fell in front of the window once more.

My attention was drawn more urgently to a thin man in his early twenties who was gesturing wildly towards Adam and Peace whilst quickly turning his head to check which of those in his immediate vicinity were listening to him. I couldn't hear what he was saying, but he appeared to be causing those around him to feel uncomfortable, a fact he seemed to notice, as he stopped talking all of a sudden and laughed a strangely high-pitched laugh for someone of his age and gender. He raised a shaking hand to his mouth and began to chew on a fingernail as those around him moved closer to Adam and Peace, leaving him standing by himself.

The teenage girl, the elderly couple, the woman at the window and the young man – they were all me. Every single one of them. I could feel it in my skin as surely as if they had pinched me, and my heart went out to them all. They wanted Peace's counsel, but they wouldn't approach Adam and his Bond-Partner in a million years. Those out on the street may have convinced themselves that they would this time, but they wouldn't, any more than I would have done.

I noted the location of the blond woman's cottage, glanced between the girl and the elderly couple until I was sure I would recognise them if they were to drift back home before I could return, then walked towards the young man with Noble at my side.

I knew what it was like to have to pretend to be someone I wasn't in order to cope with being around people. But where I had chosen a quiet but confident persona as my alter ego, this young man had made life much harder for himself by choosing a loud, brash persona that was so far at odds with whom he really was, those around him sensed he wasn't whom he pretended to be and found him unnerving to be around. His eyes were full of desperation and darted around as he wondered what to do; he clearly wanted help from Peace and Adam, but having been rejected and left on his own, I knew he would now be feeling exposed and increasingly panicky.

He didn't notice my approach to begin with, so intent was he on watching everyone enjoying Peace's attention. He was wishing he was one of them and yet knew he never would be, I knew it as surely as I knew that Noble was walking at my shoulder. When my horse and I were almost upon him, the young man straightened, his eyes widening.

'Walk with us?' I said. 'We'll leave the hullabaloo behind, shall we?' Noble and I continued on past him.

The man looked even more nervous but my and Noble's movement drew him to follow us. We slowed until he was beside me.

'I'm Quinta and this is Noble,' I said. 'We'll walk with you a little way and then if you want us to, we'll leave you in peace.' Out of the corner of my eye, I saw his shoulders relax slightly, and continued, 'I used to hate crowds too. I never knew who to talk to or what to say, I just felt like an outsider. Whatever you'd like to say to Noble and me, we'll be glad to hear it. You won't sound daft or offensive.'

'How do I tell my parents I don't want to get married and I definitely don't want them to help me find a partner?' the man blurted out. 'How do I get them to leave me alone to get on with my life?'

Noble?

By telling the whole truth. Being dishonest with oneself is the surest way to convince others that one does not know one's own mind and that intervention is necessary.

I relayed Noble's advice to the man, who slowed his footsteps and eventually stopped in the street and crouched down, his head in his hands. His shoulders heaved as he began to sob. I glanced around and was relieved for him that the whole village appeared to have gravitated to Adam and Peace. I put a hand on the man's shoulder until he stopped crying. He wiped his face hastily and stood up.

'I know how it feels to be scared,' I said. 'I spent my whole life being terrified of everything until I bonded with Noble, and I wouldn't say I'm entirely over it all now, but Noble helps me. He can help you too, if you'll let him?'

The man glanced sideways at me. 'Can he help me be a completely different person?'

'You don't need to be a different person, you're absolutely fine as you are. You just need a little help with a few things, that's all.'

He shook his head firmly. 'I'm a mess. My life is a mess. I can't do anything without going over and over it in my head first until I'm so tired I can't do it anyway. I get nowhere, I get nothing done unless it's tasks I've done a thousand times before so I don't have to think, but then I just think about everything else while I'm doing it, so work is all I can do. My parents are frustrated with me, but nowhere near as frustrated as I am with myself.'

'Can you tell me your name?' I said.

'It's Tark.'

'Okay, Tark, you're struggling because you're living in fear. The best way to not do that is to live your life one moment at a time, so tell me, what can you see, hear, smell, taste and touch right now?'

He looked all around us all and then back to me with an incredulous expression on his face.

'I know it doesn't seem like a big thing to do, but it will help, I promise you,' I said.

He stared at me for a moment longer and then said, 'Okaaaaaay then, I can see you and, um, Noble. I can hear all those people shouting and cheering behind us. I can smell Noble, it's, um, it's a good smell.' A ghost of a smile touched his mouth.

'I can't taste anything but I can feel the cobbles under my feet.' The words spilled out of him and when he stopped talking, he flushed and glared at me, daring me to laugh.

I nodded. 'Do you want to meet Noble properly? He's a lot more gentle than Peace. Hold your hand out and let him sniff it, then you can stroke him.'

Tark's hand shook as he slowly lifted it towards Noble, who sniffed it and then nuzzled each of its fingers with their fingernails bitten down to the quick. Tark gulped and then smiled. He stepped closer and stroked Noble's shoulder. Then he said to me, 'Noble said to tell the whole truth. Fine, I do want a partner, I do want to get married, but it'll never happen. No one will want me, I never know what to say or what to do. I'll never get married, so why go through the humiliation of allowing my parents to get involved? I'll only disappoint them more. I'll always be alone, that's how it needs to be, I just need to be able to tell them that, to make them believe it.'

'Or you could do as Noble counselled, and tell them exactly what you've just told me? Maybe ask them to help you practise living your life one moment at a time until you find that people start being drawn to you because they see who you really are, and they like you – maybe even want to be like you?'

'But what if Noble's wrong? What if being honest only makes them more determined to interfere, and they just make everything worse?'

'Noble is never wrong, Tark. Never.' My conviction both surprised and shamed me as I realised I was telling someone else to overcome their fear by doing as my horse counselled when I wasn't prepared to do it myself.

'Would you... would you both come with me?' Tark whispered as he continued to stroke Noble's shoulder. 'Mum and Dad are both at home in the workshop, pouring candles.'

'Of course. Just walk at Noble's side and keep stroking him. Feel his warmth beneath your fingers, and the softness of his coat. Listen to his hooves on the cobbles. Breathe in the scent of him, because you're right, it's a good smell. That's it, you're doing brilliantly. Keep allowing everything that is Noble to fill your senses. Ah, this must be it?'

Tark's feet had stopped by a gate that opened onto a cobbled path identical to those of the rest of the cottages, while their front gardens all reflected the personal tastes of their particular occupants. Tark's parents clearly loved gardening, for even before spring had been given a chance to fill the flower beds with blooms, there was colour from a huge variety of shrubs with different coloured stems and evergreen leaves.

He nodded. 'The workshop is out the back.' He glanced at Noble and then at the front door.

I said, 'I'll go and fetch your parents out here so you can stay with Noble. There's no one else around, so just keep focusing on him as he stands there next to you, and everything will be okay.'

Tark nodded uncertainly. 'Go on in, straight down the hallway, past the kitchen and you'll come to the back doors. The one on the left leads into the Chandlery.'

I returned with Tark's very surprised parents a few minutes later.

'Tark has something he'd like to explain,' I said to them, and nodded to the young man standing with one hand on Noble's neck and the other clasping a handful of his mane. I mouthed, 'The whole truth,' and smiled at him.

Noble and I left the three of them less than half an hour later with Tark smiling as his parents hugged him on the front doorstep while promising him and me that they would help him to follow my instructions for living each moment to its fullest. It wouldn't be easy for the three of them, I knew that, but I could see how dedicated Tark's parents were to him, how relieved they were to have a way to help him, and how determined they were that he should be happy. I would check in on them again before I left the village, and would be sure to pass their way often in the future to help more if I could, but for now, there were others I needed to find.

Chapter Nineteen

*T*here was something of a street party in progress when I got back to where I'd left Adam and Peace, who had barely moved from where they had stopped when they were first mobbed. Chairs and tables had been brought out and Adam sat at one, tucking into a meal with people sitting and standing around him, chatting and laughing with him. Peace ate from a huge pile of hay nearby, next to which had been placed a half barrel full of water. He was being brushed and stroked by many hands at once, and when he paused his munching to nudge someone off balance, clear his nose over someone else, or wiggle his lips on yet another, there was laughter and delight. It seemed that everyone wanted the chance to spend time with the pair before they went home with whoever's invitation of lodgings Adam accepted.

I checked in with Noble, feeling guilty I hadn't thought to ask Tark and his parents where I could get hay and water for my horse, and hoping he wasn't in desperate need of either.

My need for both is far less than the need of some for our assistance, I was informed.

I looked around for the elderly couple and the teenage girl, but could see neither. Then I spotted movement down a side street; the couple were shuffling away, still hand in hand even though they were both unsteady on their feet and looked as if a walking stick each would have been more use.

I hurried after them with Noble clopping along beside me on the cobbles. His small feet slipped down the sides of the stones that were newer and more rounded than those on the main street, and I felt the strain it was putting on his legs.

Their struggle is far greater than mine. Worry not.

Is there anything you can tell me about them that will help?

It will be far more beneficial for them if they are given the opportunity to explain.

'Hello there,' I called out when I judged that I was close enough to be heard.

The couple shuffled onward, I thought a little more quickly. Then I remembered. They were like me. Interaction with others was uncomfortable, even more so when it was the others who were instigating the conversation.

Noble, I need to run to catch them up before they reach their cottage and disappear inside. Don't you trot, okay? You'll hurt yourself. I felt his agreement and jogged away from him.

I quietened my breathing and tried to slow it as I drew alongside the couple. The lady flinched as I appeared next to her, and almost fell against the man. I reached for her and then withdrew my hand just as quickly. Inflicting myself on her in any way wouldn't help.

'My name is Quinta, and my Bond-Partner's is Noble,' I said as I walked next to them. 'You don't have to talk to me if you don't want to, and I know you don't really want to. I also know how much courage it took for you to leave your cottage when you heard Adam and Peace were approaching the village, and I know how exhausted you'll be feeling now as a result. You weren't able to fight your way through the crowd to get to Adam, and you know you won't be able to make yourselves go and visit him where he'll be staying, so you just want to get home and forget the whole thing, even though you still really want his and Peace's help.

'I'm not Adam and my horse isn't Peace, but we can help you if you'll allow us to. I was like you, you see, before I bonded with Noble. I'm still like you, actually. I know exactly how overwhelming other people can be.'

The couple stopped at the gate of a beautifully tended garden. Spring bulbs were shooting up along both sides of a pathway that wound its way around the garden in a smooth curve. Herbs had been recently planted in clumps with plenty of room to grow and spread, white cloth protected fruit bushes from the frost that still tried to nip at them at night, and neat circles of soil had been cleared and prepared inside the bends of the pathways, ready for the spring planting of vegetables. Around the outside of the garden was an untended strip of wildness; a refuge for the plants and creatures that would be discouraged within the rest of the garden. There was a sense of flow and harmony in the garden, of beauty combined with function – of love for all that nature could provide.

'You were Farmers,' I breathed. 'It must be difficult for you now that you don't have the refuge of your fields to escape to.'

'It is,' the lady said in such a quiet voice, I only just about heard her. 'We don't have children and we could never cope with having any Apprentices, so the land that Bert's family have farmed for generations has been left fallow. It doesn't matter really. Once we're gone, other Farmers will claim it and tend it, but it shouldn't be like that, it should be looked after now, it should be loved the way we always did, but it's all too much for us to manage now.'

I put myself in her place and was immediately overwhelmed by the thought of having to interview, train and manage Apprentices, or even worse, interview and choose newly qualified Farmers to take on the land.

'What did you want to ask Adam and Peace?'

'We've neither of us got very long left here,' Bert said. 'We want to know that our land is in safe hands before we go, but we're neither of us strong enough to do anything about it. We don't know what to do.' He reached out a trembling hand to the gate and clutched it to steady himself just as Noble joined us.

My beautiful, gentle horse inserted himself between the couple and whickered.

'Oooooh, he's beautiful, isn't he Bert?' the lady said.

Bert lifted his other hand and stroked the end of Noble's nose. 'He is. Hello, lad, Dee and I are glad to see you, but what will you do with a silly old pair like us? Eh?'

They have longer than they think and are stronger than they know. There is an Apprentice who will provide as much for them as they can in return for her.

I repeated Noble's counsel and they both stared disbelievingly at me.

'But I've already said, we don't have it in us to take on an Apprentice,' Dee whispered.

'Not even one who needs you as much as you need her?' I replied, sensing Noble's meaning and intention.

They looked back at Noble standing between them as if he were a member of the family, and their eyes softened.

'Why would anyone need us?' Bert said.

I flung an arm towards their garden. 'Because of this. You know what needs planting where so that everything flourishes, because you feel it. That isn't something you can teach anyone, but for someone who already has the potential to be able to do it, someone who is as sensitive as you are and who struggles with life as much as you both do, it can be encouraged and valued so that they learn to see their sensitivity as something to embrace, something to use actively rather than seeing it as something to hide from.' I stopped talking and frowned to myself.

Noble gazed at me and blinked, his long, dark eyelashes sweeping down over his lower eyelids and then back up to reveal his eyes now boring straight into me. *You teach that which you are ready to recognise.*

Bert and Dee peered at one another around Noble's nose. Bert let go of the gate and stood a little straighter. His eyes, dull and milky only seconds previously, were a little brighter.

'Who is this someone?'

'I'll be back here with her in a little bit, if you'd like to get the kettle on,' I replied. 'If you have any containers Noble can drink from, he'll be glad of some water by then too.'

Bert and Dee looked worriedly at one another. Noble poked his nose out, blocking them from each other's view, and snorted.

Dee almost smiled. 'Yes, he'll need a drink. I have some buckets that are currently full of chicken feed but I can scrub them out and fill them ready for when you get back.'

'Thank you. We won't be long.' *Noble, do you know where she is?*

Of course. As do you.

I nodded to myself as much as to him. *What would I have done if I were her. I'd have given up any idea of getting near Adam, and gone to lick my wounds somewhere I would normally have avoided because of all the people I might meet, but where it's currently safe since practically the whole village is now having a street party in a known location. We'll look for her at the centre of the village; if it's anything like Lowtown, and it definitely appears to be, there'll be a village square.*

I waved to Bert and Dee and set off with Noble, taking care to walk a lot slower than I wanted to so that he could pick his way.

When we reached the main street, the party was still in full swing, the sunshine that was now pouring down on everyone an added cause for celebration. Noble and I turned away from it and I broke into a jog with Noble trotting beside me.

We followed the main street until it opened into a square much larger than that of my home village, at the centre of which was a beautiful fountain surrounded by flowerbeds that were green with spring shoots. The young girl I had seen when we first arrived, stood amongst the shoots, one of her hands brown with soil, the other clutching what appeared to be strands of grass. Her eyes were wide with horror at the sight of Noble and me imposing on her peace and quiet, and she looked frantically all about her, considering her options. I knew she wouldn't move; she was every bit as paralysed by all of the choices and their possible consequences as I had always been.

I was desperate to relieve her agony as soon as I could. 'You wanted to ask Adam and Peace what you should do,' I called out breathlessly, 'but there are too many people with him.' Noble and I slowed to a walk. 'There are always too many people everywhere except at your home, where you hide away. But it's stifling there. You love to be outside. You didn't test for the Skills because you don't want to be in demand by anyone, but you want to contribute, to be useful.' Noble and I stopped in front of the flower bed in which she still stood clutching a tuft of grass, its roots still intact. I nodded to it. 'You're going to plant that somewhere else, because although it doesn't belong in a flower bed, you value its life, its colour, its tenacity in daring to grow where it isn't wanted. You're sensitive and as such, you're every bit as valuable as that grass. You just need to find where you belong, and I can help you with that.' I put a hand to Noble's neck. 'We both can.'

The girl looked at the grass in her hand and then back at us. 'I can't be useful. It takes me so long to pluck up courage to leave the house, the day's half gone by the time I manage it. I only did it today because the noise of Adam and Peace arriving blew everything else out of my head, and before I knew it, I was standing in the street. Then I didn't know what to do, so I ran here where it's quiet.'

I nodded. 'I know. I found you here because it's where I would have come and for exactly the same reason.'

She frowned. 'But you're Horse-Bonded.'

I smiled. 'I am now, but before I was Horse-Bonded, I was just like you. I've learnt that being sensitive is as much a blessing as a curse if you can just figure out how to use it instead of letting it overcome you.'

The girl brightened. 'It is?' Then her shoulders slumped. 'It doesn't feel like it.'

Noble wandered over to her, picking his way between the shoots until he stood directly in front of her. He stretched his neck out ever so slowly and rested his chin lightly on her shoulder. I had to bite down on my lip so as not to cry. So often, I had focused on the fact that Noble provoked me, pushed me and hurt me, but the sight of him with someone so like me was like looking at our bond how it really was, from the outside in. Noble was more sensitive than either I or the girl, and living away from his herd and amongst the noise, confusion and complications of humans, yet he was a constant source of wisdom, patience and calm, always with me in body and mind whenever I needed him, just as he was being for the teenager in front of me.

The girl lifted a hand to Noble's nose, a look of disbelief on her face as she allowed him into her world, as she allowed him to let her know that she was fine just as she was. It was humbling and heart-melting to watch, and I felt something shift within me.

How many other sensitive people were there out there who struggled to get through each day as the four I had already met here did – as I had used to? I could reach them because I was like them. Noble could reach them because he was who he was. Between us, we could help so many people in so many villages – but it would be a slow process if we walked everywhere.

I would ride.

You have found a reason to be noble, my horse observed. *That is all it takes.* Love blasted through our bond, as if he had been holding it back and suddenly released it. He had. I could feel it. He had made himself smaller in my mind so as to not pressure me any more than his constant presence and patience had. He had given me the space to realise for myself that when I chose love over fear, I could do anything… and I couldn't wait to start.

'You know how much Noble thinks of you, don't you?' I said to the girl. 'You feel it. I feel things in my skin, as if they're sitting there as part of me. I know someone who feels it as a sort of stirring inside. How do you feel it?'

She looked at me with wonder on her face, which then dropped. 'I, er, I feel it in my scalp. You can laugh if you want.'

'Why would I laugh? How does it feel, when you know things in your scalp?'

'Like an itch that wasn't really there has suddenly stopped itching.'

I nodded and smiled. 'I know exactly what you mean. Noble always tells me to feel more and think less, so my advice to you is to follow whatever you feel in your scalp. I know of a couple of retired Farmers who struggle with the world in the same way you and I do. They desperately need an Apprentice they can train to look after the land they love, now that it's too much for them. If your scalp tells you that sounds like a good way for you to go, then come with me and Noble and we'll go and have a chat with them together. They'll understand you. They won't pressure you, they'll just guide you. You can work outside doing something you love, for people who know you need your space because they need theirs too.'

Noble turned away from her and picked his way back over the flowerbed to me. He turned and watched the girl, whose eyes began to dart from one place to another as she considered her options.

'Think less. Feel more,' I said softly.

Her eyes locked with mine and then with Noble's. She walked towards us.

'Who do I introduce you to Bert and Dee as?' I asked her.

'Blair,' she whispered. 'My name is Blair. Bert and Dee? I've never heard of a Bert and Dee in Beechfield.'

I chuckled. 'They keep themselves to themselves, much like you do. You'll like them. Come on.'

Blair turned away from the main street down which Noble and I had come, and headed for a side street. 'This way will be quieter,' she said.

We emerged onto Dee and Bert's street a long way down from where it joined the main street. I stood still for a moment, trying to figure out which way to turn, but Blair immediately turned left, saying, 'This way.'

'How do you know where they live if you've never heard of them?' I asked her.

'I don't but you said to feel more and think less, so it's this way.'

I was glad she was several steps ahead of me – both literally and figuratively – and so didn't see my eyebrows shoot up into my hairline. How was she finding it so easy to follow my advice?

She is sensitive to the voice of her soul without possessing such a strong tendency to be fearful as you do. Before you apply judgement to yourself remember that your makeup is necessary for you to do what you must. One cannot teach that which one has not had cause to learn.

Okay, fine, but wow, she's amazing.

'It's here, isn't it,' Blair almost whispered as she stood by Bert and Dee's front gate, taking in every detail of their garden. 'This is beautiful, the curves, the right plants in the right places, everything flows, everything goes, it all works.' A smile spread across her face and her eyes were bright as she looked back at me.

'Shall I knock on the door, or would you like to?' I asked her.

She could barely answer, she was so keen to get through the gate. 'I will.' She lifted her hand to knock on the door, but then hesitated. I held my breath, but heard her murmur, 'Feel more, think less,' and let it out again. She knocked softly on the door. I smiled. A louder knock than that would have made Bert and Dee hesitate to answer it. A quieter one and they wouldn't have heard it. This was all going to work out just fine.

I left Blair, Bert and Dee chattering excitedly about Blair's apprenticeship, having had a cup of tea and a piece of cake with them all while Noble grazed in the paddock behind the couple's cottage.

By the time Noble and I reached the main street, Adam and Peace's welcome party had dispersed. I was glad of the lack of people in the street outside the cottage that was my last call of the afternoon, as I knew the blond woman would never have come to the door while there was still so much going on outside it.

I opened her front gate and was about to ask Noble to follow me up the path when I shook my head and grinned to myself; of course he already knew what would be required of him.

The clopping of his hooves echoed against the cottage as we got closer to it, and the curtain of a ground floor window twitched. Good. The knowledge that my horse was there would make the woman more likely to open the front door. I raised my hand to knock on the door, but it opened before I could make contact.

The woman standing in the doorway was beautiful. Her bright blond hair framed an oval face with almond-shaped, dark blue eyes that held so much misery within them, it was all I could do not to gasp – yet as she fixated on Noble, whose head now hung over my shoulder, her eyes brightened slightly and I almost believed she might smile.

'This is Noble, and I'm Quinta,' I said softly. 'We felt that you might like Noble's counsel, so please ask him anything you want to.'

The woman's eyes left Noble and filled with panic as they darted past us both to the street. 'Can you come around to the paddock at the back?'

I smiled and nodded. 'Of course. We'll be there in a tick.'

Immediately, Noble turned around nimbly on the narrow path, ensuring that his feet didn't stray to the carefully tended flowerbeds. I followed him down the path and around the front garden to a path leading to the cottage's back paddock.

The woman hurried to open the paddock gate for us both with one hand while holding a tiny, sleeping baby against her chest with the other.

'Congratulations,' I said, nodding at the baby.

She shook her head and began to cry.

I spotted a bench encircling a large tree in the paddock, and said, 'We'll go and sit there, shall we, so that Noble can stay nearby?'

She nodded and hurried towards the bench, on which she then sat, still holding her baby close.

I sat down beside her, and Noble, ignoring the paddock's ungrazed, lush grass, took up a place directly in front of her and lowered his nose to gently sniff her baby. All of the tension left her body and she reached a hand up to stroke him.

'I'm terrified all the time,' she whispered to him. 'I've always been like it. I can't go out because I see the potential for danger everywhere and I convince myself I'll cause it all to actually happen. If I see someone up a ladder, I can't get away fast enough in case I walk too close and bump it so the person on it falls. If I see someone carrying something heavy, I can't go near them in case I cause them to strain or drop it. I didn't test for the Skills, because I'd only use them to kill someone. I couldn't even think of learning any of the Trades for fear I'd poison someone if I were a Baker, or make furniture that would collapse and hurt people if I were a Carpenter, or make candles that would flare too much and cause fires if I were a Chandler – whenever a Trade was suggested to me, all I could think of was how I'd just use it to hurt someone.

'My husband and I were at school together. He was my best friend and still is. He accepts me as I am and is more than happy for me to stay at home where I feel safe. But now I have Rosa, and I'm terrified I'm going to hurt her if I stay home alone with her, and I'm terrified I'll hurt her and everyone else if I take her out and about. What sort of a mother does that make me? I can't go on like this, I have to change, for her, for my husband. I need your help.'

I could barely hear her by the time she had finished. I knew exactly how hard it had been to say what she had, and how exhausted she would now be.

Noble?

I need add nothing to that which you are preparing yourself to say.

I shifted to face the woman. 'Being a horse, Noble is completely honest and extremely sensitive – he reacts to everything around him immediately and accurately according to what he senses. If you were capable of harming him, he wouldn't be standing almost on top of you, like he is now. If you were capable of harming your baby, he would have let me know. Look at him, he's perfectly relaxed and happy in your company.'

The woman immediately shrank back from Noble and peered up at him in disbelief. Eventually, she whispered, 'How is this possible?'

'He trusts you, just like you immediately, instinctively, trusted him. Noble is ten times your weight and could easily crush you and Rosa at any moment, yet you trusted him the second you saw him. Your instincts are accurate, you just need to get used to acting on them, on how you feel, instead of on all the horrors you've created in your mind. He and I can help you to do that, if you'll let us?'

Her beautiful eyes were full of desperation as she looked at me. 'Yes, please.' She grabbed my arm. 'Please.'

'Would you tell me your name?'

'Della.'

'Okay, Della, I want you to tell me everything you can see, smell, hear and touch.'

By the time Noble and I left Della and Rosa an hour later, Della was able to walk up the path from the paddock to the street with us, and then stand waving to us as we walked away. She rubbed the fingers of one hand against Rosa's blanket and stroked her baby's hair with the other. Twice, she lifted Rosa higher so that she could smell her. I smiled. Which sensations could better ground a new mother in the present than those emanating from her baby?

I had turned down Della's offer of lodgings for my horse and myself – whilst I appreciated her gesture, I knew my constant company would be too much for her – so Noble and I had nowhere to go and yet everywhere to be. I couldn't wait to get started.

Noble pranced beside me as we headed back down the main street and out of the village. I had never seen him so vibrant, so spirited, but rather than scaring me, his excitement invigorated me, fuelling my sense of purpose as I flew high on the knowledge that between us, we had already managed to help Tark, Blair, Bert, Dee and Della. How had I ever believed that I was the only one who was sensitive, that I was the only one who was ever paralysed with anxiety, that I was the only one who felt like a failure as a human being, however hard I tried not to be?

It is a human trait to assume that the only events that occur are those of which you are aware, Noble informed me. *All humans of The New are descended from those who had the sensitivity to hear the voices of their souls even though their culture forbade it. Is it so surprising that the trait has become even more pronounced in some of you as the generations have passed?*

I guess not.

It is human nature to resist change. To see those who are different from the majority as having a problem rather than an advantage. But change is coming at a rate that is unprecedented and those with the advantage of increased sensitivity will be much needed. We are merely one bonded pair who will prepare the way for everything that is to come.

Adam and Peace are another, aren't they?

We will focus on the part we must play. Noble stopped by a fallen tree whose trunk was of sufficient girth that I would easily be able to mount him from it.

This is a beech. It was enormous, I thought as I climbed onto it. *I hope it isn't the tree the village was named for, now that it's fallen.*

The quickest way to accept that which is unfamiliar is to forego attachment to that which is familiar, Noble told me.

You're going on as if we need to prepare for an apocalypse.

I sensed amusement from my horse, which was new and far from unwelcome. *There are some who will see it that way while there are others who will feel that which it is in truth.*

Which is?

Advancement.

It's exciting! It really was. I could feel it in my skin and through all the nerves in my body. They tingled as I sat down in my saddle and wondered how I could ever have felt fear at the thought of doing it.

As when I'd ridden before, I felt as if Noble wasn't just beneath me, but above me, around me and throughout me as I asked him to move forward. Immediately, I felt for the adjustment in my body that I had made during our last lesson with Mistral but had been unable to maintain in the face of danger. The adjustment that I needed to make now. I sat into my pelvis as if it were the most natural posture, and immediately felt immovable, as if nothing could shake me from my balance, my strength, my confidence.

The thunder of hooves preceded a cacophony of shouting and

cheering as Peace burst into the field with Adam astride him and a crowd of people running behind. Noble leapt to one side at the sudden noise and movement, and then twisted and spun around to face Peace. I was with my horse in every movement of his body, in every breath. Whatever happened, he and I were inseparable, unshakeable and immovable from our quest. I couldn't stop smiling as I looked up at Adam sitting his horse as if he were born there.

'Sorry for the intrusion, but Peace was adamant that our kind of commotion was needed here,' Adam called out.

'It was, thank you,' I yelled back. 'You knew what would happen if you brought me here, didn't you?'

He grinned and winked. 'I don't know what you mean.'

Chapter Twenty

*N*ow that I was on Noble's back, I never wanted to get off. We trotted, cantered and galloped around the field to the cheers of those looking on, until my muscles began to protest. My horse slowed to a walk. I asked him to stop and then slid from his back and hugged him.

Thank you for being you, I told him. *Thank you.* I put all of my feelings for him into the thought, while knowing that they didn't come close to covering how much he meant to me.

Noble didn't recognise my gratitude as a necessity and merely snuffled in my hair, sanguine as ever.

I wandered over to where Adam had long since ceased riding Peace and now stood with a small crowd of people, one of whom stepped forward with his hand outstretched.

'I'm Kole, and I'd like to apologise on behalf of everyone in Beechfield. We were all so excited to see our dear friends again that we completely neglected you and your Bond-Partner. Won't you and, Noble, isn't it?' I nodded and he continued, 'Won't you and Noble come and stay with me, my wife, Ossel and our son?'

He waved towards a smiling, red-haired woman carrying a small child.

I shook his hand. 'No apology is necessary. It was lovely seeing Adam and Peace welcomed so warmly, and Noble and I were soon occupied with one thing and another. Thank you, we'd love to come and stay with you.'

Kole nodded and turned to those standing with Adam and Peace. 'Do you hear that, everyone? Pass the word around that Quinta and Noble will be staying with us, next door to Adam and Peace, so if anyone needs the horses' counsel, our end of the village is where it's at.'

'Your end of the village is always where it's at,' someone called out. 'I feel a street party coming on.'

'Didn't you just have one of those?' I whispered to Adam as Kole beckoned me to follow him and his wife.

'That?' Adam chuckled. 'By Beechfield's standards, this afternoon's event was a quiet get together. Brace yourself, Quinta, you're about to learn what the word party really means.'

He wasn't wrong. When I woke the following morning, it was only just about morning still and when I looked out of my bedroom window, I was mortified to discover that there were people queuing down the street, presumably waiting to see Noble and Peace.

I checked in with Noble to find that he was snoozing under a beech tree in Kole and Ossel's paddock – despite Noble's counsel the previous day, I was relieved that the village's name didn't rely on a single fallen tree – having grazed to his heart's content.

I quickly washed and dressed, then flew down the stairs to find a note on the kitchen table informing me that Kole had left for a day's work in the fields, and Ossel for a morning shift in the village Tailor's shop, after which she would be back to make me some lunch. I added milk to some cereal left out for me, bolted it down and then shot out of the front door and down the path to the street.

'Hi, everyone,' I said to the people waiting there. 'I understand completely if you're waiting to see Adam and Peace, but if you're happy to have counsel from Noble, I'm, er, now available. I'm so sorry to be appearing so late in the day.'

A woman standing nearby smiled knowingly. 'To be honest, we're all surprised to see you up and about this early, considering who you're staying with. I'd love to come and see Noble, but there are ten in front of me, so I'll wait my turn. ISSY!' she yelled to a woman standing at the front of the queue that led up to the gate of the cottage next door. 'GET YOURSELF BACK HERE, QUINTA'S AVAILABLE.'

The woman waved and hurried towards me.

Noble and I stayed in Beechfield for just over a week, during which time I passed on Noble's counsel to so many people that I lost count of them all, and not just because of their number; I was more tired than I had ever been due to constant late nights as a result of the full diary of social events Kole and Ossel hosted, apparently as a matter of course and all of which I thoroughly enjoyed.

When the queue of people wanting Noble's and Peace's advice shrank to a trickle arriving at intervals during the day, I left Adam to it and went with Noble to visit Bert and Dee, only to find that they weren't at home.

'They've gone up to their old farm, love,' a woman called out of an upstairs window of the cottage next door. 'I saw them leaving just after dawn, dressed in their farming gear and with a young girl in tow, I think she's Blane and Cair's girl? All three of them had a proper spring in their step, they did, it was lovely to see.'

I smiled and waved my thanks, then Noble and I headed for Tark's house. We passed Della and her husband and baby on the way, who were all, her husband explained excitedly, out for their first ever family stroll.

Della's eyes were warm as she smiled at Noble and me, but she didn't speak, for which I was glad as I could see the concentration it was taking for her to stay rooted in the present when her thoughts wanted to drag her into any number of improbable futures. Her husband, on the other hand, was full of joy and gratitude, and couldn't stop thanking me and my Bond-Partner. When I could see that Della was becoming exhausted from her efforts, I explained where Noble and I were going, and left the family to continue on their way.

Tark's mother opened the door, wearing an apron with wax down it, and smiled warmly when she saw me standing on the step with Noble just behind me. She turned and called for her son, then said to me, 'He has times when he can do as you said, and times when he can't, but he's trying. We all are. Thank you, Quinta, for giving us hope that he can live a normal life.'

I glanced at Noble and instantly knew what I needed to say. 'Please don't hope for that. Tark is more sensitive than most people, and that's a good thing. It doesn't always seem like it because the world is brighter, louder and more overwhelming to him than it is for most people, but Noble tells me there'll come a time when you'll be glad he's as he is. Help him to cope, but please, please don't try to change him, he's perfect as he is.'

Tark appeared at his mother's shoulder and she glanced up at him with tears in her eyes and said, 'Quinta and Noble are here to see you.' She looked back at me and mouthed, 'Thank you,' then turned and went back down the hall.

Tark stepped past me, holding his hand out to Noble. 'I'm so glad to see you,' he said softly.

'I hear you're doing brilliantly,' I said.

'Sometimes,' Tark replied without looking at me. 'Sometimes it's easy, sometimes it's hard. Too hard.'

'But sometimes is more times than previously, so you're doing brilliantly,' I insisted. 'It takes practice to live every moment instead of letting them all pass by while your attention is somewhere else. I, of all people, know that, but it gets easier.'

He put his forehead to Noble's and whispered, 'I hope so.'

'Know so. I wanted to let you know that Noble and I will be leaving soon, but we'll be back to check on you every now and then. If you're finding it tough, hang in there, take each moment as it comes, and before you know it, we'll be back. Okay?'

'You promise?'

I nodded. 'I promise.' I reached up and pulled some loose strands of Noble's mane away from the hair that was still attached, and gave them to Tark. 'When you're finding it hard, hold these in your hand and think of Noble. Remember how he smells, how he sounds, how soft his coat is under your fingers. He'll know you're thinking of him and he'll be with you as surely as he's with me. You can do this, Tark, Noble wouldn't be ready to leave here if you weren't.'

Tark stood straight, rubbed Noble's forehead and then stepped back from him. He glanced sideways at me and whispered, 'Thank you.'

'You're welcome. We'll see you soon.'

Noble reversed down the pathway and into the street, and with a wave to Tark, I followed him and then walked beside him back to Ossel and Kole's cottage, leaving my heart with Tark.

He has his life to live and you have yours, Noble advised.

I know. But I also know how hard he'll find it and I wish I could do the hard bit for him.

Because you think you could do it better?

Yes. No. I don't know, exactly. Is it wrong to want to spare someone else from fear, pain and hardship?

Right and wrong do not exist. It is more a case of discriminating between actions that are helpful and those that are unhelpful. When someone has attracted challenges into their life so that they may gain from overcoming them then stepping in the way is unhelpful.

Which is why we need to leave.

We have been helpful. Our continued presence would be unhelpful, Noble confirmed.

I'll let Adam know that we'll be leaving tomorrow.

I saw Noble back to his paddock and he immediately trotted to the fence over which Peace was leaning from the paddock next door, and began to nibble at his friend's shoulder, dislodging mouthfuls of hair and spitting them out, while Peace did the same at Noble's withers.

I climbed through the paddock fence and tapped on the back door of the cottage in which Adam was staying. One of his hosts opened the door, a basket of washing at her hip.

'Quinta, how lovely to see you again. Do you need me or Adam?' she asked.

'Adam, please, if he's not busy?'

She came out and pointed back through the doorway. 'Go on in.' She nodded down to her washing basket. 'Wish me luck with this lot, Peace pulled the last load back off the line as soon as I was back indoors after hanging it out. I'm glad to see he's currently occupied with Noble.'

'He didn't, did he?' Adam said, appearing in the doorway.

'I'm so sorry, we'll be out of your hair at first light in the morning.'

'That's what I was just coming to tell you,' I said to him. 'It's time for me and Noble to go.'

'I'll leave you both to it,' Adam's host said and hurried off towards the washing line that hung down one side of her paddock.

Adam nodded to me. 'You and that incredible little horse of yours have an important job to do, I think, and I wish you all the very best with it all.'

My face fell. 'You and Peace aren't coming with us?'

The twinkle didn't leave his eyes, but even so, the sadness I had seen in him before appeared behind it. 'We can't move at the speed you'll need to if you are to reach all of those craving the help that you are so uniquely placed to give. And besides, Peace and I have our own work to do, much of which is unpleasant and uncomfortable and should not have to be endured by any other than he who caused it and his ever tolerant Bond-Partner.'

I frowned in confusion. 'I can't imagine you ever having caused anything unpleasant or uncomfortable.'

'I don't suggest you try, but rather that you dedicate all of your focus to your mission. Go and help all of those who slip beneath the notice of the Horse-Bonded less able than yourself to recognise them, Quinta, and know that you and Noble take my love and best wishes with you.'

I hugged him. 'Thank you, Adam, for everything you've done for me. I'm going to miss you and Peace, and so will Noble.'

He hugged me back. 'Our paths will cross both out on our travels and back at The Gathering, don't doubt it. And before that, I rather suspect that we'll be thrown together as guests of honour at another of Kole's street parties. I've never known him allow any Horse-Bonded to leave Beechfield without first having endured a leaving party.'

I grinned and was immediately shocked to discover how much I looked forward to the thought of yet another social event, and further, how much I relished the thought of travelling alone and at speed with Noble, even though it meant leaving Adam and Peace behind.

'Did I really say I was leaving at dawn?' I groaned at Ossel as she poked her head around my bedroom door, her face lit up by her lantern. 'How are you up already when you only went to bed a few hours ago? My head feels as if someone's sitting on it.'

She grinned. 'Practice and determination. Without them both, I'd never have kept up with Kole long enough to marry him, let alone coped with having his son, who's been every bit as lively as his father from the first moment he moved in my belly. Come on, the day is about to begin, and it's going to be a nice one, I felt it in the air when I went out to get some eggs.'

'You've already been outside?' I put the pillow over my head and said, 'Is there something in the water of Beechfield that reaches you and doesn't reach me?'

She laughed. 'If it's any consolation, the chickens were no more pleased to see me than you are. I've got breakfast on the go…'

'Of course you have.'

'…so come on down when you're ready.'

I washed, dressed, stripped the sheets off the bed and left them in a neat pile, then packed my back-sack with the freshly washed clothes Ossel had left on top of it the previous day. I shook my head as I pulled the drawstring tight. The woman and her family were forces of nature.

They merely act on how they feel in any given moment. They well demonstrate how much energy one may utilise when it is not wasted by excessive thought, Noble observed.

I obviously still think waaaaaaaay too much then, I replied, looking around for my saddlebags. Unable to locate them, I went downstairs and into the kitchen, dumping my back-sack by the door to the paddock where I knew that Noble was dozing under the beech tree.

'I don't suppose you've seen my saddlebags anywhere, have you?' I asked Ossel. 'I may have left them out in the shed with Noble's saddle, but I thought I brought them inside.'

Ossel pointed towards a kitchen chair that had been pulled back from the chunky wooden kitchen table. 'Over there. I packed them with enough food to last you for a few weeks. I don't know where you're heading and you don't appear to be carrying any hunting equipment, so I hope that'll be enough?'

'It'll be more than enough, thank you. I really can't thank you enough for this and all of the other food you've given me, for your hospitality, for doing my washing... you've been so kind and generous.'

Ossel turned around in surprise. 'Honestly? The Horse-Bonded give up any idea of a normal life – of marriage, children, homes of your own – and travel around the villages of The New, helping us all to stay true to what our forefathers put in place for us, and you think you owe any of us thanks? It's the least we can do. Thank you, Quinta, for all of the time you and Noble have spent with us all. Adam and Peace pass through here often to help us, so we never tend to have that much need for any of the other Horse-Bonded, but you and Noble have really made your mark here. Don't be strangers, please?'

'Um, we won't be. You know, I never had any chance of a normal life anyway before Noble tugged me. I've given up nothing and been given everything, so please, don't feel sorry for me or for any of the other Horse-Bonded. Our horses are more to us than it's possible to describe, and we all thank the light for them every single day.'

She smiled and pointed at one of the kitchen chairs for me to sit down. 'I think we all see how much Noble and Peace mean to you and Adam. He's leaving today too, isn't he?'

'Who is?' Kole said, breezing into the kitchen with his son on his hip, whom he deposited in a high chair whilst moving to open a cupboard door in one fluid motion. He took out four bowls and put them on the table as Ossel said, 'Adam.'

Kole nodded out towards the paddock and then back to me. 'We'll miss the four of you. Where are you heading?'

'We're going to feel our way and see where we end up, and then keep doing that until we've been everywhere,' I replied.

Kole grinned and said, 'That sounds like an excellent plan to me.'

Ossel poured porridge into each of the four bowls, and then pushed one towards me. 'Get that down you and be off with you then, before we all decide we aren't ready to let you go.'

I laughed. 'I'll be out of that door the second I've finished, I can't keep up with you three a minute longer.'

Kole said, 'You'll miss us once you're gone.'

I knew he was right, but then I thought of all of those I needed to reach, and felt a sense of anticipation and excitement. I hurried to finish my breakfast.

Adam and Peace were ready to leave at the same time that I was. As Noble and I walked along the track between Ossel and Kole's cottage and that in which Adam had been staying, I caught sight of my friend and his horse in the street, saying their goodbyes to their hosts. The early rays of sunshine glanced off the white of Peace's back, making him look even larger and more magnificent than he was. I swallowed hard, trying to force down the lump that appeared in my throat at not knowing when I would see him and his Bond-Partner again.

They have their mission, whatever it is, and we have ours, I told Noble as if it were he who needed reminding rather than I.

We reached the street and Adam held his arms out to me. 'Fare well, both of you, until our paths cross again.'

I bit down hard on my bottom lip so as not to cry as I hugged him, but then began to laugh as a big tongue slapped against my cheek. I pulled away from Adam to find Peace with his head in the air, curling up his top lip, and laughed even harder. I reached up and hugged the big horse and he nuzzled my back.

'You fare well too, Adam,' I managed to say. 'You and Peace. I'll miss you both.'

'They're a hard pair to say goodbye to, aren't they?' Ossel said, drawing me into a hug of her own. 'Remember what I said,' she whispered in my ear. 'Don't be a stranger.' She passed me to Kole, who almost suffocated me in a bear hug and then bent down by Noble and cupped his hands ready to give me a leg up.

Once I was in my saddle, my hosts and Adam's crowded around and patted and hugged Noble, leaving Adam and Peace standing alone, Adam with his hand at his horse's shoulder. I lifted a hand to them both, unable to stop a tear sliding down my cheek. Adam nodded and winked at me, and Peace pawed the ground. They wanted to be off.

'Bye, everyone,' I said as Noble walked carefully backward away from them. When he was clear of them all, he spun around and trotted across the cobbles as they called their goodbyes.

As soon as the last cobble was behind us, Noble sped up to a canter, his hooves pounding on the ground below me, and his tail, my hair and my cloak, all long and black, streaming out behind us. The cold morning air still had a little bit of bite, and my cheeks were soon numb and my eyes streaming. I didn't care, I didn't need to see where we were going; it was the right way, I could feel it in my skin.

Chapter Twenty-One

Noble and I visited village after village during the months that followed. I never had any idea where we were headed as we left one village for the next; we just went whichever way felt right to me, my horse or us both. I could never quite determine which it was, not that I tried very hard, for I loved the feeling of freedom that moving in an unknown direction with no consideration whatsoever, afforded me.

I revelled in every single moment while my horse and I travelled together, whether the sun was shining or hidden behind clouds that poured their contents down upon us; whether the wind blew or was still; whether we crossed plains or negotiated mountains. Noble's dainty legs carried us at a speed that I suspected would have been difficult for horses of heavier builds to maintain for long, and his nimble feet picked their way across ground that others may have avoided, enabling us to follow our sense of the direction to take almost exactly until we arrived at the next village.

As time went on, I grew less and less surprised when yet

another community appeared before us, but I still smiled at the miracle – as it seemed to me – of what could be achieved as a result of following feelings rather than plans and thoughts.

Some of the villages we visited hadn't seen any Horse-Bonded for months, a few for almost a year, and as a result, their occupants needed Noble and me to stay for a week or two in order to be able to work our way through all of those wanting my horse's counsel. Others had been visited recently and so my Bond-Partner and I were needed far less, but we stayed nearly as long in those villages as in the rest, so that I had time to find the villagers who wanted but could never ask for help; those whose sensitivity manifested in a variety of different ways while all sharing the common thread of them struggling with human interaction. I could always recognise them upon sight regardless of where they were or what they were doing, and from passing comments made by others, but it took time.

My skin would always tell me they were there, by feeling a little too tight for my body. Only when I had found each and every one of them – whether they worked during the night, or left before dawn and returned after dusk, or worked in workshops at home, or had to be walked to and from school to make sure they went, or had the Herbalist called to visit them by worried parents more often than was normal, or even were overly loud when interacting with others despite their hunched shoulders, bitten fingernails, or a hundred different mannerisms that gave them away – and offered them assistance in a way they could accept, did I feel comfortable in my skin and able to leave.

Usually, all that was required was for me to listen to them describe their feelings of being constantly worried and overwhelmed, relay Noble's counsel to them regarding humankind's need for those with a greater degree of sensitivity to their surroundings, and then recount my own experiences and explain how to fully occupy each moment so that the mind could be calm and better able to process what was happening without rushing backwards and forwards as it related all of its sensory input to past experience and fears for the future.

Occasionally, more direct input was required, such as accompanying one young woman out for walks with Noble until she felt more confident to do it with just me, then with a family member and even by herself, and in one case, taking a ten-year-old girl out on Noble's back. I didn't question what might have happened had my horse jumped at something and thrown her, because it felt the right thing to do, and therefore it was.

As it happened, the girl was so full of her experience with Noble, it eclipsed everything else from her mind and before she knew it, we had left the village, and spent several hours exploring the surrounding countryside before returning to her parents. Having done all of that, going to school a few buildings along from her home was far easier for her, and we left a happy family behind us. It wouldn't always be easy for her, and I knew that Noble and I would need to return regularly to give further assistance in the future, which we were more than happy to do.

With every person who listened to me as I told them of my own experiences and struggles, and allowed Noble and me to help with theirs, I felt stronger in myself, as if the more I gave of myself, the more I received in return.

You are all connected. The more balanced one of you becomes the easier it is for the rest to follow. The more who follow the more established becomes the new level of balance, Noble told me as I rode him away from yet another village, pondering on the phenomenon.

I didn't see how we could all be connected – we were individual people occupying our own bodies and completely independent of one another, after all – but I could feel he was right. *So we're all helping one another? I feel stronger because more people like me are coping better?*

Because you are all strengthening the pattern for embracing your sensitivity so that it is helpful rather than unhelpful.

Because everything can be either helpful or unhelpful, I remembered. *Except fear, that's never helpful, it's just crippling and horrid.*

Fear in the short term can be helpful, Noble corrected me. *It can be necessary for survival since its presence endows the body with a greater ability to react. It is fear of imagined future events that is unhelpful since it distracts from the present with its ability to make those events seem real.*

I nodded to myself. *It seems so simple to understand now I'm not consumed by it. I wasted so much time and energy imagining up all sorts of scenarios to be terrified of, none of which actually happened.*

Had you not then you would not understand those whom we seek out and help. No time is ever wasted, Noble informed me.

So am I nearly ready to help those you told me are coming? Those who will change everything for us all? How will I know when I am? How will I recognise them?

I felt Noble's amusement. *They will be difficult to miss. It is unhelpful to dwell on the future. We will continue to negotiate the path upon which we have embarked and trust that it will take us where we need to go.*

Months turned into years – seven to be exact – during which my horse and I continued to travel between villages. Every now and then, we would return to The Gathering to rest and catch up with friends for a few weeks or months before heading back out either to villages we had visited before or those that were new to us, always following our sense of where we needed to go. In all that time, I was never drawn to go to my home village.

I had sent monthly letters to my parents via Heralds ever since I had left Lowtown, from wherever Noble and I happened to find ourselves, knowing that it may take them some time to reach their destination, but that eventually, they always would. Whenever we arrived back at The Gathering for a rest, there was always a pile of letters waiting for me in return, so I knew my mother and father were both well and had two Weavers working with them, both of whom had been Apprentices and then had stayed on in the village to carry on gaining knowledge and experience from the Master Weavers my parents were. I knew they missed me but were proud of me and thrilled to hear about my and Noble's travels and life together.

So it was that when Noble and I topped a hill and I found myself looking down on my home village, I blinked in disbelief. I looked all around us both, wondering how on earth I could have spent the last few weeks travelling to Lowtown without even realising it.

The answer came to me, and to begin with, I couldn't believe it. Had I really never left the village except to take the path up to Hightown and back? I couldn't relate the well travelled life full of experience and interaction that I was now living, to the insular, restricted one I had left behind; it was as if they were completely separate lives, lived by two different people.

My heart leapt with excitement at seeing my parents, and then sank a little. Would they recognise me? Would they relate to me? Would they even like me?

Noble increased his presence in my mind, and I frowned as I recognised the reason. What was happening to me? Was I actually worrying? And about how my parents would respond to me, of all things?

You have stepped away from your previous patterns of thought and behaviour but you have not released them entirely, Noble told me. *We visit this village with the same purpose as all of the others we have visited over the years but with the added opportunity for you to discharge that which you are now ready to release.*

I couldn't wait to get started. I barely had the chance to touch my ankles to Noble's sides before he shot down the hill towards Lowtown, so that by the time we reached the valley, we were both breathless and sweaty under the warm spring sun.

Noble cantered alongside the river that had given me so many nightmares, and I felt an echo of the churning in my stomach that had once been part of my daily existence. I just needed to feel it so that I could release it, I told myself. Even so, when Noble turned away from the river and cantered up the gentle slope towards Lowtown, I felt relieved. I questioned my feelings and decided that I was just relieved to be close to finally seeing my parents after all this time. I had got over my fear of rivers long since, indeed Noble and I had been given cause to travel alongside and traverse many during the past years, and this one was no different from all of those.

Shouts reached us from the nearest cottages of Lowtown, and I caught glimpses of people waving from windows before others began to appear at the end of the main street.

'There's a Horse-Bonded and her horse coming!'

'Wow, I've never seen a horse that small, isn't he glorious?'

'Lucy, stop shrieking or they'll turn around and go and visit a village whose children are less noisy.'

'Flaming lanterns, that looks like Quinta, but it can't be, can it?'

I heard each and every voice; their different tones, volumes, inclinations and meanings, and smiled at every one. By the time Noble stepped onto the cobbled street, there was a crowd waiting to greet us, just as there had been at every other village we had visited so far.

Out of habit, I scanned the crowd as I smiled, waved and returned the copious greetings that came my way, looking for those who I knew would never come and see me. I didn't expect to see anyone; I had been the person who fulfilled that part of the spectrum of different characters in Lowtown, and I was here, sitting astride my horse. There couldn't be anyone else, could there?

But there were. There was a young mother carrying a baby and holding tightly to the hand of the small boy standing beside her, looking every bit as if she were about to turn and run away. And there was a man with more grey hair than black, standing right at the back of the crowd. I could see that he wanted to reach me, but knew he would never manage it even though he had more reason than anyone else there to be the first to properly greet me – for he was my father.

Chapter Twenty-Two

*M*y mouth dropped open. How could that be? My father was… my father. He had always been there to help me, to protect me – because he knew what it was like to be me, I suddenly realised. It was as if he and I were the only two people present as I was transported back to my life before Noble tugged me.

It was my mother who always took me to school. When she couldn't go to Hightown for supplies or to deliver cloth to the Dyers, I had to go; my father never went, in fact, I couldn't remember him leaving the house or its attached workshop to go anywhere or do anything. When I failed to return to Lowtown after having been swept away by the river, it was my mother who brought a search party to come and find me. When I went walking at nighttime, it was always my mother who came with me. My father was just like me, or rather, I was just like him.

But he was here now, and without my mother. Where was she, and what was he doing out of the house by himself? I smiled. He had heard everyone shouting about the approaching horse and Horse-Bonded and he had known who it must be.

Love transcends fear, I told Noble, knowing he didn't need me to tell him.

I came back to myself. It would be excruciating for my father being out here. I blew a kiss to him and pointed in the direction of our cottage. He nodded, turned around and practically ran home.

I jumped down from Noble's back and greeted all of those who had turned out to welcome us. I recognised some of them from my reluctant forays out of the house, but the rest were strangers. I extended the same invitation to all of them to come and knock on my parents' door if they needed me or Noble for anything, then began to walk down the main street with Noble at my side, waving to those who called out welcomes and greetings as we passed their cottages.

When we reached the much larger building that was the village school, I had a vision of myself clinging to my mother as she tried to prise my hands from her skirts and hand them to whichever kindly teacher's turn it was to take me, crying and screaming, inside, where once the terror of being separated from my mother had passed, I would settle down at a desk to work.

When the first bell rang, I would make my feet take me outside to the playground, knowing that if I didn't go, I would have to stay behind after school. Sometimes, I would walk straight into a game of tag, in which I was instantly included, and would forget how overwhelming the playground was and enjoy myself. When the bell went to end playtime, I would run in with everyone else, full of happiness and confidence that I had got over my fear of the playground… only to endure it all over again when the bell rang to signal the end of the next lesson.

As I got older, I learnt to cope with school from day to day using a variety of coping strategies – counting everything, from the cobbles on my way there, to the windows of the school building, the number of children I could see at any one time, the floor and ceiling tiles in my classrooms, the railings of the fence that surrounded the school building and playground, the books on each shelf in the book corner; pretending I was someone else, as I later employed in order to visit Hightown; volunteering for plant watering duty or library duty or animal care duty in order to avoid the playground between lessons – and I stopped hanging on to my mother at the gate, sometimes even managing the short walk to school by myself.

But then during the school holidays, I would get used to the safety of being at home with my parents, and on the first day of term, I would be hysterical. My mother would walk me to school, accompany me inside and leave me to cry in the library until I had recalibrated myself and could venture out to join whichever lesson was in progress.

I blinked as the clatter of Noble's hooves on the cobbles brought me back to myself, and looked back at the school we had just passed. Now, it looked just like any other school building, and, strangely, a lot smaller than it had only a minute before. The gate was just a gate, and the playground just one of hundreds I had passed during my travels.

We retraced the steps I had taken every school day for ten years and with each, I remembered more of the person I used to be. My footsteps slowed as I shrank back in on myself, feeling nauseous and panicky, but where before I had found only more fear inside myself, now I found Noble.

Immediately, I remembered whom I had become, and calmed down. But I couldn't hold everything that bombarded my senses away from me. My previous life hadn't just collided with my new one, it was as if the two were both trying to occupy my attention at the same time, fighting for recognition, for existence.

Had we returned here before now you would not have been able to hold to all you have become, Noble advised me. *As it is you are balanced and strong. You are able to distinguish between that which is helpful and that which is not. You are able to release that which is not.*

I took a deep breath and believed him. I stopped trying to hold away everything of my old life and allowed it to filter into my mind. The fear over what the day would bring collided with my confidence that whatever happened, Noble and I would deal with it, and then floated away from me as if it were never mine to begin with. The nauseating vulnerability of being away from home was obliterated by my love of travelling to different villages, meeting people and helping those who asked for it. The desperation I had felt to interact with as few people as possible was overcome by my keenness to find the young woman with the baby and toddler, and anyone else who came to my attention as possibly needing Noble and me to seek them out to offer the help for which they couldn't ask.

Slowly, Lowtown transformed in my mind from a place that held aspects of myself with which it could torture me, to just another village among the many that my horse and I had enjoyed visiting.

My parents' home was another matter entirely. As soon as it came into view with its rose growing up and over the front porch from one side, and most of its frontage obscured by a ferocious and determined ivy, I was bombarded with memories. There, I had felt safe. I had dragged my feet as I left it, often trembling and crying, and then raced back towards it as fast as my legs would carry me as soon as I could. I had made it and the workshop that jutted out from behind it into a prison, somewhere I convinced myself I wanted to be, but was unable to leave.

Yet you did. And now you have returned, Noble observed.

I put a hand up to his mane and ran my fingers through it. *Now I've returned,* I agreed, and my memories dissolved to nothing, leaving a grey stone cottage covered in rambling, overgrown plants standing before me. It was no prison, but merely a building in which lived two people whom I loved dearly. *Come on, we'll go around the back. Unless things have changed considerably, the paddock will just have a few chickens in it, so there'll be plenty of grass for you.*

Noble followed me along the narrow, stony track between my parents' cottage and the one next door, and into the paddock which was just as I remembered it. My horse immediately dropped his head down to graze the lush spring grass. I found the bucket my mother used to take water to the chicken coop, filled it and put it out near where Noble stood munching contentedly. Then I made my way to the cottage, listening to the clacking sound of a loom being operated that drifted through the open door of the workshop, just along from the back door of the cottage.

I poked my head into the workshop and saw two unfamiliar people working with their backs to me. One was operating my mother's loom while the other was attaching new warp strings to the loom that had been mine.

I stepped inside and called out, 'Hi, I'm Quinta.'

Both of them stopped working and turned to look at me.

I smiled. 'I've heard so much about you both.' I nodded to the red-haired lad at my mother's loom. 'You must be Tolston, it's good to meet you.' Then I looked at the dark-haired, heavy-browed girl. 'And you must be Yelda, it's great to meet you too.' They both came over and shook my outstretched hand.

Yelda said, 'It's good to meet you too, we've heard all about you from your parents and just about everyone else here. You're something of a legend, you know, in fact I'm pretty sure the younger kids don't even believe you're real. Where's your horse?'

I nodded towards the paddock. 'Just out there, he'll be pleased to see you if you want to go out and meet him. I think my dad's probably in the house, but where's my mum?'

'She's gone up to Hightown,' Tolston said. 'She'll be back in a few hours, I should think.'

I nodded. 'Okay, great. Um, how's my dad been?' A pang of something I couldn't yet face bit at my heart.

Tolston looked at Yelda, who said, 'He's the same as always. Sometimes he comes out and works while we're here, other times we know he's been out here during the night when he can be alone. He's a lovely man and such a good teacher. When Tol and I qualified, we both felt we owed it to him to carry on here to help with all the orders, so he and your mum wouldn't have to take on new people. You know, so he wouldn't have to cope with anyone new.'

I couldn't hold it back any longer. Guilt pulled down on my heart until I felt weak with it. How had I not seen that my father struggled every bit as much as I did? Where he and I had worked easily, happily, laughingly alongside one another, I had left him to have to take on people who, lovely as they were, weren't my mother or me; weren't the easy, safe company we were. He felt vulnerable in his own workshop because of me, and my mother would have had to take on more of the work when he couldn't work alongside Tolston and Yelda. Because of me.

Now you can help him as you have helped so many others, Noble interjected.

I should have come back here before, I could have helped years ago.

We have already discussed this. Had we returned years ago you would have been no help. You would have been drawn back into your old patterns and been unable to find a way out other than by leaving with both your and your parents' issues unresolved. You are always where you need to be. You know this.

I felt the two Weavers' eyes on me. 'Sorry,' I said, 'I just needed to listen to Noble for a moment. Thank you, both of you, so much, for everything you've done and continue to do for my parents. Is this truly where you want to be though, because if not, I can put the word around while I'm on my travels, that you're looking to relocate?'

Yelda smiled and glanced shyly at Tolston. 'We're happy here now, thanks. We're actually getting married in a few months' time and we're happy to settle here permanently and take on more of the running of the workshop as your parents want to do less. We both came here looking for apprenticeships because the Master Weavers in our home villages already had enough Apprentices, and somehow, we managed to find ourselves learning from the best, as well as finding each other. How lucky are we?'

I smiled and murmured, 'You're always where you need to be.' My guilt ebbed away as if it had never been. *It all worked out for the best, I get it, but I need to help my dad.*

I sense no one standing in your way, Noble informed me.

No. Right. Fine. I'll go to him now. So why was I still standing there?

'Are you okay?' Yelda said. 'Oh, you're listening to Noble again, aren't you? You have that same faraway look on your face.' She looked towards the workshop door. 'I need to meet the horse I've heard so much about. What do I do?'

I walked to the door with her. 'Just hold your hand out for him to sniff. When he's finished, if he stays near you, you can stroke him. If he moves away then he wants his own space.'

She nodded. 'Come on, Tol, we're due a quick break.'

A thought struck me. 'It's nearly lunchtime and you're due far more than a quick break. Take the afternoon off, Dad and I'll take your places later.'

'Really? Are you sure?' Tolston said. 'We should square it with him.'

I shook my head. 'If he was up for your company, he'd be out here, you know that. He'll be fine with it, I know he will. Please, go and enjoy the sunshine, goodness knows, it's been long enough since we all saw it.'

'Thanks, Quinta. Let your parents know we'll be back bright and early tomorrow?' Yelda said.

'I will. Go and meet Noble, then enjoy the rest of your day. I'll see you tomorrow.' I headed towards the back door with purpose, turned the doorknob and then kicked the door at the bottom to get it to open as I had done so many times before. 'Dad, I'm home,' I called out, closing the door behind me.

Hurried footsteps sounded in the hallway and then the kitchen door was flung open and my father appeared. Without speaking, he opened his arms and drew me into one of his bear hugs, evoking memories of my time growing up with him and my mother; he had always held back from me when I was having a meltdown, leaving me to my mother to deal with, but he had always been ready with a hug for me when I was on an even keel as I was now. When I was like this, I realised, I didn't frighten him; I didn't remind him of his own fears and make his own problems worse.

Well, now I was here to try to make them better.

'I've missed you and Mum so much,' I said when I finally pulled back from him. 'I haven't been at The Gathering for months, so I haven't been able to pick up your most recent letters. How are you both?'

He smiled. 'Your mum is fine, and I'm all the better for seeing you. I knew you were coming, you know. I don't know how, but I did. Then when I heard people shouting and cheering, I knew it was because of you.'

'And you left the house to come and see me. I know how much that will have taken out of you,' I said, looking deeply into his dark eyes, so like my own. In that moment, I understood why Noble looked so deeply into me at times; I knew that my father would feel my words as well as hear them, that he would understand.

He nodded slowly. 'I can see that you do. But you know, Quinta, when I saw you riding into the village on Noble, when I saw for myself everything you have become, I forgot everything. For the first time in my life, I felt like I was normal. Just for a few moments, all I could feel was pride in my daughter.'

I smiled. 'That's all it takes, Dad. Focus on what you love and fear can't find a way in.'

He shook his head and smiled ruefully as he led me to the kitchen table and pulled out a chair for me. When I sat down, he sat down next to me with a sigh. 'If only it were that straightforward.'

'It really is that straightforward, but that's not to say it's easy, I of all people know that.' I took his hand. 'You know what I was like, and you see me now. It works, Dad. You're sensitive and you get overwhelmed easily, but if you choose where to put your focus, you can learn to use your sensitivity to help you instead of allowing it to frighten you.'

My father looked at me as if I were telling him the sky was, in fact, green.

'You knew I was coming,' I said. 'Where did you feel it?'

He frowned. 'What do you mean?'

'Where in your body did you feel confirmation of your thought that I was coming? I feel it in...'

'My skin,' my father said.

I smiled. 'And when you have something bugging you, something you feel you need to do, or need to know, it feels like your skin is tight. Then when you've resolved whatever it is, your skin suddenly feels comfortable again.'

He nodded slowly. 'I would never have thought to explain it like that, but yes, that's it exactly. I know your mother's okay right now, as surely as I knew you weren't when you nearly died in the river. I told your mother, but she thought I was just being neurotic like always. Then when you didn't come home, I begged her to get a search party together and go and look for you. Even then though, I couldn't go with those who volunteered to go.' He put his head in his hands. 'I'm so sorry, Q, I'm your father and I let you down so badly that day, just like I let you down every other day of your life. I can't tell you how relieved I was when you were tugged. I knew I was bad for you, and your mother was so protective over you because she knew how much I struggled and she wanted to try to help you past it, but the more she protected you, the worse you got.'

'Dad, look at me.'

He obeyed me with bloodshot eyes.

'You did everything right. I needed to know how it feels to be frightened of everything so that I could learn to move past my fear and then help others do the same. There's a lot of change coming. Noble won't tell me what it is, but it's to do with humankind advancing. He says that those of us who are sensitive are important to the process, that we'll be needed by everyone else because we'll be able to adjust to the changes more easily. It's hard being sensitive, but it's also a blessing if you can find a way to manage it, and I can help you to do that now Noble's helped me.' I looked deeply into his eyes again. 'You can feel that I'm telling you the truth, I know you can. Let me help you, Dad, because Mum and the rest of Lowtown will need you and whoever that woman is who's like us.'

'Eleri,' my father said without hesitation. 'Your mother recognised that she's like me when she and her husband moved here, and she does as much for her as she can.'

I smiled. 'I've missed Mum so much.' I flicked my eyes up to my father's. 'Let's go and meet her with Noble. Can you imagine her face?' His eyes lit up. 'Good, now hold that thought and don't let your mind stray from it. Imagine her face while you get your shoes on, come on.'

He managed it, but as his hand settled on the metal doorknob, panic flickered across his face.

I put a hand on top of his. 'It's cold in your hand, isn't it. Focus on the cold spreading through your palm and up your wrist. Listen to the doorknob squeak as you twist it, and feel the spring inside resisting you. That's it, now notice the difference beneath your feet as you step from the flagstones to the earth outside. Feel the sun on your face, hear – really hear – the birds singing and try to see how many different voices you can pick out from them all. When you're ready, focus on Noble. See him over there? Let him fill your senses, and let your senses fill your mind as you make your way over to him.'

He did everything I said. My father's love for me was practically visible as he listened intently to my voice and chose to follow my instructions over his urge to stop in his tracks and think himself out of what he was doing. My heart swelled when he reached out a shaking hand for Noble to sniff, and then held it in place while Noble gently nuzzled the back of it before sniffing all along my father's arm, up to his shoulder, neck and face, and then blowing in his ear.

Before I knew it, he was walking between Noble and me, along the track to the street and then down it and the next street until we reached the main street and turned to walk out of Lowtown.

The sight of my beautiful Bond-Partner walking step for step beside my father almost choked me several times, but I managed to swallow quickly and concentrate so that the second my father began to struggle, I could remind him to stay in the present with me and Noble, rather than straying to fearing for his immediate future as his mind so badly wanted to.

Everyone we passed caught the meaning of my smile, nod and hand held out at hip height out of my dad's sight, and kept their distance. They smiled and nodded in return and some blew kisses.

Once we had left the village behind us and were walking alongside the river, my father began to find it a little easier to maintain his concentration, while I found it harder than I cared to admit. I had grown used to effortlessly being in the present, but now I found that I needed to focus almost as intensely as he did.

Yet focus you do. Learning To Soar you do well, Noble told me. He had known I would manage in the presence of the fear that lingered within me, I could feel it through our bond. He had complete confidence in me, which only served to highlight that I didn't; that I wasn't as confident in myself as I had thought I was.

It was a relief when we finally saw a dot in the distance, moving along the path towards us all.

'There she is,' my father said and then looked around himself frantically.

'Focus,' I reminded him. 'The sound of the water. The sparkles bouncing off it when the sun comes out from behind the clouds. Noble's footfalls beside you, his warmth, his presence.' *Feel more, think less,* I reminded myself as the sound of the water caused a lurch in my stomach.

My father clenched his fist, breathed in and out deeply, and nodded. He was back with us. If he could do it, I could do it.

We continued on towards the dot that had just resolved into a line as it moved in our direction more quickly. I smiled. My mother knew who it was that approached her. I so wanted to run to her, but I wouldn't leave my incredibly brave father, and I wouldn't use her as the crutch she had always been for me. I would get myself completely together before we reached her.

A large bush to the left of the path jogged my memory and I stopped in my tracks as I suddenly realised where we were. I tried to focus on the memory of Noble's family herd milling around between the bush and the river, but my eyes were drawn down to where a baby Noble had perched between the river and its bank, then to the river that had pulled me away from him. I felt as if it were doing the same thing again; as if I were being drawn to the river and couldn't help myself from jumping in headfirst so that it could do with me as it willed. My stomach churned and I thought I was going to vomit.

I gasped as a strong hand closed around my arm and held on tight. 'I've got you, Q.'

I blinked and realised I was standing on the edge of the bank; any loss of balance and I would be in the river. I began to shudder and pant as my father pulled me gently away. I turned to him and collapsed into his embrace, sobbing.

His voice rumbled in his chest as I cried into it. 'It's okay, I've got you.' He stroked my hair as he had when I was a child and had hurt myself. When I managed to stop crying, he said, 'Dry your eyes, now, your mother's nearly upon us. You don't want her to see you like this, do you?'

I pulled the sleeves of my jumper down over my hands and rubbed at my face. 'No, of course not, I'm sorry, Dad, I don't know what came over me.'

'Yes you do,' he said softly. 'It was here that you went in, wasn't it?'

I couldn't do this, not now, when he needed me.

You are always where you need to be. The thought was so faint, I only just caught it. I glanced at Noble and relaxed as his eyes bored into me. What were the chances that I should be at this exact spot with my father, Noble and very soon, it appeared my mother? Of course I was here because I needed to be.

I pointed. 'Noble was trapped just there. I jumped down beside him and then when he braced against me and jumped up here, I ended up out there.' My voice shook almost as much as my finger as I pointed out into the river. 'And then...' my voice caught in my throat. 'And then it took me with it down there.'

My father enfolded me in his arms again and held me tightly. 'And I knew. I felt you were in danger, and I did nothing.' As he hugged me, I felt some of the hold the river had over me begin to dissipate.

I hugged him back fiercely. 'It doesn't matter now. We're both here with the horse who caused it for a good reason.' I pulled back from him. 'We have to let it go and move forward, otherwise it'll hold us back. Noble wasn't trapped, Dad. He put himself in that position so I would prove to myself that when I feel love, I can't feel fear. I didn't think twice about jumping into the river to help him get out, just as you haven't had to focus on being present now that I've given you reason not to need to. And now, here we both are. We can do anything.'

My father looked between Noble and me. 'He risked your life on purpose?'

'There's more than my life at stake, Dad. He did what was necessary to prepare me to learn what I needed to learn. To demonstrate that when I have a reason to be noble, I can be, like he always is.'

'And what's his reason?'

'Me. Us. Humankind. Like my reason is now. We're both here

because I'm finally strong enough to release the fear of the river I've been holding on to, and because you need to release the guilt you've been holding on to so that you can hear the voice of your soul more clearly when it speaks to you.'

I stopped and frowned. How did I know that?

You have cleared the majority of your fear. The voice of your soul speaks through you more easily. You taught that which you needed to learn.

I felt a surge of strength. 'I'm who I am now because of what happened, Dad, not in spite of it. Thank you for worrying about me, and for making sure a search party was sent out for me. You gave me all the help I needed, and you always will, I can feel it in my skin.'

He nodded slowly. 'I can too.'

'So help me now? Focus on staying in the present, where I'll always be?'

'I'll give it everything I've got.'

I squeezed his hand. 'Then everything will be okay.'

'Quinta!' My mother's excited voice reached us. 'And Birch, what a lovely surprise this is! And that must be the amazing, the magnificent Noble!'

'Come on,' I pulled my father with me as I ran to my mother. I flung my arms around her and hugged her for all I was worth, then put an arm around my father as his strong arms encircled us both. When we finally pulled away from one another, I turned to properly introduce my mother to Noble, only to find him grazing a little distance away. He passed wind loudly and then snorted.

'Um, yes, that's Noble, believe it or not,' I said. 'And he's clearly off duty.' I smiled as I sensed my horse's contentment both at the grazing and at that which had transpired.

'Well, since he's got food and water, and I'm carrying some delicious pasties I got in Hightown, why don't we have lunch here by the river, and you can both explain how you come to be here?' my mother said, looking at my father with such love and amazement in her eyes, I almost felt as if I were intruding. Then she looked at me with exactly the same expression.

'That would be lovely,' I said. 'Before we start though, I should probably tell you that I gave Tolston and Yelda the afternoon off, and promised them that Dad and I would make up their work.'

My father sighed. 'This is what we're dealing with now, Sabrina,' he said to my mother. 'Our Quinta is Horse-Bonded, and that means whatever she says goes.'

My mother hugged him and winked at me. 'If this is the result, I'd say it's a very good thing.'

Chapter Twenty-Three

The days that followed were bizarre yet wonderful.

While I was proud of my father for occupying his mind with the sensations that accompanied operating his loom so that he could tolerate both his fellow workers' company in the workshop, and the presence of those villagers wanting Noble's advice in the paddock, I wanted to give him a break from at least one of those situations when I could, and that meant Noble and me taking to the streets.

It was more than strange to walk the streets of Lowtown while they were full of people; they took on a completely different feel and appearance from when I had hurried along them early in the morning or late in the evening, and I began to feel as if my previous time in the village had been some weird dream.

We were stopped frequently by people who told me they had known me since I was a baby and were proud that one of their own was now one of the Horse-Bonded. I smiled and thanked them for their kind words even though I had no clue who most of them were. I didn't need to for them to affect me. It was as if with every hand I shook, whether of people coming to see Noble for counsel or of villagers we met in the street, I settled into the person I had become; as if being recognised by those who had known me before, as someone different, finally cemented the new version of myself.

Every street along which I rode Noble or walked with him at my side, rapidly became somewhere of which I was now fond, replacing entirely my previous memories of them as routes to be negotiated as quickly as possible. I noticed for the first time that the gardens were every bit as beautiful as all of the other villages I had visited, and that the front doors were painted in a variety of bright colours, all of which complemented the colours of those either side.

I smiled at the laughter and merriment emanating from the open windows of many of the cottages as my horse and I passed by one sunny afternoon, and winced at the sound of someone – a young child, I supposed – practising with a violin in another. My stomach rumbled at the smells of freshly baked bread wafting from one cottage, gravy from another, and what could only be bacon sizzling on the stove of another.

I waved at a horde of children as they skipped past Noble and me, towards the school building, presumably having been home for lunch. I heard the school bell ringing in the distance and grinned ruefully with the knowledge that those still on their way there would be held behind after the last lesson of the day for the exact number of minutes they were late. While I was capable of experiencing so much of Lowtown differently from when I had lived there, some things were not subject to viewpoint and interpretation.

Noble remained quiet as far as my learning was concerned, only venturing counsel when it was requested by those who sought him out. I could sense his satisfaction that all was proceeding as necessary, and I was content to allow the friendly, vibrant version of Lowtown to replace the one I had created in my mind and to which I had held on for such a long time.

I located Eleri after following my mother's directions to her home. Having already heard from my mother about the challenges Noble had helped me to overcome, Eleri was more than eager for my help, so I began to visit her almost daily. When I found myself too busy with those who came to visit Noble and me, I was overjoyed that she found herself able to come and see me.

No one who had been resident in Lowtown for any length of time was surprised when the spring rains arrived; they were as much a constant as the snows that tended to arrive just in time for The Longest Night Festival. When the heavy showers became longer than the breaks between them, as happened in some years, the Lowtown ritual was evoked of joyfully referencing the river in place of normal greetings and farewells.

'The strength of the river to you,' replaced 'Good morning.'

'May the river bestow gifts upon you,' referred to the flotsam and jetsam that the river hurled up onto its banks, and replaced 'Goodbye.'

When several days passed with rain falling constantly in huge, head-pounding droplets, we were all forced to stay inside as much as possible, even Noble, who was usually indifferent to the weather but was grateful for the stone field shelter to which he was given access in an adjacent paddock when the trees in his own failed to protect him from the onslaught. The greetings and farewells of those of us who did venture out from time to time became more subdued.

'The strength of the river to you,' became 'Mighty are we who still stand.'

'May the river bestow gifts upon you,' became 'May the river spare us from her path.'

After a further day and night of unabating rain and a now rapidly rising river that lapped mere metres from the top of the slope upon which the lowest cottages had been built, we were all reduced to foregoing any attempt to be cheerful, merely uttering, 'Glad we're all still here,' as we hurried past one another across the shining, dirt-stripped cobbles between which ran rivulets that spilled over the stones in places as the water hurried down to the rapidly swelling river.

'It's never been this bad,' my mother said, standing, dripping in her long coat on the mat by the back door. 'Not so as anyone can remember, anyway. I saw old Parsons on my way to get this.' She handed me two bottles of milk. 'He thinks it'll only get worse for us even if the rain stops today. Apparently, the dam up at Hightown has grown weak in several places, so much so that the Carpenters up there were going to be working on it this summer. He reckons they'll have to open the floodgates to let more water through and relieve the pressure on it before it gives way completely. They'll send a messenger to warn us before they do it, and he's expecting one by lunchtime, so he's organising help for everyone in the lower cottages. They're packing up and moving as much of their stuff as they can up to the school hall this morning, then they'll be needing beds with those of us higher up until the water level drops. I'm going there now to help Keith and Hara. I said you'd help Eleri, Quinta, she'll feel much more comfortable with you than anyone else.' She glanced at my father as he sat at the kitchen table next to me, sipping his tea.

I nodded and said, 'Then we could have her and her children to stay here, couldn't we, Dad? Her husband went to visit his sister over at Farcreek a few days ago as she's not long had a baby, so it'll just be the three of them. What do you think?'

My father froze for a moment but then his eyes emptied of their concern and glazed over slightly as he refocused on the information relayed to him by his senses, so that his mind emptied of thought. He didn't look at me as he felt his way forward.

'That will be fine,' he said finally.

My mother beamed. 'Okay, Birch, would you go and make beds up for the three of them in the spare room, while Quinta and I go and help everyone move out?'

My father surprised us both by shaking his head. 'You make up the beds, I'll go and help Keith and Hara.'

I so wanted to hug him, but didn't want to break his concentration; I knew how much effort it would be taking him to keep his focus on both my mother's voice and his love for her so that his anxiety was kept at bay.

I got to my feet and took my breakfast bowl and mug to the sink. 'I'd better get going, Eleri's a fair way away from the school, this isn't going to be a quick job.'

I will assist, Noble informed me.

No, you should stay where you are. I can layer waterproof layers on to keep me dry, and I have a hat that will keep the water out of my eyes. You'll get soaked and you won't be able to see for the water running into your eyes. And besides, the lower part of the village could suddenly flood from the river even before the flood gates are opened. I can get upstairs in any of the cottages at short notice if I have to.

I have already proven that I can do likewise. I had a brief glimmer of Noble climbing the two flights of stairs to my room at The Gathering before he added, *Were my kind unable to endure water falling from the sky then we would be easy prey for predators whenever such conditions arise. I will assist.*

A sense of calm determination wove its way through our bond and I knew he wouldn't be talked out of it, so I donned my ankle length, waterproof coat and a wide-brimmed, waxed hat, and went out of the back door, intending to walk to the neighbouring paddock where he had been taking shelter.

I had a sudden sense that he was on the move, then jumped as he splashed through the rain and skidded to a halt at my feet, spraying water all over my coat. I grinned. *Okay, point taken, you're far less affected by the rain than I am.*

He blinked and then turned towards the path to the street. As soon as we reached it, I could hear the river charging along the valley floor below. My heart skipped a beat but then steadied. I was no longer afraid of the river. I could do this – Eleri needed help.

I focused on the sound of the water crashing and thundering past Lowtown as it roiled and turned in on itself, and found a strange sort of peace within it; it had no malign intent, it just was. I put a hand to Noble's withers so that I wouldn't stray from his side, and we walked along the street a little way before taking a narrower street between two cottages, down to a lower street, then another side street off that to the lowest street upon which stood Eleri's cottage.

There were people garbed similarly to me dashing around everywhere, pushing barrows full of possessions, or rushing back with empty ones to various cottages for their next load. The river was deafening as it hurtled along just below the cottages with an urgency that only increased our own.

I hurried along to Eleri's cottage and knocked on the door, calling her name and hoping she could hear that it was me. Judging by the wary look on her face as she opened it, she hadn't been able to.

She relaxed and smiled. 'Oh, thank goodness it's you. Is that Noble standing up there on the street?'

'It certainly is. When he knew I was coming to help you, he wouldn't be deterred. Have you gathered together the most important stuff?' Eleri nodded. 'Great, we'll take that first. Once we've cleared out everything you need, you and the children can come and stay with us. We'd better hurry.' It was as if my words hung in the air between us without reaching their destination, as Eleri's eyes suddenly widened in concert with my own.

A roaring sound was descending upon us, as if the sky were falling in from above… only it wasn't coming from above exactly. Where was it? I spun around. It was coming from further up the valley.

I felt as if my heart leapt into my throat, blocking my voice so that I was only able to squeak, 'I think the dam might have given way. Get the children, quickly, we have to get out of here now.'

Eleri immediately disappeared up the stairs of the cottage. I turned and tried to shout a warning to Noble and anyone nearby who might not have registered what the noise meant, to run to the streets higher up, but my words were taken by the roaring as soon as they left my mouth so that not even I could hear them.

You need not speak or even think for me to know your intent, Noble told me, standing calmly in the street as if there were nowhere he would rather be.

So, move! Go back the way we came, Noble, I'll be right behind you with Eleri once she's fetched the children. Please, run, you're in danger.

Where there is danger there is possibility. My beautiful boy stood hoof deep in water with rain hammering down so hard on his head and back that the droplets bounced and collided with those lashing down behind them before cascading from him in a circular waterfall. He seemed to occupy far more space than my eyes told me that he in fact did, as if he were bigger than the village, the river, all of it. I had never felt safer.

Eleri appeared beside me, carrying her baby wrapped in a cloak, and holding the hand of her elder child, who was crying.

I held out my hands. 'I'll take Ethan, you'll need both hands for Ewan in case you need to pick him up and run with him. Come on, hurry.'

She handed her baby to me, and I crouched over him, sheltering him from the rain as much as I could whilst hurrying to the gate where Noble still waited. He turned and walked calmly towards the side street down which he and I had walked only minutes before. I splashed next to him, wanting to run but unable to for fear of slipping and falling on Ethan.

The roaring became a booming noise, and my heart hammered in my chest at the realisation that the water from the dam must have hit the cottages at the far end of the village. I looked around but could only see people ahead of us and hoped that meant everyone had left the lowest cottages behind us.

Blood pounded through my body, driven by my heart which was now driven, despite my efforts to stay calm, by fear.

Counsel that Noble had given me mere weeks previously entered my mind unbidden. *Fear in the short term can be helpful. It can be necessary for survival since its presence endows the body with a greater ability to react.* It was very necessary in that moment and the fact that it was actually helping rather than hindering me gave me a boost.

My legs found more strength and speed, and my senses sharpened. I held out a hand behind me to Eleri, who immediately clasped it. I pulled her along in my wake as she pulled Ewan along in hers, but as the booming sound split into the splashing of water and the crashing of the debris being hurled against the cottages further along the street, we still hadn't reached the side street up which everyone else in the vicinity had disappeared.

'Pick him up, Eleri, I'll pull you and keep you moving, but you'll have to carry him or he'll be swept away,' I shouted. We stopped for a second while she heaved Ewan onto her hip, then we all began to move more quickly.

We reached the side street and almost threw ourselves up it behind Noble and the other villagers who were running to safety, glad that it rose steeply, and hoping it would take us out of harm's way. We were almost at the top of it when the river hit the cottages below us. It was as if an unseen force stopped all of us in our tracks and spun us around, panting and gasping, to watch in horror as the water boomed past, swamping the cottages on the far, lower, side of the street, including Eleri's.

Eleri moaned and allowed Ewan to slide down her sodden skirt to the ground. She grabbed hold of his hand as an awful scraping, grinding noise sounded above that of the water. An enormous tree came into sight, juddering across the width of the street as it was alternately trapped and then liberated by the force of the water. Its near end freed when it reached the gap in the cottages provided by the side street, and the water it had held up thundered past. But then the trunk wedged between the first cottage after the side street, and the one opposite, and the water behind it slammed against it... and surged up the side street behind us.

It was as if everything happened in slow motion as the water seemed to reach out to Ewan and gently enclose him before sucking him from his mother's grasp, drawing him back down to the flood.

There was no time to think. I handed Ethan to his mother and told her to stay where she was, hoping upon hope that my words would reach her through the paralysis of her shock and horror. Then I ran after a screaming Ewan with Noble trotting at my side.

Like all children of both Hightown and Lowtown, Ewan had been taught to swim before he could walk, but I suspected it was terror combined with survival instinct that was responsible for him flailing around with his arms so that his head remained above water.

How my noble horse and I remained on our feet whilst racing downhill on slippery cobbles, I'll never know, but we were united in our strength of purpose. Between us, we made it to the torrent flowing below, in one piece.

Ewan had been carried by the water to the tree trunk that was still wedged across the street, and was clinging to a branch sticking up in the air as water gushed around and occasionally over the top of him.

'Well done, Ewan,' I shouted with no confidence whatsoever that he could hear me. 'Hold on tight and I'll climb on this end of the trunk and come and get you. Just hang on until I get to you.'

I quickly pulled off my boots and was just undoing my coat with the intention of shedding it, when there was a dreadful splitting sound. I looked up as the tree trunk split in two and was swept away by the river, taking the little boy with it.

I knew what I would need to do and in that instant of realisation, I froze. But then Noble stepped forward and the last tendril of fear of the river that had lurked within me, fled. I dropped my coat and stepped into the water beside my horse. I just had time to wrap a chunk of his mane around my hand before the river took us both.

Chapter Twenty-Four

*J*ust like the previous time I had been swept away, I had no control whatsoever over my physical circumstances and was subject to the current and any obstacles in its way. But this time was so different. This time, I had allowed myself to be taken by choice. This time, I could feel my Bond-Partner's fear as his survival instinct vied with his soul's purpose. This time, my love for my horse and my concern for Ewan endowed me with a calm sense of strength – and an ability to hear the voice of my soul with utmost clarity.

I knew that my ability to go with the flow of the river would both reflect and affect my ability to go with the flow of life, and as such made no attempt to struggle or try to resist either; I had to focus on Ewan and Noble and everything else would take care of itself.

I gasped and spluttered alongside my horse as I pulled myself closer to him and then kicked hard with my legs whilst pushing down against his withers, so that I momentarily rose up out of the water.

I spotted Ewan just ahead of us and to the right, still clinging to his section of tree trunk. Noble and I sensed, thought and responded as one. As soon as I landed back in the water, he used his greater weight to steer us to the right and then kicked hard beside me, swimming with and slightly across the current, towards the bank where I thought I could make out some of the villagers from Lowtown running along behind us.

I sent all of my love for my horse along our bond, and felt his strength and determination surge to match mine, eclipsing the instinct of his species to save himself at all costs. There was nothing we couldn't do.

We both wheezed and snorted as we swam with the current towards Ewan, and slowly, we gained on him.

'HANG ON,' I managed to shout to him, and he turned towards us, his face ghostly pale, his blue eyes wide and terrified. His hold on the branch slipped and my heart plummeted as he plopped into the water. The sound of screaming reached us from the riverbank as he disappeared from sight, eclipsing the noise of the river with the heartbreak it carried.

Noble and I continued to swim, and when Ewan popped back up into sight, he was just in front of us. I reached out and grabbed him, and was relieved when he coughed and then yelped in fright.

'Ewan,' I spluttered. 'I'm going to… get you onto… Noble's back, and he'll… swim you to the bank, to your mum, okay?' I gasped for more breath. 'Kick with your… legs against the… water, that's it and I'll… heave you up.' I gasped and spluttered again. 'That's it, now hang on to… Noble's mane with… both hands, and… squeeze your legs around him.'

All of a sudden, the current felt different and the sounds around us changed. I looked downriver and saw that the water had flooded into some trees, against which it was smashing with a vengeance – and we were heading straight for one of them. I pushed against Noble with everything I had, in the hope that I would be carried around one side of the tree and he and Ewan around the other. Water rebounded off the tree and slammed into my face.

By the time I could see again, I had indeed been carried around the tree, but into faster flowing water while Noble appeared to be swimming in what looked like far slower flowing water – he was almost at the bank! He was tired, but he would make it. I relaxed and looked back to see where the current was taking me.

I was hit by another wall of water and then it was as though someone had suddenly turned the lights out. Darkness, choking, and excruciating pain were all of me.

It occurred to me that maybe I should feel fear, yet I couldn't find any to feel. Everything was okay. I would either die or survive, and either was fine. Yet it wasn't my time to die, the voice of my soul told me through my skin, my heart, my stomach, my mind. I remembered that Noble had told me I had work to do in the future, and that all of my experiences and everything he had taught me would enable me to do what I would need to do. That meant I would live.

I kicked my legs and reached upward with my arms, despite the pain in my head warning me that I was far from well. Light forced its way through my closed eyelids, and my eye sockets felt as if they were on fire, obliterating the pain of coughing water out of my lungs and their subsequent desperation for air. I opened my eyes and blinked water out of them even as the river carried me at impossible speed towards goodness knew where.

The tree with which I had collided was no longer in sight, and it didn't appear or sound as if there were any more in my immediate vicinity. All I could hear was the thundering and splashing of the untamed water thrashing all around me... and a rhythmic pounding coming from over to my right. I blinked more water out of my eyes and winced as my eyeballs rotated in their sockets towards the bank where my amazing, stunning, noble Bond-Partner galloped apace with the river. He whinnied shrilly, and I felt his confidence in me – which was my confidence in me.

I turned my body and kicked out to the left so that I moved with and across the current to the right. Just as when Noble had been at my side, I wouldn't fight the flow of the river, I would just steer myself within it towards the horse who galloped relentlessly alongside me, reminding me of our bond, our purpose and our strength.

When I reached shallower water and the current slowed, Noble's hoofbeats slowed in concert. I kicked a little harder towards the bank. When the current slowed further, I stretched my feet down and managed to touch solid ground. I continued to paddle with my hands as I walked to the edge of the water, noting with concern the blood that dripped from both of Noble's nostrils along with the rain that continued to pound down on him.

I staggered towards him and rested my forehead against his withers as he heaved and blew. I almost thanked him for leaving me alone in my mind so that I could be sure of the voice of my soul, whilst remaining as close to my side as he could get so that I was reminded of my confidence and strength when I needed it the most. Then I realised that I had steered myself, my life, towards him without pausing to think, because he was my life and I was his. Gratitude was irrelevant.

The blood dripping from his nose was not, however. Neither was the fact that he was rapidly becoming chilled by the rain that had already washed away his sweat and now took his body heat with it as it flowed to the water lapping at my ankles. My horse needed a Tissue-Singer to heal the bleed in his airways from over-exerting himself, and he needed to keep warm.

Come on, we need to get back to Lowtown, I told him. *We can't stop. Not yet.*

I put a hand on his neck and began to walk, drawing him with me back towards the village while gradually moving up and further away from the floodwater in case it rose even further.

I refused to allow my mind to wonder how far the river had taken us both before Ewan got out, and then me once the deeper, faster-flowing water took me. It didn't matter. We just had to keep moving one foot after another until we could stop.

Just as the rain began to ease slightly, the sound of voices reached us. Noble whickered, spraying blood all over my legs.

'OVER HERE!' I yelled over the river's gurgling and thrashing. 'HELP, OVER HERE!'

I blinked water out of my eyes, wondering if it were my imagination that it was my father's voice who answered, 'QUINTA! I KNEW YOU WERE ALIVE, I JUST KNEW IT, THIS WAY, EVERYONE.'

Both my footsteps and Noble's slowed as a whole crowd of people swarmed out of the sheeting rain before us.

'Is Nethin here?' I said weakly, 'Noble's bleeding and he needs a Tissue-Singer.'

'I can see that, love,' my father said, wrapping a cloak around me, 'but he's not bleeding nearly as much as you are. Nethin, come over here, would you?'

I shook my head. 'I can wait. Noble's bleeding because he galloped far beyond where he should have stopped so I wouldn't give up, so I would keep steering for the bank. Please, have him seen to first. Please?'

Nethin's voice sounded by my ear as the lights began to dim again. 'My Apprentice is already seeing to him. It's a nasty pulmonary haemorrhage, but will be quickly healed, unlike your skull, which is fractured again. Gable's on his way, so I'll just sing your face back together while we're waiting for him, shall I?'

As she began to hum, I whispered to my father, 'Ewan. Is he okay?'

My father caught me as my legs gave way, and lowered me to the ground. 'He's shocked but otherwise fine, thanks to you and Noble.'

'Where's Mum?'

'She'll be coming along behind with Gable. I'd only just reached Lower Street when I heard the river coming. I ran the way I knew you'd have gone to Eleri's, and heard what happened. I came after you and met Eleri coming back with Ewan. Everyone said there was no way you'd survive the force of the flood, but I knew they were wrong. I knew you were alive, I felt it. I sent your mum to fetch Gable, and ran to Nethin's and persuaded her and everyone else here to come after you.'

'You did?'

He chuckled. 'Hard to believe, isn't it.'

'I love you, Dad,' I whispered.

'I love you too, Q. Close your eyes now, it'll take your energy as well as that of the Healers' to sort your injuries out. Was it a rock again?'

'A tree,' I whispered and then winced as my eyes followed his suggestion and closed. I flicked them back open and winced again. 'Noble. I have to get him back to his shelter. He'll get a chill if he keeps still for long, he got so hot racing along beside me. His healing will have exhausted him too, I have to get him back to shelter so he can get warm and dry, and he can rest. Help me up, Dad, we can't wait here for Gable, we need to get moving.'

There was a pause. Then my father said, 'You're not moving anywhere.' He turned away and said to the people crowded around Noble and me, 'We need to get her and Noble back to Lowtown but she can't walk. We'll need to carry her in my cloak. Would three of you please help me?'

I couldn't decide whether I was more shocked by his continuing determination to take charge of the situation, or by the speed with which those nearest to me leapt to pick up a corner of the cloak in which I was nestled. Regardless, I was soon in transit back to Lowtown.

Noble, are you okay?

You are as aware of my physical condition as am I.

I know your bleed has stopped, but the healing has taken energy you didn't have to begin with. Can you follow okay?

It is not possible for energy to be taken from me. It has merely been directed towards something other than that for which I had intended it.

I could sense his weariness as well as surmise it from the faintness of his thought.

The effect is the same. A thought occurred to me. *If energy can be redirected, then I can direct that which I'm saving by being carried, towards you.*

That would be inadvisable. You are fatigued and you require much healing.

I would have laughed if I hadn't felt nauseous at how much it would hurt. *Since when was our partnership about doing what's advisable? We're about feeling our way and welcoming the possibilities that accompany difficult situations, and that doesn't change just because it's you who needs help rather than me. I love you, Noble.* It wasn't just a statement, but a declaration of intent. *I love you.* It was as much of myself as I could give him.

You do, Noble agreed. *You are She Who Is Noble.*

I smiled as I felt his vitality increase far more than I could have hoped, and sensed him stepping along behind me with slightly more strength and conviction.

'Quinta?' my father's voice was urgent. 'Q, stay with me.' His voice rose. 'Nethin, her eyelids are fluttering.'

'S'okay, Dad,' I whispered.

His ear appeared in front of my face. 'What did you say? Q? What did you say?'

'S'okay. I'll be okay. I can feel it in my skin.'

Chapter Twenty-Five

*I*t was a close run thing, apparently, but I pulled through as I knew I would; it wasn't my time to go. Even if I hadn't felt comfortable in my skin despite being badly injured, even if I hadn't heard the voice of my soul assuring me I would live, even if I had resorted to wondering, to thinking, I would have arrived at the same conclusion, because Noble always told me the truth. Always. He had told me I would be needed in the years to come, so I would be there.

He too recovered well. By the time I awoke, having slept for the best part of two days and nights following our return to Lowtown, the rain had finally stopped, Noble had ploughed his way through several bales of hay in between resting in the deep straw bed my parents' neighbours provided for him in their field shelter, and he was standing in the mud below my bedroom window, resting a hind leg and snoozing while he waited for me to come back to myself.

Feeling weak, I sat on the edge of my bed and put a hand up to my face. I pressed and prodded around my eyes, nose, mouth, jaw, and then all around my head. My eyes felt a little swollen, as did my nose, but there was barely any tenderness anywhere; Nethin and Gable had done an amazing job of singing me back together for the second time.

I felt Noble register that I was awake, and smiled. I got to my feet and walked unsteadily to the window. When I opened it, I was bombarded with the sounds of birdsong, leaves rustling in the fresh, spring breeze, and voices both near and distant. I looked down and instantly, my heart filled with love.

Noble whickered but didn't look up.

You should still be resting, I told him.

I am resting.

I guess. At least it's stopped raining, but that mud is irritating your heels, I can feel it.

Noble stretched his neck and back, then turned and made for the grass. It glistened as the sunlight highlighted the water still clinging to each and every blade, stalk and flower. As Noble began to tear at it, I sensed its sweetness; now that the sun had finally managed to pierce the clouds, the grass was flourishing and would nourish my weary Bond-Partner.

His dark coat shone and his black forelock, mane and tail hung as masses of separate hairs without a tangle in sight. Someone had groomed him.

The back door slammed and heavy footsteps squelched towards where Noble grazed. My father appeared clutching several carrots in one hand and my grooming kit in the other. He towered above my horse as he fed him the carrots one by one, then took out a brush and set about grooming Noble's already gleaming coat. I sat on the windowsill, too weak to stand but enjoying the sight of my father with my horse too much to go back to bed.

The bedroom door creaked open and my mother rushed to my side. 'Quinta, thank goodness you're back with us, what are you doing out of bed? You should have called out to me and I'd have brought you some soup.' She grabbed a blanket from my bed and wrapped it around my shoulders.

I snuggled against her. 'I'm fine, Mum. Seeing those two together is all I need at the moment.'

She stood with her arm around me, watching my father and Noble. 'He's done that several times since the rain stopped yesterday. He loves being with Noble and he wanted to look after him like you do.'

'He's been amazing, hasn't he?' I said.

She hugged me. 'He really has. I love your father, Quinta, you know that, but it's been... difficult at times. Now, a whole new side of him has come out, and that's all thanks to you.'

I nodded down to my horse. 'It's thanks to him.'

More voices sounded downstairs. Ewan ran over to my father, followed by Eleri carrying Ethan in her arms. Immediately, Noble stopped grazing and reached out to Ewan, snuffling all around his face and neck and making him giggle.

'How are they all doing?' I asked.

'Ethan is fine, as is Ewan physically, but he only smiles and talks when he's with Noble. The rest of the time, he's either silent or he cries, and he won't go any further from the house than the paddock. Eleri's doing better than I expected, I think all her attention is taken up trying to make Ewan feel safe.'

'And the rest of the village?'

'Amazingly, no one was killed. There were a few minor injuries from people slipping while running from the flood, and the lowest row of cottages is still underwater, but apart from that and shock at what so very nearly happened to you, Ewan and Noble, everyone is coping well. The Hightowners are mortified at the dam giving way, and have promised that their Rock-Singers will be here as soon as the water recedes, to help our own Rock-

Singers rebuild the lower cottages along a new street further up in the hills. I think their inhabitants all need a bit of distance from the river after what happened.' Her voice softened as she said, 'How are you feeling, love? After everything?'

I grinned. 'Hungry, now you mention it.'

She stroked my forehead as she had when I was a child. 'You know that isn't what I meant. I know how much you suffered after the river took you last time, and then it happened all over again, only this time it was worse because Noble was taken too…'

I reached for the hand resting on my shoulders and squeezed it. 'I'm fine, Mum, in fact I'm better than fine. Noble has helped me to see the world so differently, to experience it so differently, that I can pretty much take anything that comes at me.'

'But you must have been terrified.' I felt her shudder.

'You'd think, wouldn't you, but I wasn't.' I squeezed her hand again. 'I'm not the same person who left here.'

She touched her head to mine. 'No, you're not. But you'll always be my daughter and there are some things I can still do for you, so I'm going to get you something to eat. I've got soup on the go, and while you're having that, I'll make you anything you like.'

My stomach gurgled at the thought of food. 'Scrambled eggs on fried bread, with fried mushrooms, onions and tomatoes?' I said hopefully.

She chuckled. 'I made sure I had a good stock of them all as soon as you got back here. Coming up. Keep that blanket wrapped around you if you're going to stay there, okay?'

I rolled my eyes and grinned. 'Yes, Mum.'

It was the following day before I had enough energy to get dressed and go out to Noble, who was still being superbly cared for by my father and his neighbours. My horse had a huge pile of hay in the field shelter to which he still had access even though the sun continued to shine, as well as grass and plenty of available water, and he was immaculately groomed. As I stroked him, I thought I caught a whiff of lavender, about which I asked my father when I returned to the cottage for breakfast.

He and Eleri both flushed slightly and my father said, 'Um, well, I went to see Nethin to ask whether there was anything Noble needed other than food and water while he was recovering, and she said that although she'd healed the few of his muscles that were a little strained, massaging lavender into his legs and back would ease any residual soreness. I tried a little on a small area of his back and he seemed to like it, so Eleri and I have been doing it twice a day.'

'I hope that's alright?' Eleri said, flushing redder.

I smiled. 'I think it's lovely. Thank you, both of you, for everything you've done for him.'

'It's nothing compared to what you and he did for me,' Eleri said, reaching out to Ewan sitting next to her and stroking his hair.

'And I enjoy doing it,' my father said. 'I've enjoyed all the time I've spent with Noble. I like to think I'm looking after him, but I'm pretty sure I get more from it than he does.'

I took a seat next to him and helped myself to a bread roll. My mother cleared her throat and pushed the bread basket closer to me. I chuckled and took a second roll, then spread them both with butter and jam. A mug of steaming tea was placed in front of me, then as I ate what I thought was my breakfast, the smell of what would apparently be my second breakfast made me look away from the conversation I was having with Eleri and my father, to where my mother was indeed frying bread, mushrooms, onions and tomatoes in one pan while scrambling eggs in another.

'So, once I've digested enough of all the food I'm about to be practically force fed,' I said, pausing to wink at my mother, 'I was thinking that I'd saddle Noble and go for a wander around the village. He could do with stretching his legs.' Ewan froze and Eleri immediately put an arm around her son and pulled him closer. 'Would you like to help me get Noble ready, Ewan?' I asked.

His big blue eyes moved to the window that overlooked the paddock where Noble was grazing and then back to me, but he remained frozen.

'How about if your mum comes and helps?' I added. 'We could give him a little groom and then I can show you how to put the saddle on and do up the girth.' His eyes flicked back to the window and he nodded.

Eleri smiled at him. 'Let's get you upstairs and dressed then, shall we, young man?' She took his hand and waited for him to get down from his chair.

I bolted down everything my mother put in front of me, and was just wiping my mouth when Eleri and Ewan reappeared.

'Ethan's still asleep,' Eleri said to my mother. 'Would you mind giving me a shout if he wakes?'

'I'll do no such thing,' my mother said with a smile. 'If he wakes, I'll take care of him until you get back. You take your time.'

I held out one of Noble's grooming brushes to Ewan. 'There you go, it has nice soft bristles, Noble will love being groomed with it.' Ewan took it from me and practically dragged his mother out of the back door. She looked over her shoulder at me, grinning with delight.

I groomed Noble's head, neck and back while Ewan did his legs and belly. My horse moved not a single muscle as the young boy moved around and underneath him.

I fetched my saddle and showed Ewan where on Noble's back

to put it, then asked him to reach underneath for the girth and hold it for me while I did it up. My horse knew of my intention for it was also his.

'There, he's all ready,' I said. Noble turned his head and nuzzled Ewan's cheek. 'What's that, Noble? You want Ewan to sit on your back? Wow, he's never asked for anyone other than me to ride him before, that's amazing. What do you think, Ewan, do you want to?' I glanced quickly at Eleri, who nodded.

Ewan giggled as Noble continued to wiggle his upper lip gently against the boy's cheek.

'The saddle looks very comfy, doesn't it?' Eleri said gently. 'I'd love to sit on it, but Noble hasn't invited me to, he's invited you. Would you like to sit on his back?'

Ewan nodded. Eleri lifted him up and then gently lowered him into the saddle.

Just as happened whenever I rode him, I felt as if Noble extended beyond his body, his energy reaching up and around the boy like it had when he carried Ewan to the river bank to safety.

Ewan smiled. When Noble began to walk around the paddock, the little boy's smile stretched until it lit up his whole face.

'Will you trust Noble and me?' I breathed to Eleri.

'How can you even ask that?' she replied.

'Come on then, you and I'll follow behind. Noble won't allow anything to happen to your little boy, but Ewan might need you.'

Noble made his way carefully towards the open paddock gate and then up the path between the cottages. The mud was deep, but my horse was careful to make no movement that could unseat his passenger. He carried Ewan to the street and then along it to the end, where he turned down to the street below. The little boy never looked back at his mother, not even when we reached the second to lowest street, from which he could see the water from the end of each side street. He smiled and waved to everyone who called out and waved to him, which was every single person we saw.

When Noble turned for home, I whispered to Eleri, 'Okay, so I was wrong, he doesn't need us.'

Eleri shook her head in agreement, her smile nearly as wide as her son's. 'He just needs Noble.'

So did most of Lowtown, as it turned out. The villagers were shocked by what had happened, and many came to see Noble for counsel once word got about that he and I were available again, while many more just came to bring him carrots and to be near him after hearing how much his calm presence affected their friends.

My horse and I went for a walk around the village every afternoon, sometimes with me in the saddle but more often with Ewan riding. Eleri always came with us, sometimes carrying Ethan and always smiling as she watched her elder son come back to himself. She trusted Noble implicitly with Ewan and never interfered, not even when her son began to answer questions from the villagers about how much hay Noble ate, how much time he spent eating grass, and who had groomed him to get such a shine on his coat. When he continued to talk upon our arrival back home, however, she couldn't contain herself. She hugged her son, then tickled him until he cried with laughter.

My feeling was that Noble and I would be needed until the river had returned to normal and the ruined homes were well on their way to being rebuilt, so he and I remained at my parents' home throughout the spring.

We travelled to Hightown regularly and were besieged by its villagers wanting Noble's counsel each and every time.

During our early visits, we found Hightown's Rock-Singers busy using their voices and intentions to lift rocks into the reservoir, precisely placing them to form a wall in front of the dam. Our subsequent visits revealed the village's Carpenters working behind the safety of the wall to remove the old dam, and our later visits found them working with the Rock-Singers to build a new one made mostly of stone with some wooden elements.

There was often a Herald watching the work in progress, sometimes two. As carriers of news, letters and messages between villages, they were welcomed and given detailed drawings of the plans to take with them when they left, in the hope that other villages that had a similar requirement for water management could benefit from the lessons learnt by Hightown and Lowtown.

The Heralds always made sure to approach Noble and me before we left for Lowtown, without exception wanting confirmation that the – often grossly exaggerated – tales they had heard of Ewan's rescue were true. I was embarrassed by many of the descriptions of the event that they repeated to me, and made sure to give them the factual, unembellished story.

It was heartening to witness the two villages recover from their trauma, especially when they had a huge party halfway between the villages – very near to where I had first met Noble – to celebrate the river finally having shrunk back between its banks, to which every single household contributed and every single person attended, even my father, Eleri and Ewan, who was the guest of honour.

He was a different child as a consequence of his time with Noble, and lapped up all of the attention showered upon him. When the fiddlers began to play, he and his mother were invited to take to the floor first, and were cheered on as they whirled around one another, shouting and laughing.

You did this, I thought to Noble. *Without you, Ewan would have died and there would be no celebration, no laughter, no joy.*

My horse looked up from where he grazed, his role in carrying the 'Champion of the River', as Ewan had been pronounced on his invitation to the party, concluded. *We will leave soon.*

It wasn't a question or even an instruction, but an acknowledgement that I would finally be able to get some relief from my skin feeling tight, as it had for some weeks. *We will,* I agreed as I watched my mother lead my father onto the dance floor. *They don't need us anymore. We need to go back to The Gathering, don't we?*

You need not ask a question to which the voice of your soul has already given you the answer, was all my horse told me before dropping his head back down to graze at the edge of what was rapidly becoming a hullabaloo.

I grinned. It was slightly difficult to take his gentle reprimand seriously while he wore a large, white, pink and yellow garland around his neck and four small ones around each pastern, courtesy of Eleri and my mother.

'You'll be off soon, won't you?'

I turned around and looked up at my father. I grinned and nodded towards the dancing. 'How did you escape?'

'Tolston saved me. He wanted to dance with your mother, and old Parsons stepped in to take Yelda's hand before she could make me stay, so I ran for it.'

I laughed. 'We'll be on our way in a few days' time. You'll be okay?'

He put an arm around my shoulders. 'I will. I won't ask about you.' He looked over to where Noble was walking further away from the rapidly expanding dance area. 'As long as you're with him, you'll be fine.'

I nodded my agreement.

Immediately, Noble spun around and looked right into me as he had so often. *Your wellbeing is no longer dependant on your proximity to me as is appropriate and necessary.* There was no mistaking the importance of his message, and my heart fluttered.

What? Why? Where are you going that I can't go?

Such a place does not exist in truth.

So then, what are you referring to? You're scaring me.

I merely point out that you are She Who Is Noble regardless of where you are or who you are with.

I nodded and relaxed.

Chapter Twenty-Six

*N*oble and I left Lowtown a few days later, as planned. We hadn't planned on the sight that greeted us as we reached the street outside my parents' cottage, however.

Since I had left to find Noble without the traditional Quest Ceremony – where villagers all turned out to send the member of their community chosen by a horse, on their way with all good wishes for their quest to find their future Bond-Partner – everyone resident in Lowtown, and it seemed a good many resident in Hightown, had decided that they would hold one on my departure this time, even though the object of my supposed quest was present.

I hugged my parents, Eleri, her newly returned husband and their children goodbye, then I waited while they all stroked and patted Noble, all the while reassuring Ewan – and as a consequence reinforcing to my tearful parents – that we would return soon. Then, Noble and I walked between two opposing lines of cheering villagers, all of whom wished us well and hung little ornaments of metal, fabric or grass from my clothes and my horse's mane and tail. Some of the ornaments were horseshoes as was normal, but most were fish, in line with the 'Big Fish' title Noble had been awarded on carrying the Champion of the River to the festivities several days before.

The corridor of people extended far beyond the end of the village, continuing out onto the pasture across which so many of the villagers had raced, first when Ewan was carried away and then when my father begged them to help him find me. A garland was gently lowered around Noble's neck by the final villager, this one of red and purple.

'Goodbye, Big Fish, and thank you,' Eleri's husband said as he stepped away from my horse. 'And you, Quinta. Thank you.' He was panting from having jogged to the end of the corridor in order to be in position when Noble and I arrived there.

I understood, and hugged him. 'Take care of them, Nave, I'll see you all before too long.'

I turned and waved to everyone now crowding behind Noble and me, then put my foot in my stirrup and mounted so that I could wave to my parents at the back of the crowd. I looked over their heads to the village of Lowtown as Noble began to walk away. It felt more like home than it ever had when I lived there, and I was sad to be leaving everyone there, but we had somewhere else to be.

Noble agreed and moved up to a trot and then a fast canter before I had fully turned around and settled into my seat. I laughed out loud. *You would have me fall off in front of the whole of Lowtown and half of Hightown?*

She Who Is Noble you cannot fall. His thought was accompanied by his usual confidence but also a hint of something else that I couldn't quite identify – almost like a warning even though I knew he didn't hold with the idea of me ever needing one. Reassurance in advance of something happening? No, he didn't hold with my needing that either.

I merely afford you the means to succeed where many others will fail when the time comes. Do not linger upon our conversations. Merely accept them and store them so that when you need them their purpose becomes clear to you.

Can't you just tell me that now?

I have. Repeatedly. She Who Is Noble follow my counsel.

I nodded and concentrated on doing just that.

We could have visited four villages on our way to The Gathering, but when I thought of stopping off at them, I felt uncomfortable in my skin and when I thought of continuing on our way I felt comfortable, even though it meant washing in cold lakes, ponds and streams, sleeping on increasingly hard, sun-baked ground, and eating travelling rations once I had exhausted my fresh food parcels.

As summer wrestled us firmly away from spring, the discomfort of travelling in the steadily increasing heat was a small price to pay for my peace of mind, both as a result of following my feelings and of being alone with Noble after months of constant company. I had loved being with my parents and everyone else, but the time alone with my horse allowed me the opportunity to catch up with myself, to really know myself – to soar, now that I had progressed from learning to soar. Whenever Noble's recent cryptic announcements made their way into my mind, I did as he had told me and allowed them to settle further in my mind each time so that when I wanted to remember them, I would find them part of me.

When the buildings of The Gathering loomed into sight, I

couldn't decide whether I was ecstatic to be within shouting distance of my friends, or disappointed that my time alone with my horse was over. But when we turned away from the river and rode between the paddocks, and first Hannah waved to me from where she was working in one of the crop fields, then Newson came rushing to the fence of Integrity's paddock accompanied both by his graceful, tall grey mare and a black stallion with a torrent of black hair for a mane, I knew I was ecstatic to be back.

I jumped down from Noble and rubbed first Integrity's forehead and then that of the black horse. 'Hi, Resolute, so, Ellie's back too, is she?' I said to him. 'Do you and Integrity have room for one more?' Noble and Resolute began frantically grooming one another over the fence. 'I'll take that as a yes. Thanks, Newson.'

My friend stood holding the gate open. He stepped aside as Noble trotted into the paddock and resumed his grooming with Resolute.

'Did you really need to ask? These three would travel the world together if circumstances allowed it,' Newson said with a chuckle. 'Welcome back, Quinta. Tales of your heroism reached here weeks ago, but I didn't expect you to arrive so close behind them, you're normally gone longer than a few months. Is everything okay?' He shut the gate.

'Yes thanks, I just had a feeling I needed to get back here.' I unsaddled Noble, and Newson handed me a bucket of water and a sponge.

'I'd be the last person to argue with those feelings you have. Should we be worried?'

I grinned. 'There's never a need for that.'

He shook his head as he dunked another sponge in a bucket by his feet. 'So, the Heralds weren't exaggerating. You're actually invincible.' He winked at me over Noble's back as he squeezed water where my saddle had sat, and rubbed my horse's sweat away.

I groaned. 'I told them all what really happened.'

He laughed. 'Don't worry, they told us your version, but I'm afraid they also repeated the versions the villagers are telling, and they're far more entertaining. How are you coping with your new status as a legend?'

I rolled my eyes at him.

'That well, eh?' He stopped laughing and said, 'When Integrity knew you were near, she told me that She Who Is Noble was approaching. Good on you, Quinta. For saving the boy, for all you've achieved and for who you are now.'

I smiled up at him. 'I'm still me and you're still you. As long as Mason is still himself, the world can carry on turning.'

He chuckled. 'Come on, it's nearly lunchtime. I'd get there early if I were you; when the hordes descend, wanting to hear what happened from the horse's mouth, as it were, you won't get a chance to eat.'

'If only Noble could just tell them all via their horses, it would save my digestion,' I replied, scraping the excess water from my horse whilst wondering if I should bother as Resolute was rapidly making his way to the same spot.

Newson chuckled. 'If only they'd take a whole load of our complications on for us, our lives would be simpler. We may be Horse-Bonded but we're still human, aren't we.'

'Is everything okay with you?' I asked him as we patted our horses. Noble didn't pay me any attention and, deprived of equine company as he had been for months, I couldn't blame him.

'Yeah, I think so,' he replied as we both climbed between the fence rails. 'I just get frustrated with myself that I don't change as much as Integrity tells me I can. As much as I want to,' he corrected himself.

'Change can be slow or fast, it's still change,' I said.

'Adam said that.'

'Adam's here? Now? He and Peace don't usually get back here until the winter. Are they alright?' I asked, looking around to see if I could see them as we began to walk towards the buildings.

'Peace looks even more ancient than he has the past few years, but he's okay. Now you mention it though, Adam did seem a bit melancholy over breakfast.' He sighed. 'Do you see what I mean? I was so busy trying to sort out in my mind what to do today, I didn't ask him what was wrong. I meant to, but then it slipped my mind.'

'It's unusual for Adam to be anything other than cheerful,' I said. 'Hopefully I'll find him at lunch.'

But Adam didn't appear in the dining room at lunchtime. I sat at the table nearest the door and looked up every time anyone came in or went out, but there was no sign of him.

I apologised repeatedly for being distracted when those crowding around me to welcome me back and ask about my and Noble's 'swim in the river' as many of them referred to it, had to repeat their questions. Eventually, I made my apologies and went back out to the paddocks to see if I could find Peace, all the time feeling as if my skin didn't fit. There was no sign of him. Noble, however, gradually increased his presence in my mind until I noticed it above my concern.

You know where they are.

I will take you to them, he told me by way of agreement.

I'll fetch your saddle.

I ran to the tack room where I had deposited Noble's saddle only an hour or so previously, but couldn't find it. I ran along the saddle racks, checking the hundreds of saddles upon them even though I knew exactly where I had left Noble's, then came to a stop and stood with my hands on my hips, rechecking all of the saddles near the empty rack where I had put the one I sought, and from which still hung the bag containing my grooming kit.

Like Noble's, all of the saddles had images, symbols or in some cases, initials, stitched into the back of their cantles. I frowned as I spotted a large, brown saddle with an image of a dove – the sign for Peace. So, they hadn't left again, then. Adam may have stopped riding Peace some years before, but they rarely left without Peace's saddle and its attached saddle bags. They couldn't be that far away. Maybe I should just walk with Noble to find them, and hope my saddle reappeared as suddenly as it had disappeared, while I was gone.

'Well, that's fair ruined my surprise,' Mason said from the doorway.

I turned to see him walking towards me, carrying my saddle. 'I wondered where you were when I didn't see you at lunch. Hi, Mason.' I gave him a hug and then took my saddle when he offered it to me.

'Hi, yourself, and congratulations, She Who Is Noble. When I heard you were back and had headed for the dinin' hall, I nipped out here and took your saddle back to my workshop for a minor adjustment. I hope you don't mind.'

I inspected my saddle. 'It looks the same as before. What did you do?'

He grinned. 'Put it on the rack.'

I did as he instructed, and gasped. Where before the image on the cantle was of me standing with Noble, there was now also a small boy sitting on Noble's back. 'It's Ewan. Mason, I can see it's him as surely as I recognised myself and Noble when you stitched our likenesses in such amazing detail. How could you possibly have known what he looks like?'

'Heralds have their uses,' Mason said, 'and there've been a good many arrivin' here over the past few weeks, desperate to tell us all of your and Noble's escapade. They all gave the same general description of the Champion of the River, as I gather he's called, and each gave a few extra details besides, when I asked them. I planned this little adjustment as soon as I heard what happened. Somethin' like you and Noble did should be commemorated so it's never forgotten. I'm proud of you, Quinta. I have no right to be, but I am.'

I hugged his ample frame and said, 'You have every right to be, you've been an amazing friend to me, Mason.' I stepped back from him. 'As has Adam. Do you know where he and Peace have gone?'

Mason shrugged. 'I can't say as I do. You're worried, I can see it. Come on, we'll look for him together.'

I picked up my saddle and grooming kit. 'Don't worry, it's probably nothing. Noble knows where they are and he said he'd take me, but then I couldn't find my saddle. Not that it's an issue; I can't tell you how much your thoughtfulness, not to mention your skill, mean to me. I'll go to them, though, if you don't mind? Noble can carry me quicker than if we walk.'

Mason held up his hands. 'Sure, you go. Let me know they're okay when you get back though? Adam won't want a fuss.'

'Will do. See you later, and thanks again.' I hurried out of the tack room and on to Noble's paddock.

When I reached my destination, Noble was grooming with Integrity. He left her side immediately, leaving her looking after him, her long, white lashes batting against her cheek as she blinked and then dropped her head to graze as if Noble's departure were of no consequence.

My horse whickered to me as he trotted over, and despite my concern for Adam and Peace, I couldn't help but grin at him. 'Is there anywhere you haven't rolled? If my dad could see you now, he'd be horrified,' I told him, reaching out to stroke his dirty, dusty neck.

I got to work with my brushes, and when the dirt that had covered him had mostly been transferred to me, I saddled him and opened the paddock gate. He waited for me on the pathway, and as soon as I was on his back, he walked a few steps and then took off at a fast canter.

I didn't question him. He had said he would take me to find Adam and Peace, and I was relieved not only to be doing that, but at the fact that finally, after weeks of feeling restless and uncomfortable, I had settled back into my skin. More than that, I now felt a sense of anticipation, as if today were the beginning of something new.

The sun was hot as we reached the river bank and turned right, cantering with the flow of the water. I smiled. Everything felt right.

Noble surprised me by suddenly turning right, into the hills. He cantered between two of them and then partway up another, before making his way around its side to the base of yet another. He whinnied, and a deep whinny sounded in response. I frowned. That wasn't Peace; he'd always had a relatively high-pitched whinny for such a big horse. I looked up the hill we were now ascending and just about made out a large, black horse standing, looking down at us.

Noble tore up the hillside, only slowing to a trot and then a walk when we were nearing its brow. I recognised the large black horse as he whickered his welcome. 'Oak! Hello, gorgeous boy, what are you doing here?'

The answer to my question materialised in front of Noble and me as we reached the brow and found Adam and Oak's Bond-Partner, Rowena, sitting by a large mound of soil. Adam smiled up at me, his hand resting on the mound.

'Where's Peace?' I said, looking around.

Rowena scowled as she was wont to do, and glanced at the mound of soil.

'Oh, Adam.' I jumped down from Noble and ran to my friend, crouching down by his side and putting an arm around his shoulders. 'I'm so sorry.' I withdrew slightly and looked at him more closely. 'But I don't need to be. You're okay. And you're different. Something's changed.'

He Who Is Peace is an example to you all, Noble informed me. I didn't need to look up to know that his eyes were boring into me. *Cloud In The Storm's presence is no coincidence.*

'He Who Is Peace,' I said to Adam, who nodded, still smiling.

'Cloud In The Storm,' I said to Rowena, whose eyes widened. She opened her mouth to say something and then hesitated; Oak was communicating with her.

She relaxed and nodded to me. 'She Who Is Noble. You're another forerunner, aren't you? Like me and Adam. That's why Noble's brought you here.'

I stood up slowly. 'I suppose I am. I know all the lessons I've learnt have been necessary for me to be able to help those who can put humankind on the right track when it reaches a crossroads.' I looked above Adam's and Rowena's heads to where Noble and Oak now grazed side by side, and nodded. 'I should feel as if I'm intruding here, but I don't. I feel as if here is exactly where I need to be, as if the three of us being here together is necessary.'

Adam nodded and patted the ground next him. 'Sit down here awhile.'

I unsaddled Noble and then took my place next to Adam. He, Rowena and I sat in silence, looking across Peace's grave to where the river sparkled below.

Finally, Rowena said, 'I can be strong because of my bond with Oak. Adam has peace coming out of every pore in his body

because of the dear old boy we've just buried. You've become...
noble? What does that mean?'

I smiled. 'It just means that whenever the situation calls for it,
I'll choose love instead of fear.'

Rowena raised her eyebrows. 'Always?'

I glanced over at Noble and nodded. 'Always.'

Epilogue

$\mathcal{A}$dam left The Gathering within days of Peace's death, having decided to travel to a village he knew well and loved, and settle into a quiet life there while he, Rowena and I awaited that for which our horses had prepared us.

'Quinta and I will be checking up on you regularly, so you be sure to behave yourself,' Rowena told Adam with a shake in her voice as she hugged him goodbye.

'It's Coolridge you're going to, isn't it?' I said as I took my turn at hugging him. 'I know it. There are a couple of people I'm due to revisit there, so Noble and I will be there very soon.'

'You have no need to check on me, either of you, I'm fine, I just can't be here at the moment,' Adam said, stepping back from me and standing tall despite the size and weight of his back-sack. 'I have friends in Coolridge and since it's recently found itself without a resident Herbalist, it's an ideal location for me. You'll be welcome to stay whenever you happen to be passing that way, but please don't go out of your way.'

Rowena grinned. 'Quinta's just told you she needs to be there soon anyway, and I have a strong feeling I'll be needing to pass through there shortly after.' Her grin faded and she looked at me. 'Unless we should stay around here in case whoever it is that we're the forerunners for arrives and starts creating turmoil without us?'

I shook my head and said, 'I think we carry on as normal. Noble has always assured me that we're always where we need to be. We won't miss anything.'

Rowena nodded slowly. 'Oak has just confirmed Noble's advice.' She brightened. 'So then, Adam, you'd best go and enjoy the peace at Coolridge before Quinta and I start descending on you, hadn't you?'

He returned her grin. 'I'll consider myself on my way then, shall I? Fare well, both of you.'

'Oh, come here.' Rowena hugged him again and then turned him around and gave him a little push. 'You look after yourself, do you hear me?'

'I wouldn't dare do otherwise.' His chuckles drifted back to us as he walked away.

Weeks turned into months and then into years as the three of us continued with our lives – Adam as Coolridge's Herbalist, and Rowena and I splitting our time between being at The Gathering and travelling around the villages with our Bond-Partners, helping where we could and being sure to drop in regularly on Adam.

During that time, I often wondered whether any other 'forerunners', as Rowena had called the three of us, would become apparent. When they didn't, the feeling I'd had that something settled into place when the three of us were gathered at Peace's grave, proved to be accurate.

Strength, peace and love were united and ready for whoever and whatever were coming.

Other books by Lynn Mann

**Humankind is ready for change and
Quinta has a part to play...**

The Horses Know Trilogy

The Horses Know

Amarilla is one of those chosen by a horse as a Bond-Partner. She looks forward to a lifetime of learning from her horse and of passing on the mare's wisdom to those seeking help. But then she discovers that she is the one for whom the horses have all been waiting. The one who can help them in return.

In order to give the horses the help they need, Amarilla will have to achieve that which has never been attempted before. Only her beloved mare can give her the motivation, the courage and the strength to believe she can succeed. If she does, a new era will dawn for horses and humans alike...

The Horses Rejoice (The Horses Know Book 2)

Amarilla and Infinity have been the catalysts for change that they agreed to be, but they know there is more to be done. If they can befriend the Woeful and persuade the rest of humankind to do the same, then the destructive ways of The Old will forever be in the past.

Amarilla, Infinity and their friends set out on a journey to find the Woeful but their search becomes something so much more due to a courageous chestnut mare, a lone Woeful youngling and numerous herds of wild horses who seek their help along the way. But the friends never forget what they agreed to do. They must reach the heart of the Woeful community. And then they must be willing to risk losing everything...

The Horses Return (The Horses Know Book 3)

It has been more than twenty years since the Kindred came to live in Rockwood. Most of the villagers have embraced the Kindred and all that they have to teach, but there are those who fear the Kindreds' influence, and so have drifted away to live as outcasts. The outcasts suffer, living as they do, but they refuse help, even from the Horse-Bonded.

Will is adamant that he can succeed where the Horse-Bonded have failed, and bring the outcasts home. But his forceful personality constantly gets in his way. He is the key to the future, but if he is to play his part, he must allow a herd of wild horses to show him how to be the person he needs to be. Only then will he fully understand the lengths to which Amarilla and Infinity have gone to ensure that he can fulfil his destiny and reunite the human race...

Horses Forever (A Sequel to The Horses Know Trilogy)

It has always been believed that the people of The Old obliterated themselves generations ago, but when horses begin to amass at one of the city sites of The Old, the villagers of Rockwood discover the truth – an underground city, full of people, has survived.

Supreme City's inhabitants have been waiting for the conditions to be right for them to come up to the surface and claim dominion. They believe the time has come. They are genetically enhanced, armed and aggressive, and they are certain that nothing can stand in their way. But they haven't counted on Will, Maverick, the Horse-Bonded and several hundred horses…

In Search Of Peace (A Prequel to The Horses Know Trilogy)

Adam is on the verge of grief-induced insanity when a horse chooses him as a Bond-Partner and refuses to leave his side. He tries to rid himself of his unwanted companion as he has everyone else, but finds it more difficult than he could have imagined.

Just when it seems as though the horse has managed to find a way through Adam's grief and bring him back to himself, Adam rejects him in the worst possible way, resulting in catastrophe. In order to save the Bond-Partner who has tried so hard to save him, Adam must remember what his would-be saviour tried to teach him. And he must do it soon, before it is too late for both of them…

In Search Of Peace, like A Reason To Be Noble, is a prequel to The Horses Know Trilogy and can be read before, alongside or after the other books.

The Strength Of Oak
(A Prequel to The Horses Know Trilogy)

Unloved and unwanted by her parents, Rowena is desperate for a way out of the life she hates. When a horse chooses her as his Bond-Partner, she thinks she has found one – but she soon discovers that while she can leave her family behind, there is no escaping herself.

With patient guidance from her horse, Rowena begins to accept the truth of her past, and to believe she can change. But then her past catches up with her at the worst possible moment, leaving her with a choice. She can be the person she was, or she can be the person her horse has shown her she can be. One choice will give them both a future. The other will be the death of them…

The Strength Of Oak, like In Search Of Peace and A Reason To Be Noble, is a prequel to The Horses Know Trilogy and can be read before, alongside or after the other books.

Tales Of The Horse-Bonded
(Companion Stories to The Horses Know Trilogy)

A collection of short companion stories to The Horses Know Trilogy, Tales Of The Horse-Bonded is available to download free. To find out more, please visit www.lynnmann.co.uk.

Did you enjoy A Reason To Be Noble?
I'd be extremely grateful if you could spare a few minutes to leave
a review where you purchased your copy.
Reviews really do help my books to reach a wider audience,
which means that I can keep on writing!
Thank you very much.

I love to hear from you!
Get in touch and receive news of future releases at the following:

www.lynnmann.co.uk

www.facebook.com/lynnmann.author

Acknowledgments

Enormous gratitude goes, as always, to my editorial team – Fern Sherry, Leonard Palmer and Caroline Macintosh – without whom I would be utterly lost! Thanks also to Amanda Horan for her cover design, I love it when she brings the horses and settings in my head to life.

This book would have been much harder to write had it not been for Marcus, my dark bay Welsh Cob x Thoroughbred who was with me from 1995 until his passing in 2014. He was uncompromising in his ability to teach me about fear, constantly poking and prodding the parts of me deep inside that I really would have preferred remained buried, so that I had little choice but to work towards achieving a stronger, more stable frame of mind. We travelled a long and tricky path together, and I will always be immensely grateful to him for hanging in there with me until I understood.

Printed in Great Britain
by Amazon